CW01475646

LPC Accounts Online

LPC Accounts Online

James Catchpole

The College of Law

OXFORD
UNIVERSITY PRESS

OXFORD
UNIVERSITY PRESS

Great Clarendon Street, Oxford OX2 6DP

Oxford University Press is a department of the University of Oxford.
It furthers the University's objective of excellence in research, scholarship,
and education by publishing worldwide in

Oxford New York

Auckland Cape Town Dar es Salaam Hong Kong Karachi
Kuala Lumpur Madrid Melbourne Mexico City Nairobi
New Delhi Shanghai Taipei Toronto

With offices in

Argentina Austria Brazil Chile Czech Republic France Greece
Guatemala Hungary Italy Japan Poland Portugal Singapore
South Korea Switzerland Thailand Turkey Ukraine Vietnam

Oxford is a registered trade mark of Oxford University Press
in the UK and in certain other countries

Published in the United States
by Oxford University Press Inc., New York

© Oxford University Press, 2010

The moral rights of the author have been asserted
Database right Oxford University Press (maker)

First published 2010

All rights reserved. No part of this publication may be reproduced,
stored in a retrieval system, or transmitted, in any form or by any means,
without the prior permission in writing of Oxford University Press,
or as expressly permitted by law, or under terms agreed with the appropriate
reprographics rights organization. Enquiries concerning reproduction
outside the scope of the above should be sent to the Rights Department,
Oxford University Press, at the address above

You must not circulate this book in any other binding or cover
and you must impose the same condition on any acquirer

British Library Cataloguing in Publication Data
Data available

Library of Congress Cataloging in Publication Data
Data available

Typeset by Newgen Imaging Systems (P) Ltd., Chennai, India
Printed in Great Britain
on acid-free paper by
Ashford Colour Press, Gosport, Hants

ISBN 978–0–19–954098–3

1 3 5 7 9 10 8 6 4 2

Preface

The reaction of most law students upon realizing that they are required to complete a course in accounts is one of appreciable concern. This resource has therefore been developed to help ease the perceived pain of accounts and to place greater emphasis on the learning and application of accounts through participation and continued practice. Drawing on my experience of teaching and co-ordinating both Solicitors' and Business Accounts on the LPC, I have sought to develop a resource that focuses its tuition, exercises, and feedback towards those undertaking the Legal Practice Course.

I would like to thank Lucy Read of Oxford University Press for being the architect behind the development of this resource. I would also like to extend my special thanks to Cheryl Cheasley, formerly of Oxford University Press, whose tireless enthusiasm, continued encouragement, hard work, and overall contribution has ensured that this resource has reached completion. My thanks also go to those who have reviewed the drafts and concepts associated with the resource, and I hope that their suggestions have been satisfactorily incorporated into the final product.

James Catchpole
September 2009

Note: In November 2008 the Chancellor of the Exchequer introduced a temporary reduction in the VAT rate, reducing it from 17.5 per cent to 15 per cent. This reduction of 2.5 per cent was announced to last until 31 December 2009. Given the temporary nature of this VAT reduction, all calculations requiring the application of VAT in *LPC Accounts Online* will continue to require you to apply VAT at the rate of 17.5 per cent.

Acknowledgements

Grateful acknowledgement is made to the Law Society for permission to reproduce extracts of the Solicitors' Accounts Rules 1998, copyright © The Law Society.

Publisher's acknowledgements

Each section of this resource was reviewed prior to publication by a number of LPC lecturers and students. In particular, we would like to thank the following people for their constructive feedback throughout the development of this resource:

Margaret Arrand, Birmingham City University
Jennifer Buckett, BPP LPC student, 2007–2008
Lucy Crompton, Staffordshire University
Michelle Cumming, College of Law LPC student, 2007–2008
Kathryn Devonald-Davies, School of Law, Swansea University
Rosemary Evans, Staffordshire University
Rachel Haffner, London Metropolitan University
Saima Hassan, Manchester Metropolitan University LPC student, 2007–2008
Russell Hewitson, Northumbria University
Byron Jones, Cardiff University
Phil Knott, Nottingham Law School
Ruth Lawson, Manchester Metropolitan University LPC student, 2007–2008
Nicholas Longworth, Manchester Metropolitan University
James Mendelsohn, University of Huddersfield
Peter Owen, BPP LPC student, 2006–2007
Sheree Peaple, De Montfort Law School
David Stewart, University of Westminster

We are also grateful to the following people for sharing their time, expertise, and experience in contributing to the practitioner video interviews which form a key part of this resource:

Daniel Bluett, Solicitor
Kathy Pinney, Solicitor, Boodlehatfields Solicitors

Outline contents

Detailed contents

Guided tour of this product

LPC Accounts Online is a unique and innovative learning resource. This book will give you information on how to apply the Solicitor's Accounts Rules 1998 to the work that you will do when in practice, and the exercises you will find online will provide you with an opportunity to put this knowledge into action. The varied and engaging online exercises complete with feedback are designed to help you to practice the accounting skills required on the Legal Practice Course. The web site will give you feedback on your performance, help you track your progress, and enable you to reflect on your learning. Above all, the exercises will support your classroom or workshop sessions and provide an interactive environment in which to prepare for your LPC assessments.

An animated Guided Tour of this product can be viewed on the homepage. Simply click on the 'Guided Tour' link on the *LPC Accounts Online* homepage at **www.oxfordinteract.com/lpcaccounts.**

What can I find online?

Interactive exercises

100 interactive exercises covering all aspects of accounting as required on the LPC can be found at: **www.oxfordinteract.com/lpcaccounts**

Once you've registered (for details on this, see p xx), you'll be able to access all of these exercises. The web site is divided into two main areas: Solicitors' Accounts and Business Accounts. At the start of these two main areas you can see film of a practitioner talking about how they use their accounting skills in their day-to-day life as a practitioner. Use these sections to help you understand why it will be important for you to master accounting skills during your LPC.

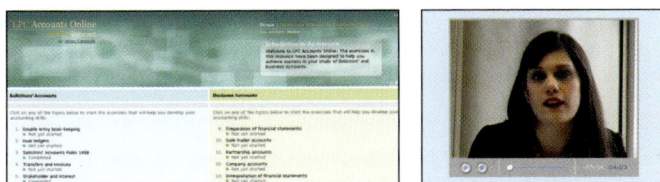

Each of the two main areas is sub-divided into a number of sections containing exercises on different topics. The different sections can be opened in any order, at any time during your course. Once you've started on a topic, the web site will track your place, so that next time you log in you will be able to start again where you left off or choose to start somewhere new. This enables you to work through more than one topic at a time, and makes sure that the web site is useful to you regardless of the structure of your LPC.

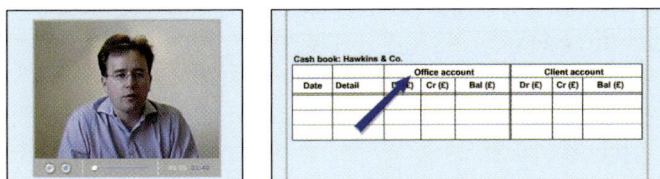

At the start of each of the topics, you will see a film of the author, who will introduce the skill. Before you start any exercises, you'll be given the opportunity to watch an 'Animated Demonstration'. These animations provide a worked example of the topic to be covered, ensuring that you understand as much as possible before starting on the exercises.

You will then be guided through a series of exercises which will help you develop and practice your accounting skills. For more information on the types of exercise that you can expect to undertake, see page xv. If you score less than 50% in some exercises, you will be recommended to undertake a supplementary exercise which will give you more practice before you move on. You can 'skip' this supplementary exercise if you want to, but in order to get the best from this resource it is recommended that you undertake the exercise. If you score over 50%, you will still be given the opportunity to undertake the back-up exercise, but you will not be recommended to do so.

Your scores

The scores you achieve in each exercise will be recorded and can be viewed in the panel on the left of the screen on by clicking on the 'My Scores' link (see p xvii for more details). Use this facility to check on your progress and identify areas where you may need to ask for more support or help from your tutor.

Your account

Once you've registered your account, you can change your password at any time by clicking on the link to 'My Account' at the top of the page.

Reflective diary

Whenever you're online, you'll be able to reflect on your learning using the reflective diary that is built into the web site. Sometimes, the feedback in the exercises will prompt you to use this facility, but you can click on the link to the reflective diary at any point. The link will open a document for you to use to record your thoughts; this document can then be saved wherever you choose for future use. Reflecting on your learning can help you keep a record of your progress and this can be particularly useful in preparing for assessments or even for training contract interviews.

How should I use this book?

This book is divided into thirteen chapters, which mirror the arrangement of the exercises online. To get the most from the resources available online, it's advisable to read the relevant chapter in this book *before* attempting the relevant exercises.

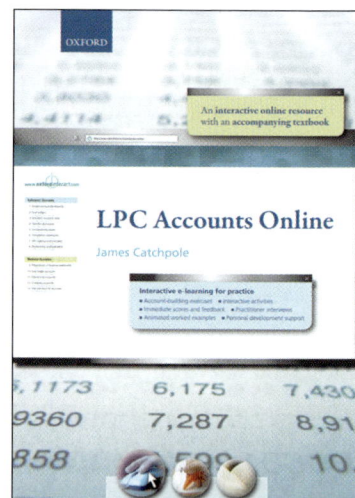

The online exercises

LPC Skills Online features features a range of exercise types. All of the exercises have a practical focus and use realistic, but fictional scenarios, typical of situations that trainees would come across during their training contract. All exercises also provide feedback on the answers chosen, so you can understand why your answer was correct or incorrect.

Use the following pages to familiarise yourself with the types of exercises you will undertake online.

Matching

This exercise will require you to match a series of statements to a correct answer. For example, in Exercise 1 in the section covering VAT on expenses and disbursements, you'll be asked to identify which of various types of money are expenses and which are disbursements.

True or false?

You'll be asked to identify various statements or words as correct (true) or incorrect (false). Exercise 5 in the section covering the Solicitors' Accounts Rules 1998 requires you to identify which of a series of 'mantras' are true or false.

Multiple choice questions

It's likely that you will be familiar with this type of exercise. You'll be given a question, followed by a choice of answers. Select the answers which you think is most appropriate.

Complete a flowchart

These exercises enable you to identify various stages of a process. For example, Exercise 1 in the section covering Sole trader accounts, you'll be asked to place the various headings of a sole trader's profit and loss account in the correct order.

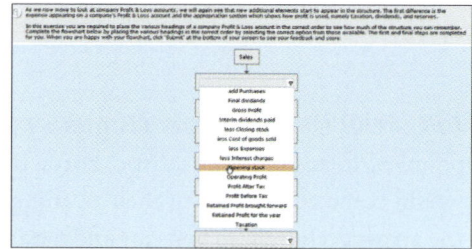

Drop-down boxes

These exercises will give you a scenario, followed by a list of transactions. You'll then be asked to input these transactions onto the relevant blank ledgers by selecting the correct answers from a drop-down box.

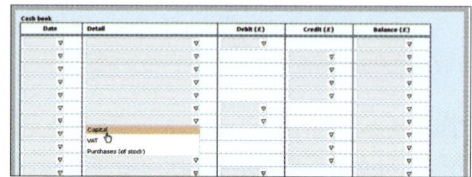

Fill in the boxes

Like the exercise described above, these exercises will give you a scenario, followed by a list of transactions; you'll be asked to input these transactions onto the relevant blank ledgers. However, instead of selecting the correct answers from a series of drop-down boxes, you'll be able to complete the ledgers by typing directly into the relevant place. The web site can take account of different ways of typing the same answer, so your answer would still be correct whether you typed '15 May' or 'May 15'. However, refer to the guide at p xviii for more information on this.

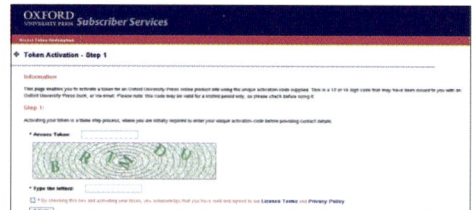

Other important features

'My Account'

Once you've registered with *LPC Accounts Online*, and have started making your way through the exercises, you can change your password at any time using the link to 'My Account'.

Remember to keep your password secret as this holds the key to your personal access of this resource, and to information about your progress.

'My Scores'

As you complete the exercises, your scores are displayed on the left of the screen, but can also be accessed via the 'My scores' link at the top of the screen. If you repeat exercises within a skill area, the site will record the most recent score only. Use the 'My scores' link to export your scores into a spreadsheet or to email your scores to a lecturer.

How to input your answers when completing 'Fill in the boxes' exercises

Some exercises in *LPC Accounts Online* require the user to type in their own answers in the spaces provided in a blank ledger. These exercises are a great way to really test your knowledge.

LPC Accounts Online is a sophisticated resource which can recognise different ways of typing the same information. For example, *LPC Accounts Online* will mark both 'May 15' and '15 May' as correct answers in a date column. However, it's wise to get into a habit of presenting information in a uniform way, in order to avoid a correct answer being marked as incorrect.

Use the table below to make sure that you're typing your answers in the correct way.

TYPE OF ANSWER	RECOMMENDED FORMAT
Dates	Dates should be presented in the following format: **May 15** **Oct 11** • *Do not* add letters after the day (e.g. May 15th, May 31st).
Abbreviations for months	When inputting dates, months should be abbreviated as follows: **Jan, Feb, Mar, Apr, May, June, July, Aug, Sept, Oct, Nov, Dec**
Figures	Figures should be presented in the following format: **5,000.00** **15,000.50** **164,234.78** • *Do* use a comma to separate the units. • Do represent pence, even if this is '00'. • *Do not* use a '£' symbol.

TYPE OF ANSWER	RECOMMENDED FORMAT
Abbreviating 'Debit' and 'Credit'	When you need to identify a balance as debit or credit, use the following format: **5,000.00Dr** **15,000.50Cr** • Do use a capital letter at the start of your abbreviation. • *Do not* insert a space between the end of the figure and your abbreviation.
Detail column	Always start entries in this column with a capital letter: **Cash** **Equipment (computer)**
Clients' names	When abbreviating a client's name in the detail column, use the following format: **Hull, C.** **Firmin, L.** • Do separate the last name from the initial with a comma. • Do use a full point after the initial.

Remember!

Take care with spelling when typing your answers – a typographical error will mean that your generally correct answer is marked incorrect!

How to register

It's easy to register to use *LPC Accounts Online*. Simply follow the steps below:

1. Tear off the perforated strip on the access token you'll find at the back of this book. Please be aware that by tearing off the strip, you are agreeing to the Terms and Conditions of Use and the Privacy Policy which can be found at: www.oup.com/oxfordinteract/iplaccounts/privacy. Once the perforated strip has been torn off, you will no longer be able to return the book to the place where you bought it. The access code you will find under perforated strip is unique, can only be used once, and is not transferable.

2. Log on to **www.oxfordinteract.com/lpcaccounts**

3. Click on the link under the 'New users' heading on the right of your screen, and then follow the instructions to register your account. You'll be able to choose your own username and password which can be used for all subsequent log-ins. You will not need to use the access code again after this.

Note: once you've entered your access code, your account will be active for two years. After this time, your account will be de-activated and you will not be able to access the web site.

4. That's it! You're now registered on *LPC Accounts Online* and can log in at any time using the 'Existing users' section on the right of the home page.

Registering your access code is very straightforward, but if you have any problems, please call: **Customer Services on +44 (0)1865 353705**

www.**oxford**interact.com

» Introduction «

Introduction

As part of your LPC you are required to complete a course in accounts. Although this may seem like an unnecessary module for a future solicitor to study, there is no doubt that a thorough working knowledge and understanding of the accounts and financial statements used by solicitors will be essential to you in your legal career regardless of the area of practice in which you find yourself. Almost all areas of legal practice will require you to receive and handle your clients' money or have an understanding of the financial statements of your clients, regardless of whether or not your firm is large enough to have its own accounts department. Some examples of areas of practice where you will be required to rely on the accounting skills learnt on your LPC include:

- Property
- Banking
- Corporate
- Litigation
- Matrimonial

To help you appreciate how accounts are encountered on a day-to-day basis in the practice areas listed above, *LPC Accounts Online* contains two practitioner interviews which you should watch before you attempt any of the online exercises.

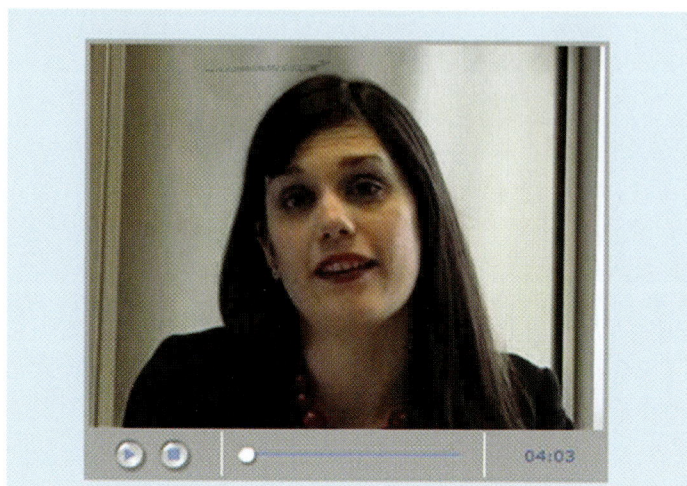

The structure of *LPC Accounts Online*

LPC Accounts Online is split into two sections: Solicitors: Accounts and Business Accounts.

In the Solicitors' Accounts section we will cover eight topics ranging from an introduction to double entry book-keeping principles, the dual ledger system of accounting and the Solicitors' Accounts Rules 1998 to preparing Completion Statements, accounting for VAT, and recording abatements and bad debts. In this section the focus is squarely on introducing the key principles which will enable you to actively create sets of accounts to record any money received into, or used by, your practice. The exercises in this section will provide you with plenty of practice in constructing your own sets of accounts.

In contrast, the Business Accounts section focuses on equipping you with a sound understanding of the variety of financial statements which must be kept by those who run businesses, either as a sole trader, partnership, or company. With this aim of enabling you to read and interpret accurately the financial statements of your clients in practice, the exercises in this section focus on testing your understanding of the key principles surrounding the construction of financial statements; the exercises will not however require you to actively create detailed sets of financial statements as this is beyond the remit of the LPC.

The book

The book is designed to provide an introduction to essential accounting principles. However, it is important to note that the book by itself will not equip you with the accounting skills which you will require in practice. Rather, the book is intended to act as a starting point for study, arming you with knowledge of the basic principles that you will need to put into practice and use to complete the interactive online exercises successfully. You should therefore read the relevant section of the book prior to attempting any of the online exercises. At appropriate stages throughout your reading you will be directed to go online and attempt the interactive exercises.

The website

The true value of *LPC Accounts Online* lies with the extensive array of resources which can be found online. Therefore once you have completed your reading of a particular section or when you are directed to do so by the book, you should log on to the website at www.oxfordinteract.com/lpcaccounts.

Once you have registered with the website using the token included at the back of this book, you will be presented with a list of the topics available. The order in which you complete the topics will depend on the structure of the course developed by your LPC provider. It is important to note that you can begin the exercises on any topic at any given time, regardless of whether or not you have completed all of the exercises in another topic. However, once you have chosen a particular topic, you will be required to complete the exercises in the order in which they appear. This is because each exercise has been designed to build up your knowledge of the subject progressively and to build on points covered in earlier exercises. Once you have successfully completed and 'unlocked' all of the exercises

00:14 02:34

in a particular topic, you can then return to attempt any exercise in any order. In particular, you may find it useful to go back and attempt particular exercises during your revision.

Once you have chosen the particular topic you wish to begin, you will not immediately be directed to the online exercises. Rather you will first be presented with a short video clip of

Cash book

Date	Detail	Debit (£)	Credit (£)	Balance (£)
Sept 5	Balance b/d			7,000.00Dr
Sept 5	Sales	4,000.00		

Sales account

Date	Detail	Debit (£)	Credit (£)	Balance (£)
Sept 5	Balance b/d			9,000.00Cr

Purchases (of stock)

Date	Detail	Debit (£)	Credit (£)	Balance (£)
Sept 5	Balance b/d			2,000.00Dr

03:19 09:56

the author which you should watch to find out what will be covered in the section you have chosen to begin and how the topics contained within the section are relevant to practice. An animated demonstration is also provided at the beginning of all but two of the topics, and you should watch and listen to each animated demonstration before you move on to attempt the exercises. Combining both video and audio elements, each animated demonstration combines on-screen worked examples with accompanying audio explanations which are designed to help you learn how to apply the principles you read about in the book to record transactions and create accounts in practice successfully.

The exercises

A key benefit of *LPC Accounts Online* lies in the wide variety of interactive exercise types which are contained online. The purpose of the exercises is twofold:

— shorter exercise types such as multiple-choice questions and true/false are designed to test your understanding of the essential principles which underpin accounting procedures;

— longer account-building exercises will require you to put your accounting skills into practice and actively create sets of accounts to record the transactions relating to realistic accounting scenarios across a range of practice areas.

To help you assess how well your study is going, all exercises are 'marked' and you will be given your score for the exercise once you have completed it and clicked the 'Submit' button. All exercises are also accompanied by immediate feedback which is designed to help you identify any errors you made and provide useful tips and guidance for tackling such exercises in future. Many of the exercises are also accompanied by additional notes and the correct answers which you can print off and file in your portfolio for future reference.

Additional supplementary exercises are also available at many points throughout the site and are designed to help you consolidate your understanding of a particular topic or offer further practice in completing accounts. An 'A' in the exercise name (e.g. Exercise 2A) in the exercise map contained at the start of all sections in the book indicates that a supplementary exercise is available. If you scored less than 50% in the main exercise you will automatically be directed to undertake the supplementary exercise. However, if you scored over 50% but you would like further practice, you can choose to attempt the supplementary exercise provided.

Reflective diary

In order to help you get the most from this resource you will be encouraged at various stages throughout the exercises to reflect on your learning and the exercises you have undertaken by completing the 'reflective diary', which is available online. This can be accessed by clicking 'Reflective Diary' at the top of your screen and contains a number of questions which you are encouraged to complete and which are designed to help you assess what you have learnt by completing the exercises you have undertaken.

Reflective Diary
LPC Accounts Online — Solicitors' Accounts

Section:

Exercise number;

- **What was the exercise about?**

- **How did I do?**

- **Did I meet my own expectations in this exercise?**

- **Which accounting principles were important in this exercise and why?**

- **Which, if any, of the Solicitors' Accounts Rules 1998 were important in this exercise and why?**

Once completed, your reflective diary can be saved anywhere you like and can also be printed off and included as part of any personal development record system which your institution may already operate.

Conclusion

Finally, it is important to stress that the exercises contained in *LPC Accounts Online* are not intended to replace the face-to-face teaching and practical exercises provided by your LPC provider. You should always approach your tutor directly if you are unsure of any of the points covered on either your Solicitors' or Business Accounts course.

Part 1

Solicitors' Accounts

www.**oxford**interact.com

Section 1

Double entry book-keeping

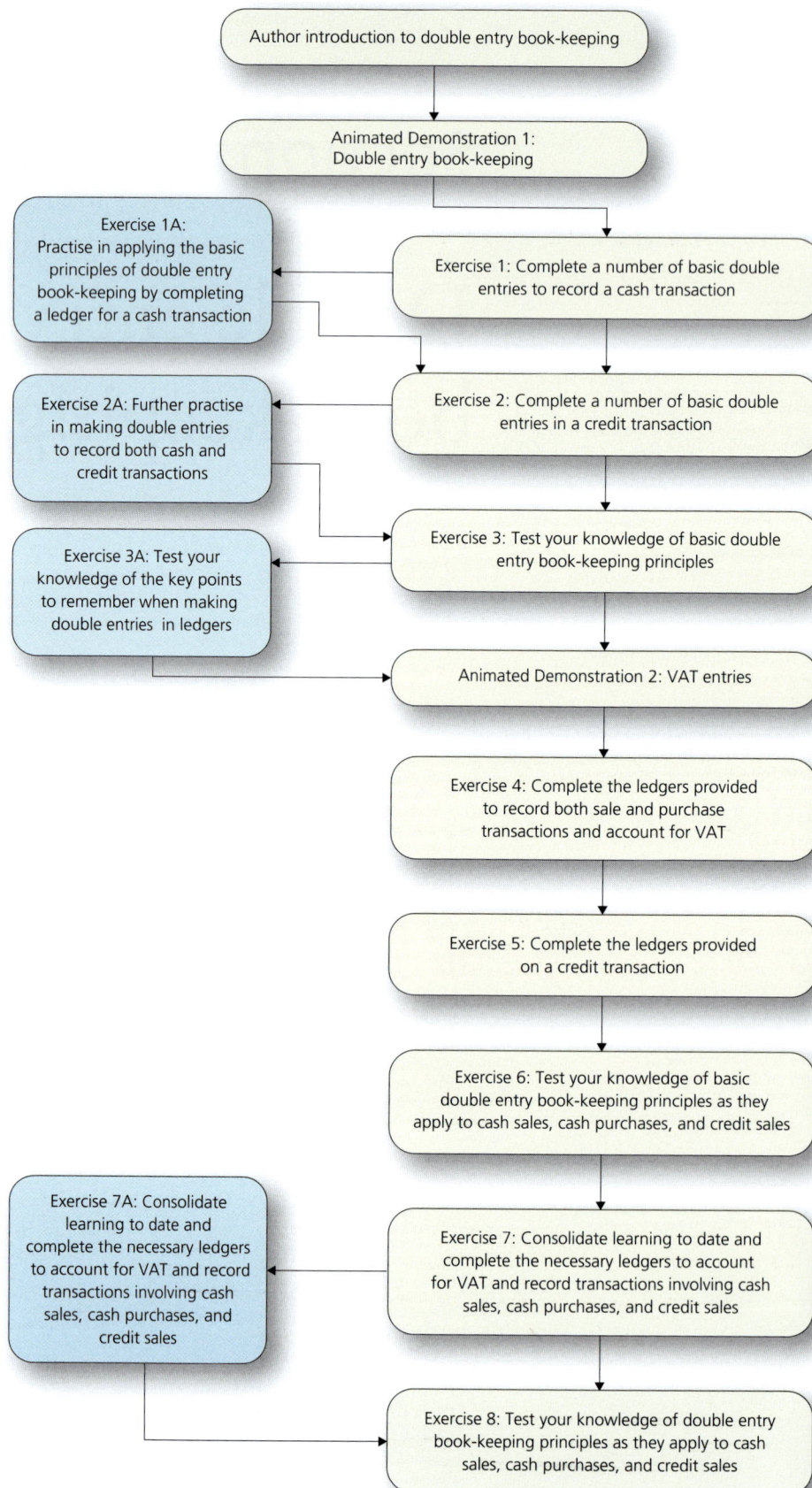

Exercise map

Author introduction to double entry book-keeping

↓

Animated Demonstration 1:
Double entry book-keeping

↓

Exercise 1A:
Practise in applying the basic principles of double entry book-keeping by completing a ledger for a cash transaction

← Exercise 1: Complete a number of basic double entries to record a cash transaction

↓

Exercise 2A: Further practise in making double entries to record both cash and credit transactions

← Exercise 2: Complete a number of basic double entries in a credit transaction

↓

Exercise 3A: Test your knowledge of the key points to remember when making double entries in ledgers

← Exercise 3: Test your knowledge of basic double entry book-keeping principles

↓

Animated Demonstration 2: VAT entries

↓

Exercise 4: Complete the ledgers provided to record both sale and purchase transactions and account for VAT

↓

Exercise 5: Complete the ledgers provided on a credit transaction

↓

Exercise 6: Test your knowledge of basic double entry book-keeping principles as they apply to cash sales, cash purchases, and credit sales

↓

Exercise 7A: Consolidate learning to date and complete the necessary ledgers to account for VAT and record transactions involving cash sales, cash purchases, and credit sales

← Exercise 7: Consolidate learning to date and complete the necessary ledgers to account for VAT and record transactions involving cash sales, cash purchases, and credit sales

↓

Exercise 8: Test your knowledge of double entry book-keeping principles as they apply to cash sales, cash purchases, and credit sales

Introduction

It is important that all solicitors are governed by the same accounting rules and that money belonging to clients, as a priority, is protected. You will be in a position of trust, and it is important you maintain that trust with your clients when you handle their money. It is with this in mind that the Solicitors Regulation Authority's Legal Practice Course Outcomes which govern the Legal Practice Course require that you complete a course in Solicitors' Accounts, and that you are familiar with the Solicitors' Accounts Rules 1998.

In fact, this requirement that you act with integrity and maintain the standard of a highly regarded and influential profession is entrenched in the Solicitors' Accounts Rules 1998, which state:

Solicitors' Accounts Rules 1998

Rule 1 – Principles

A *solicitor* must comply with the requirements of rule 1 of the Solicitors' Code of Conduct 2007 and in particular must:

. . .

As we progress through your Solicitors' Accounts course, we will look at the Solicitors' Account Rules 1998 in more detail and seek to apply them. In order that you meet and maintain such standards, it is necessary that you are introduced to the basic accounting procedures that all solicitors' practices are required to follow. In conjunction with your Solicitors' Accounts course, *LPC Accounts Online* will first introduce you to the basic concept of double entry book-keeping before moving on to consider the dual ledger system of accounting used by most solicitors' practices so as to ensure that you are able to comply with your profession's accounting standards.

Purpose of book-keeping

All businesses need to record the transactions that they enter into, recording the money they spend and receive. Book-keeping and double entry book-keeping are the means by which a business may record such transactions and the relationships they create.

Collectively, these records will then show an accumulative picture of all the financial transactions undertaken, and how the relationships they record have changed over a period of time. It is from these records that financial statements will be created; the two key financial statements are:

- *Profit & Loss accounts*: summarize transactions of a particular nature (revenue and expense transactions) to calculate profit (or loss) over a period of time.

- *Balance Sheets*: summarize the overall assets of a business as at the end of the accounting period – accordingly it is updated to take account of the performance of the business over the year.

The Profit & Loss account and Balance Sheet will be discussed more fully in Section 9.

In this section, *LPC Accounts Online* will concentrate on the recording of the transactions and the manner in which solicitors' practices are required to make such records. Once you have read the following section on double entry book-keeping relating to cash transactions, watch Animated Demonstration 1 online for a detailed explanation and worked examples of key double entry book-keeping principles relating to cash and credit transactions.

Cash book

Date	Detail	Debit (£)	Credit (£)	Balance (£)
Sept 5	Balance b/d			7,000.00Dr
Sept 5	Sales	4,000.00		

Sales account

Date	Detail	Debit (£)	Credit (£)	Balance (£)
Sept 5	Balance b/d			9,000.00Cr

Purchases (of stock)

Date	Detail	Debit (£)	Credit (£)	Balance (£)
Sept 5	Balance b/d			2,000.00Dr

03:19 09:56

Double entry book-keeping

Double entry book-keeping is so called because every financial transaction recorded requires two entries to be made in two different ledgers – one will be a debit and the other will be a credit.

> **Essential Principle**
>
> *Double entry book-keeping:* Every financial transaction to be recorded requires *two entries* (i.e. a double entry) to be made in two separate ledgers – *one in a debit column and the other in a credit column.*

Why this rule? Book-keeping is about relationships and every transaction made by a business involves a change in the status of two relationships maintained by the business. Accordingly, two entries are required to record the change in each relationship.

Corresponding ledger entries can be seen in Example 1.1 below.

Example 1.1

Cash book

Date	Detail	Debit (£)	Credit (£)	Balance (£)
Sept 5	Balance b/d			7,000Dr
Sept 6	Sales	5,000		12,000Dr
Sept 7	Purchases (of stock)		2,000	10,000Dr

Sales account

Date	Detail	Debit (£)	Credit (£)	Balance (£)
Sept 5	Balance b/d			9,000Cr
Sept 6	Cash		5,000	14,000Cr

Purchases (of stock)

Date	Detail	Debit (£)	Credit (£)	Balance (£)
Sept 5	Balance b/d			10,000Dr
Sept 7	Cash	2,000		12,000Dr

If you have not done so already, watch Animated Demonstration 1 online for an explanation of how corresponding ledger entries are made to record both cash and credit transactions.

Cash transactions

In Example 1.1, it is possible to see two sets of double entries being entered: the first made on 6 September and the second made on 7 September, recording a sale of £5,000 and purchases of stock of £2,000 respectively. Both transactions are cash transactions. Let's now look at these transactions in slightly more detail; after which it may be an appropriate time for you to attempt Exercise 1 online.

This is an introductory exercise giving you the chance to complete a number of basic double entries. In this exercise we will only work with cash transactions.

Read the question below and the transactions that follow. When you are ready, click on the 'Your ledgers' tab above or the 'Complete your ledgers' button at the bottom of your screen to see the various ledgers in which you are required to record the transactions linked to Caroline's business. For each transaction you are to input, you should start with the Cash book, and select the correct entry from the options available. As we have seen two entries will be required for every transaction, so once you have made the entries in the Cash book you should make the corresponding entries in the corresponding ledgers by selecting the correct entry from the options available. Remember, you should consider carefully the order of the headings you are picking and the figure. You will be required to calculate these as you proceed. The first entry has already been made for you. When you are happy with the ledgers you have created click 'Submit' at the bottom of your screen to see your feedback and score.

Don't forget, you can click 'Save' at any point if you want to come back to this exercise later.

During August Caroline set up a business buying and selling second-hand computer games from a market stall in Petticoat Lane and made the following transactions:

- Aug 1   Caroline invested £8,000 of her personal savings into the business bank account as new capital.
- Aug 2   Caroline pays £200 rent in cash for her market stall pitch.
- Aug 4   Caroline sells £150 of games for cash.
- Aug 5   Caroline pays £50 cash for a mobile phone.
- Aug 6   Caroline sells £250 of games for cash.
- Aug 7   Caroline pays £100 wages in cash to her casual helper.
- Aug 8   Caroline pays £15 cash for a second-hand game to one of her customers, to add to her stock.

Save   Print   Complete your ledgers

The cash sale

If we look at Example 1.1 we can see a number of ledgers being used. The first, the Cash book, will record all transactions involving cash going in or out of the business. The Purchases (of stock) and Sales accounts will be used to record the accumulative expenditure or receipt in respect of each item.

Essential Principle

When recording entries that use cash, always start with the Cash book.

- Money paid into the bank makes it a debtor of the business (the bank owes that money) so debit the Cash book – the credit goes elsewhere.

- Accordingly, money withdrawn from the bank account is the opposite so involves a credit to the Cash book (the bank is a creditor of the business for the amount it gives back).

Let's first look at the cash sale made by the business which is illustrated in Example 1.2:

- The £7,000Dr balance on the Cash book means **the bank is a debtor of the business**; it owes £7,000 to the business. Accordingly, the bank account has £7,000 in it.

- The cash sale means the business receives £5,000 from a client. This in turn is banked by the business and, in doing so, **the business makes the bank a debtor for £5,000** – a debit entry for the amount banked is required.

- After every entry has been made, the balance must be updated. In this instance a debit entry must be added to a debit balance; consequently, **two debits make a bigger debit** so the £5,000 is added to the £7,000. This then results in a new balance of £12,000Dr.

- The Detail column of the Cash book will always state the name of the corresponding ledger in which the second of the two double entries (i.e. the credit entry in this instance) will be made as a means of cross-reference. The other ledger used will be the ledger corresponding to the activity involved; on this occasion it is the Sales ledger. The Sales ledger will be used to record the accumulative sales made by the business during the year.

Example 1.2

State name of corresponding ledger

Cash book

Date	Detail		Debit (£)	Credit (£)	Balance (£)
Sept 5	Balance b/d				7,000Dr
Sept 6	Sales ◄		5,000		12,000Dr

State date

Cash book: Money in = debit entry

Debit entry on a debit balance = bigger debit balance

Once the receipt of money has been recorded in the Cash book, this completes the first of the two double entries required. The second double entry will need to be made in the corresponding ledger, i.e. the Sales ledger, which we can see in Example 1.3 below:

- Note that the balance brought down in the Sales ledger is a credit balance. This means that the business has, thus far, made sales of £9,000.
- The entry in the Detail column cross-references the name of the ledger in which the debit entry was made, i.e. Cash.

> **Essential Principle**
>
> Always put the name of the ledger used for the other half of the double entry in the Detail column as a means of cross-reference.

- As the entry made in the Cash book was a debit, a credit is required in the Sales ledger.
- When the Sales ledger balance is updated, the credit entry must be added to a credit balance; consequently, **two credits make a bigger credit** so the £5,000 is added to the £9,000. This then results in a new balance of £14,000Cr.

Example 1.3

State name of corresponding ledger

Credit entry on a credit balance = bigger credit balance

Sales account

Date	Detail		Debit (£)	Credit (£)	Balance (£)
Sept 5	Balance b/d				9,000Cr
Sept 6	Cash ◄			5,000	► 14,000Cr

State date

Credit entry in this ledger as Cash book entry was a debit

Once the entry in the Sales ledger has been made the double entry required to record a sale has then been completed: in one ledger a debit entry has been made, while the other ledger contains the corresponding credit entry.

The cash purchase

The principles applied to the cash sale will apply in reverse when a business buys goods for cash.

- In order to pay for the goods, the business will obviously need to withdraw money from the bank, so the bank is giving money back to the business – from the point of view of the business the bank **becomes its creditor for the amount withdrawn**. Or, put another way, if money going into the bank account makes the bank a debtor requiring a debit entry in the Cash book, money being withdrawn from the bank account will require the opposite entry, namely a credit in the Cash book.

Essential Principle

In the Cash book money from/to a client:

Debit = money **IN**

Credit = money **OUT**

- Accordingly, we can see in Example 1.4 that when £2,000 is withdrawn to pay for the goods, a credit entry is required in the Cash book.

- When the balance is updated, the credit entry must be subtracted from the debit balance; consequently, **a credit entry makes a debit balance smaller** so the £2,000 is subtracted from the £12,000. This then results in a new balance of £10,000Dr.

- The mathematics in updating the debit balance in the Cash book is that **if the balance is a debit and the entry is a credit, or vice versa, the entry is always deducted from the balance**.
- The entry in the Detail column cross-references the name of the ledger in which the corresponding debit entry is to be made, i.e. Purchases (of stock).

Example 1.4

State name of corresponding ledger

Credit entry on a debit balance = smaller debit balance

Cash book

Date	Detail		Debit (£)	Credit (£)	Balance (£)
Sept 5	Balance b/d				7,000Dr
Sept 6	Sales		5,000		12,000Dr
Sept 7	Purchases (of stock) ◄			2,000	► 10,000Dr

State date

Cash book: Money out = credit entry

The corresponding debit entry therefore needs to be made in a different ledger, one which records money spent on goods, i.e. the Purchases (of stock) ledger. This ledger can be seen in Example 1.5.

- Note that the balance brought down on the Purchases (of stock) ledger is a debit balance. This means that the business has, to date, purchased goods of £10,000.
- The entry in the Detail column cross-references the name of the ledger in which the credit entry was made, i.e. Cash.
- As the entry made in the Cash book was a credit, a debit entry is therefore required in the Purchases (of stock) ledger.
- When the Purchases (of stock) ledger balance is updated, the debit entry must be added to a debit balance; consequently, **two debits make a bigger debit** so the £2,000 is added to the £10,000. This then results in a new balance of £12,000Dr.

Example 1.5

State name of corresponding ledger

Debit entry on a debit balance = bigger debit balance

Purchases (of stock)

Date	Detail		Debit (£)	Credit (£)	Balance (£)
Sept 5	Balance b/d				10,000Dr
Sept 7	Cash ◄		2,000		► 12,000Dr

State date

Debit entry in this ledger as Cash book entry was a credit

Essential Principles

Remember, when updating the balance:

- Two debits make a bigger debit (add);
- Two credits make a bigger credit (add);
- A credit makes a debit balance smaller (subtract);
- A debit makes a credit balance smaller (subtract).

If you have not done so already, attempt Exercise 1 online to practise making basic double entries to record both cash sales and purchases.

Cash book

Date	Detail	Debit (£)	Credit (£)	Balance (£)
Aug 1	Capital	8,000.00		8,000.00Dr
▽	▽		▽	▽
Aug 1	▽	▽		▽
Aug 2	▽		▽	▽
Aug 3 ▽	▽	▽		▽
▽	▽		▽	▽
▽	▽		▽	▽

Capital account

Date	Detail	Debit (£)	Credit (£)	Balance (£)
▽	▽		▽	▽

Rent account

Date	Detail	Debit (£)	Credit (£)	Balance (£)
▽	▽	▽		▽

Purchases (of stock)

Date	Detail	Debit (£)	Credit (£)	Balance (£)
▽	▽	▽		▽

Credit transactions

In credit transactions, unlike a cash transaction, no money changes hands when the transaction is made. A credit transaction will (usually) involve the issuing of an invoice by one party for goods or services. It is only when payment is made at a later date that the Cash book will be used – up to this point no money has changed hands; rather a debt has been created and must be recorded accordingly.

As a basic example, let's assume that our business provided Sarah with legal services and we sent her an invoice for £6,000 on 10 September; on 25 September Sarah sent us a cheque for £6,000 to settle her debt with us.

The ledgers that we will be using to record this transaction are shown in Example 1.6.

Example 1.6

Cash book

Date	Detail	Debit (£)	Credit (£)	Balance (£)
Sept 5	Balance b/d			7,000Dr
Sept 6	Sales	5,000		12,000Dr
Sept 7	Purchases (of stock)		2,000	10,000Dr

Sarah's account

Date	Detail	Debit (£)	Credit (£)	Balance (£)

Sales account

Date	Detail	Debit (£)	Credit (£)	Balance (£)
Sept 5	Balance b/d			9,000Cr
Sept 6	Cash		5,000	14,000Cr

It is only when Sarah pays the liability, i.e. her debt to us, that we will use the Cash book. In the meantime we will need to show that we have invoiced Sarah and that our sales have increased having undertaken work for Sarah. So, the first two ledgers that we will use are Sarah's ledger and the Sales ledger.

The issue of the invoice for credit

- In issuing the invoice the business makes Sarah a debtor of the business. Accordingly, when a sale is made on credit a debit entry is required in a ledger in the name of the client who owes the money, in this case Sarah. The entries required to record this transaction can be seen in Example 1.7.

Example 1.7

State name of corresponding ledger

Debit entry on a zero balance = debit balance

Sarah's account

Date	Detail		Debit (£)	Credit (£)	Balance (£)
Sept 10	Sales ◄		6,000		► 6,000Dr

State date

Credit transaction: start with Client ledger, (debt owing) debit entry

- Now that the debit entry has been made, a credit entry must be made in the corresponding ledger. As with the sale 'for cash', this second entry will be made in the ledger corresponding to the activity involved; on this occasion the Sales ledger. The entries required can be seen in Example 1.8.

Example 1.8

State name of corresponding ledger

Credit entry on a credit balance = bigger credit balance

Sales account

Date	Detail		Debit (£)	Credit (£)	Balance (£)
Sept 5	Balance b/d				9,000Cr
Sept 6	Cash			5,000	14,000Cr
Sept 10	Sarah ◄			6,000	► 20,000Cr

State date

Credit entry in this ledger as entry in Client ledger was a debit

- Once both ledgers have been completed the balance will show that Sarah is a debtor of the business for £6,000.

Essential Principles

- The Cash book is never used to record a credit transaction.
- On issuing a credit invoice begin with the Client ledger – the client becomes a debtor of the business so debit the Client ledger – the credit goes elsewhere (the Sales/Costs ledger).

Payment of the credit invoice

When Sarah sends a cheque to settle her invoice (i.e. her debt with the firm), this will amount to a cash transaction and accordingly the Cash book will be used to make the first entry. The entries required to record this transaction can be seen in Example 1.9.

- The significance of this transaction is that it is a cash transaction and accordingly the Cash book will be used to make the first entry.

- Sarah is making the payment to the business, which in turn will be paid into the bank account – **the bank is being made a debtor** for the sum of £6,000 so a debit entry is made in the Cash book.

Example 1.9

| State name of corresponding ledger |
| Debit entry on a debit balance = bigger debit balance |

Cash book

Date	Detail		Debit (£)	Credit (£)	Balance (£)
Sept 5	Balance b/d				7,000Dr
Sept 6	Sales		5,000		12,000Dr
Sept 7	Purchases (of stock)			2,000	10,000Dr
Sept 25	Sarah ◄		6,000		► 16,000Dr

| State date |
| Cash book: Money in = debit entry |

- That now completes the first of the two double entries to be made. The second entry, the credit entry, should now to be made to give Sarah credit for making the payment, hence the need to use her name in the Detail column of the Cash book. This second entry is illustrated in Example 1.10.

- On Sarah's ledger begin by noting the £6,000Dr balance before the receipt of the £6,000. It is necessary to reach the stage where the business records show that Sarah no longer owes it any money. A debit balance is cancelled by a credit entry of an amount equal to the balance – this determines the need for a credit entry in Sarah's ledger.

- Alternatively, one can determine that a credit entry is required by virtue of the fact that a debit entry was made in the Cash book.

Example 1.10

State name of corresponding ledger

Credit entry on a debit balance = smaller debit/zero balance

Sarah's account

Date	Detail		Debit (£)	Credit (£)	Balance (£)
Sept 10	Sales		6,000		6,000Dr
Sept 25	Cash ◄			6,000	► 0.00

State date

Credit entry in this ledger as Cash book entry was a debit

Once this final entry has been made it will show that Sarah's debt has been extinguished and the business is in receipt of money from her. In total, two sets of double entries were made, the first to show the issuing of the invoice, and the second showing the receipt of payment. Example 1.11 highlights the two sets of double entries made.

Example 1.11

Cash book

Date	Detail	Debit (£)	Credit (£)	Balance (£)
Sept 5	Balance b/d			7,000Dr
Sept 6	Sales	5,000		12,000Dr
Sept 7	Purchases (of stock)		2,000	10,000Dr
Sept 25	Sarah	6,000 ◄		16,000Dr

Sarah's account

Date	Detail	Debit (£)	Credit (£)	Balance (£)
Sept 10	Sales	6,000		6,000Dr
Sept 25	Cash		6,000	0.00

Sales account

Date	Detail	Debit (£)	Credit (£)	Balance (£)
Sept 5	Balance b/d			9,000Cr
Sept 6	Cash		5,000	14,000Cr
Sept 10	Sarah		► 6,000	20,000Cr

Now attempt Exercise 2 online which will provide you with the opportunity to complete ledger entries to record both cash sales and purchases and also the recording of credit transactions.

As we have seen from the previous exercise, two entries will be required for every transaction, so once you have made your Cash book entry a corresponding entry is then made in the corresponding ledger. In this exercise we start to look at credit transactions.

Read the question below and the transactions that follow. When you are ready, click on the 'Your ledgers' tab above or the 'Complete your ledgers' button at the bottom of your screen to see the various ledgers in which you are required to record the transactions linked to Peter Brittain's business by selecting the correct entry from the options available. You should carefully consider the order of the headings you are picking and the figure as you will be required to calculate these as you proceed. You should also remember that you should only start with the Cash book if you have received cash. If an invoice has been issued, you should start with the correct Client ledger. When you are happy with the ledgers you have created, click 'Submit' at the bottom of your screen to see your feedback and score.

Don't forget, you can click 'Save' at any point if you want to come back to this exercise later.

On 1 June Peter Brittain had £7,000 in his bank account — this entry has already been made for you. Now complete the entries for the following transactions made in June by selecting the correct entry from the options available. All bills issued by Peter are payable within 28 days.

- June 1   Peter buys new stock for cash for £400.
- June 2   Peter pays his electricity bill of £240 for cash.
- June 3   Peter issues a bill to Mark for servicing his Harley Davidson for £300.
- June 4   Peter sells petrol and oil for £50 for cash.
- June 5   Peter services three motor cycles for £450 for cash.
- June 6   Peter pays £200 for his business rates.
- June 7   Peter pays £150 wages to Joan.
- June 8   Peter buys stock for £200 for cash.
- June 9   Peter sells a motor cycle tyre for £56 for cash.

You should then move on to Exercise 3 and answer a series of multiple-choice questions that will give you the chance to test your understanding of the basic principles of double entry book-keeping.

This exercise sets out a number of multiple-choice questions to help you apply basic principles of double entry accounting. Answer each of the questions in turn. When you are happy with your answers, click the 'Submit' button at the bottom of the screen to view your score and receive feedback on your answers.

Question 1
On 1 March Thomas sold goods for cash for £200. When making the entries, which of the following sequences is correct?

○ • Cash transaction, start with Cash book
   • Credit Cash book with Net sum of £200
   • Go to Sales ledger and credit with £200

○ • Cash transaction, start with Cash book
   • Credit Cash book with Net sum of £200
   • Go to Sales ledger and debit with £200

○ • Cash transaction, start with Cash book
   • Debit Cash book with Net sum of £200
   • Go to Sales ledger and debit with £200

○ • Cash transaction, start with Cash book
   • Debit Cash book with Net sum of £200
   • Go to Sales ledger and credit with £200

Question 2
On 3 March Thomas bought goods for cash for £500. When making the entries, which of the following sequences is correct?

○ • Cash transaction, start with Cash book
   • Debit Cash book with Net sum of £500
   • Go to Purchases (of stock) ledger and credit with £500

○ • Cash transaction, start with Cash book
   • Credit Cash book with Net sum of £500
   • Go to Purchases (of stock) ledger and debit with £500

○ • Cash transaction, start with Cash book
   • Credit Cash book with Net sum of £50
   • Go to Purchases (of stock) ledger and debit with £500

Essential Principles

The following 'mantras' will help you to remember some basic principles:

- In the Cash book money from/to a client:

  Debit = money IN

  Credit = money OUT

- Following the double entry principle, the opposite applies in the Client ledger:

  Debit = money OUT

  Credit = money IN

- For receipt of money, the double entry will be:

  Debit Cash book with cash received;

  Credit the Client ledger from, or for whom, the money is received.

- And for payment:

  Credit Cash book with payment out;

  Debit the Client ledger for, or to whom, the payment is made.

Accounting for VAT

The exercises that you have undertaken so far in *LPC Accounts Online* have concentrated on basic double entry book-keeping. The following section aims to build on the principles you have learnt so far and introduce you to the requirement to account for VAT.

Earlier worked examples and exercises relating to completing double entries for cash sales and purchases and credit sales ignored the issue of VAT. However, whenever a business enters into a financial transaction it is very rare for it not to incur, or be required to collect, VAT. Accordingly, we now need to consider how to account for VAT in the following types of transaction:

- cash sales;
- cash purchases;
- credit sales.

We will not be looking at credit purchases because the Solicitors' Accounts Rules 1998 only require solicitors to record expenditures with client money and office money on client matters. There is no requirement under the Solicitors' Accounts Rules 1998 to record credit purchases, even when made on a client matter, until the credit purchase is paid for. Therefore, even when solicitors incur disbursements (i.e. a payment made by a solicitor for, or on behalf of, a client) on credit, most do not actually record them in their accounts until they are paid for.

For a detailed introduction and worked examples highlighting how to account for VAT on both cash and credit transactions, go online and watch Animated Demonstration 2.

Cash book

Date	Detail	Debit (£)	Credit (£)	Balance (£)
Aug 1	Balance b/d			3,000.00Dr

Purchases (of stock)

Date	Detail	Debit (£)	Credit (£)	Balance (£)
Aug 1	Balance b/d			13,000.00Dr

Alison

Date	Detail	Debit (£)	Credit (£)	Balance (£)

VAT account (HM Revenue & Customs)

Date	Detail	Debit (£)	Credit (£)	Balance (£)
Aug 1	Balance b/d			0.00

00:55 10:14

VAT accounting

As we have already seen, whenever a business enters into a financial transaction at least two of its relationships change – hence the term 'double entry'. VAT accounting introduces another possible relationship that might change with the making of a financial transaction.

As a consequence, when accounting for VAT it is important to understand that VAT transactions must be treated as comprising two sets of double entries:

- the first entry to record the net sum; and
- the second entry to record the VAT charge.

VAT is a tax on sales that must be charged (collected) by all businesses registered for VAT; it is accounted for at the point of sale. Those businesses must maintain a record of the amount owed to HM Revenue & Customs; most do so by using an additional ledger, a VAT ledger (the VAT account).

Let's now look at two short examples; first to see how VAT is accounted for in a cash transaction, and second to see how VAT is accounted for when an invoice is issued (a credit sale).

VAT accounting in cash transactions

Starting with the recording of VAT in cash transactions, we will need to look at both cash sales and cash purchases. For example, let's assume that our business is registered for VAT and that on 15 September it sold goods for £1,000 plus VAT of £175 and that on

18 September it purchased goods for £500 plus VAT of £87.50. The ledgers we will be using to record these transactions are set out in Example 1.12.

Example 1.12

> Note the balance: if, when making a credit entry you are withdrawing money from the business, a credit (Cr) balance will mean that the Cash book is overdrawn.

Cash book

Date	Detail	Debit (£)	Credit (£)	Balance (£)
Sept 15	Balance b/d			5,600.00Cr

Purchases (of stock)

Date	Detail	Debit (£)	Credit (£)	Balance (£)
Sept 15	Balance b/d			4,000.00Dr

Sales account

Date	Detail	Debit (£)	Credit (£)	Balance (£)
Sept 15	Balance b/d			3,400.00Cr

VAT account (HM Revenue & Customs)

Date	Detail	Debit (£)	Credit (£)	Balance (£)
Sept 15	Balance b/d			300.00Dr

You will note that we now have a new ledger to record VAT that the business both collects from sales and spends on purchases.

To record the sale of goods for cash for £1,000 plus £175 VAT the sequence of entries that we must make is as follows:

- As this is a cash transaction, start with the Cash book and make a debit entry to record the net sum of £1,000.

- Then make the corresponding entry to record the sale in the Sales account with a credit entry of £1,000.

- Now record the receipt of VAT, so first return to the Cash book and make a debit entry of £175 for VAT.

- Then make the final corresponding entry in the VAT account and make a credit entry of £175.

The ledgers in which these entries have been recorded can be seen in Example 1.13.

Example 1.13

> Entry 1: record the net receipt of £1,000
> Money in = debit entry.
> Debit entry makes a credit balance smaller, so
> subtract (5,600 − 1,000 = 4,600Cr)

> Entry 3: record the receipt of £175 VAT
> Money in = debit entry.
> Debit entry makes a credit balance smaller, so
> subtract (4,600 − 175 = 4,425Cr)

Cash book

Date	Detail	Debit (£)	Credit (£)	Balance (£)
Sept 15	Balance b/d			5,600.00Cr
Sept 15	Sales	1,000.00		4,600.00Cr
Sept 15	VAT	175.00		4,425.00Cr

> Entry 2: record the net sale of £1,000
> Cash book was a debit entry, therefore
> credit entry in this ledger.
> Two credits make a bigger credit balance,
> so add (3,400 + 1,000 = 4,400Cr)

Sales account

Date	Detail	Debit (£)	Credit (£)	Balance (£)
Sept 15	Balance b/d			3,400.00Cr
Sept 15	Cash		1,000.00	4,400.00Cr

VAT account (HM Revenue & Customs)

Date	Detail	Debit (£)	Credit (£)	Balance (£)
Sept 15	Balance b/d			300.00Dr
Sept 15	Cash		175.00	125.00Dr

> Entry 4: record the receipt of £175 VAT
> Cash book was a debit entry, therefore
> credit entry in this ledger.
> Credit entry makes a debit balance smaller,
> so subtract (300 − 175 = 125Dr)

Having now recorded the cash sale, let's move on to complete and record the cash purchase by the business. On 18 September it purchased goods for £500 plus VAT of £87.50. The sequence of entries that we are required to make is as follows:

- As this is a cash transaction, start with the Cash book and make a credit entry to record the withdrawal of the net sum of £500.

- Then make the corresponding entry to record the purchase in the Purchases (of stock)/account with a debit entry of £500.

- Now record the expense of VAT, so first return to the Cash book and make a credit entry of £87.50 for VAT.

- Then make the final corresponding entry in the VAT ledger and make a debit entry of £87.50.

The ledgers in which these entries have been recorded can be seen in Example 1.14.

Example 1.14

> Entry 1: record the net withdrawal of £500
> Money out = credit entry.
> Two credits make a bigger credit balance, so add
> (4,425 + 500 = 4,925Cr)

Cash book

Date	Detail	Debit (£)	Credit (£)	Balance (£)
Sept 15	Balance b/d			5,600.00Cr
Sept 15	Sales	1,000.00		4,600.00Cr
Sept 15	VAT	175.00		4,425.00Cr
Sept 18	Purchases (of stock)		500.00	4,925.00Cr
Sept 18	VAT		87.50	5,012.50Cr

> Entry 3: record the withdrawal of £87.50 for VAT
> Money out = credit entry.
> Two credits make a bigger credit balance,
> so add (4,925 + 87.50 = 5,012.50Cr)

> Entry 2: record the net withdrawal of £500
> Cash book was a credit entry, therefore debit
> entry in this ledger.
> Two debits make a bigger debit balance, so add
> (4,000 + 500 = 4,500Dr)

Purchases (of stock)

Date	Detail	Debit (£)	Credit (£)	Balance (£)
Sept 15	Balance b/d			4,000.00Dr
Sept 18	Cash	500.00		4,500.00Dr

VAT account (HM Revenue & Customs)

Date	Detail	Debit (£)	Credit (£)	Balance (£)
Sept 15	Balance b/d			300.00Dr
Sept 15	Cash		175.00	125.00Dr
Sept 18	Cash	87.50		212.50Dr

> Entry 4: record the withdrawal of £87.50 for VAT
> Cash book was a credit entry, therefore debit entry
> in this ledger.
> Two debits make a bigger debit balance, so add
> (125 + 87.50 = 212.50Dr)

> ### Essential Principles
>
> VAT transactions must be treated as comprising a pair of double entries: one set of double entries for the net sum and another set for the VAT charge. Accordingly, the four entries will be as follows:
>
> 1. Net sum shown as deposited or withdrawn in the Cash book.
>
> 2. The corresponding entry in the associated (Sales/Costs) ledger.
>
> 3. Record the VAT element separately from the net amount of the sum deposited or withdrawn in the Cash book.
>
> 4. The corresponding entry in the VAT account.

Having now looked at both cash sales and purchases and seen the requirement to record the net amount and the VAT separately (as opposed to the gross amount, i.e. the combined sum of the net amount and VAT), you should attempt Exercise 4 online. This exercise will give you the opportunity to practise your basic double entry skills by requiring you to complete a number of ledgers to record cash transactions and account for VAT on those transactions.

(i) In the next series of exercises, we will move on to look at transactions that have a VAT element to them, concentrating initially on cash transactions and VAT, and including both sale and purchase transactions.

Read the question below and the transactions that follow. When you are ready, click on the 'Your ledgers' tab above or the 'Complete your ledgers' button at the bottom of your screen to see the various ledgers in which you are required to record the transactions linked to Udo's business by selecting the correct entry from the options available. For each transaction you should identify which ledger should be used and whether the entry is a debit or credit entry. Remember, you should only start with the Cash book if you have received cash, otherwise if an invoice has been issued, you should start with the correct Client ledger. When you are happy with the ledgers you have created, click 'Submit' at the bottom of your screen to see your feedback and score.

Don't forget, you can click 'Save' at any point if you want to come back to this exercise later.

(?) Udo starts business and carries out the transactions listed below. Record these transactions in the ledgers provided by selecting the correct entry from the options available.

- June 1   Udo invests £8,000 into the business bank account.
- June 2   Udo pays £500 plus £87.50 VAT for electricity for his premises.
- June 5   Udo buys £600 plus £105 VAT of stock for cash.
- June 9   Udo sells goods for £900 plus £157.50 VAT cash.
- June 11 Udo pays £100 plus £17.50 VAT for stationery.
- June 12 Udo pays £150 wages to James.
- June 22 Udo sells goods for £1,000 plus £175 VAT cash.

Save	Print		Complete your ledgers

VAT accounting in credit transactions

As we have seen, VAT is a tax which is accounted for at the point of sale. Therefore in credit transactions VAT is levied when the invoice is issued and, accordingly, will be recorded in the Client ledger at this time – there will be no VAT accounting when the payment is then made.

If we work our way through a basic example, we will be able to see how and where the entries are to be made. Let's assume that we have undertaken work for Sarah again, and the value of that work was £2,000 plus £350 VAT. We issued the invoice for this amount on 19 September. Sarah then sent, on 1 October, a cheque for £2,350 representing the total invoiced value.

In this example we will need to record the entries in four different ledgers: these are shown in Example 1.15.

Example 1.15

Cash book

Date	Detail	Debit (£)	Credit (£)	Balance (£)
Sept 18	Balance b/d			5,012.50Cr

Sarah's account

Date	Detail	Debit (£)	Credit (£)	Balance (£)

Sales account

Date	Detail	Debit (£)	Credit (£)	Balance (£)
Sept 18	Balance b/d			4,500.00Cr

VAT account (HM Revenue & Customs)

Date	Detail	Debit (£)	Credit (£)	Balance (£)
Sept 18	Balance b/d			212.50Dr

The first transaction to record is the issuing of the invoice to Sarah on 19 September. The only difference that we will be making in this example, compared to earlier double entries in which we issued invoices, is that we will need to show the net value of the invoice and VAT as separate entries. The sequence of entries will therefore be as follows:

- In issuing the invoice the business makes Sarah a debtor of the business, therefore a debit entry should be made in Sarah's ledger to record the net sum of £2,000.

- Then make the corresponding entry to record the sale, and credit £2,000 in the Sales account.
- Return to Sarah's ledger and make a further debit entry to record the VAT that was levied on the invoice of £350.
- Then make the corresponding credit entry to record the VAT of £350 levied in the VAT ledger.

Once both the net sum and the VAT have been recorded, this will show that Sarah is a debtor of the business for a total of £2,350. Note that we have not used the Cash book; since no cash is involved at this stage, the Cash book is not needed just yet.

The ledgers in which these entries have been recorded can be seen in Example 1.16.

Example 1.16

> Entry 1: record the net invoiced sum of £2,000
> Credit transaction: start with Client ledger
> (debt owing) debit entry.
> Debit on a zero balance makes a debit balance

Sarah's account

Date	Detail	Debit (£)	Credit (£)	Balance (£)
Sept 19	Sales	2,000.00		2,000.00Dr
Sept 19	VAT	350.00		2,350.00Dr

> Entry 3: record the VAT invoiced of £350
> Credit transaction: start with Client ledger
> (debt owing) debit entry
> Debit on a debit balance makes a bigger debit balance

Sales account

Date	Detail	Debit (£)	Credit (£)	Balance (£)
Sept 18	Balance b/d			4,500.00Cr
Sept 19	Sarah		2,000.00	6,500.00Cr

> Entry 2: record the net invoiced sum of £2,000
> Client ledger was a debit entry, therefore
> credit entry in this ledger
> Credit on a credit balance makes a bigger credit balance

Example 1 .16 *(contd)*

> Entry 4: record the VAT invoiced of £350
> Client ledger was a debit entry, therefore
> credit entry in this ledger.
> Credit entry makes a debit balance smaller/credit balance, so
> subtract (212.50Dr – 350 = 137.50Cr)

VAT account (HM Revenue and Customs)

Date	Detail	Debit (£)	Credit (£)	Balance (£)
Sept 18	Balance b/d			212.50Dr
Sept 19	Sarah		350.00	137.50Cr

As you have seen, when credit transactions are entered four entries will be required to record the debt being created (invoiced), i.e. the net sum, and the VAT. Now we need to turn our attention to when the debt is paid. As we have already addressed the issue of VAT when the invoice was issued, we only need to make two further entries to record the receipt of the total amount received from Sarah, i.e. the cheque for £2,350. The sequence of entries will therefore be as follows:

- As this is a cash transaction, start with the Cash book and make a debit entry to record the gross sum of £2,350.
- Then make the corresponding credit entry in the client ledger to record that Sarah has paid the invoice rendered and that she no longer owes the business £2,350.

The ledgers in which these entries have been recorded can be seen in Example 1.17.

Example 1.17

> Entry 1: record the gross receipt of £2,350
> Money in = debit entry
> Debit entry makes a credit balance smaller, so
> subtract (5,012.50 – 2,350 = 2,662.50Cr)

Cash book

Date	Detail	Debit (£)	Credit (£)	Balance (£)
Sept 18	Balance b/d			5,012.50Cr
Oct 1	Sarah	2,350.00		2,662.50Cr

> Entry 2: record the gross receipt of £2,350
> Cash book was a debit entry, therefore credit entry in this ledger.
> Credit entry makes a debit balance smaller, so subtract

Sarah's account

Date	Detail	Debit (£)	Credit (£)	Balance (£)
Sept 19	Sales	2,000.00		2,000.00Dr
Sept 19	VAT	350.00		2,350.00Dr
Oct 1	Cash		2,350.00	0.00

Essential Principles

- VAT is a tax that is accounted for at the point of sale. In a credit transaction the VAT is recorded when the invoice is issued.

- There is no VAT accounting when the payment is made under the credit transaction (i.e. when the invoice is paid).

- Accordingly, the four entries required to record the debt being created and that a separate amount is also due for VAT are as follows:

    1. Show debt created in Client ledger, for net amount only (debit entry).

    2. The corresponding entry in Costs/Sales ledger (credit entry).

    3. Record the VAT element separately from the net amount of the invoice (debit entry).

    4. The corresponding entry in the VAT account (credit entry).

- When the debt is paid, only two entries are required:

    1. Cash book for gross amount (i.e. all that invoiced) to show monies into business (debit entry).

    2. The corresponding entry in Client ledger to show all of debt paid (credit entry).

The completed ledgers showing the issuing of the invoice to Sarah and the receipt of the gross sum can be seen in Example 1.18.

Example 1.18

Cash book

Date	Detail	Debit (£)	Credit (£)	Balance (£)
Sept 18	Balance b/d			5,012.50Cr
Oct 1	Sarah	2,350.00		2,662.50Cr

Sarah's account

Date	Detail	Debit (£)	Credit (£)	Balance (£)
Sept 18	Sales	2,000.00		2,000.00Dr
Sept 19	VAT	350.00		2,350.00Dr
Oct 1	Cash		2,350.00	0.00

Sales account

Date	Detail	Debit (£)	Credit (£)	Balance (£)
Sept 18	Balance b/d			4,500.00Cr
Sept 19	Sarah		2,000.00	6,500.00Cr

VAT account (HM Revenue & Customs)

Date	Detail	Debit (£)	Credit (£)	Balance (£)
Sept 18	Balance b/d			215.50Dr
Sept 19	Sarah		350.00	137.50Cr

The requirements for VAT mean that an extra pair of double entries must be made to show the additional element of VAT for each transaction at the point of sale, purchase, or invoice. Now attempt Exercises 4 and 5. These exercises will help you consolidate your learning to date and give you the opportunity to practise making entries to account for VAT in transactions involving cash sales, cash purchases, and credit sales.

Cash book

Date	Detail	Debit (£)	Credit (£)	Balance (£)
▽	▽	▽		▽
▽	▽		▽	▽
▽	▽		▽	▽
▽	▽		▽	▽
▽	▽		▽	▽
▽	▽	▽		▽
▽	▽	▽		▽
▽	Capital		▽	▽
▽	VAT		▽	▽
▽	Purchases (of stock)		▽	▽
▽	▽	▽		▽
▽	▽	▽		▽

Capital account

Date	Detail	Debit (£)	Credit (£)	Balance (£)
▽	▽		▽	▽

Electricity account

Date	Detail	Debit (£)	Credit (£)	Balance (£)
▽	▽	▽		▽

In this exercise, we will work with VAT associated with credit transactions, i.e. when invoices are issued.

Read the question below and the transactions that follow. When you are ready, click on the 'Your ledgers' tab above or the 'Complete your ledgers' button at the bottom of your screen to see the various ledgers in which you are required to record the transactions on Emma's ledgers by selecting the correct entry from the options available. Remember, you should consider carefully the order of the headings you are picking and the figure. You will be required to calculate these as you proceed. When you are happy with the ledgers you have created, click 'Submit' at the bottom of your screen to see your feedback and scores.

Don't forget, you can click 'Save' at any point if you want to come back to this exercise later.

Record the following transactions in Emma's ledgers by selecting the correct entry from the options available. On 1 August her bank account was overdrawn by £2,500. You are to make this first entry in the Cash book. All invoices issued by Emma are payable within 21 days.

- Aug 1 Emma issues an invoice to Sam for £3,000 plus £525 VAT.
- Aug 2 Emma issues an invoice to Jenni for £1,400 plus £245 VAT.
- Aug 3 Emma issues an invoice to Kim for £200 plus £35 VAT.
- Aug 5 Emma issues an invoice to Jean for £500 plus £87.50 VAT.
- Aug 6 Emma receives payment from Sam of £3,525.
- Aug 9 Emma receives a cheque from Jenni for £2,101.90.
- Aug 11 Emma receives Kim's cheque for £235.
- Aug 18 Emma receives Jean's cheque for £587.50.

Save   Print   Complete your ledgers

Once you have completed these exercises, undertake Exercise 6 online to test yourself further on applying basic double entry book-keeping principles as they apply to cash sales, cash purchases, and credit sales.

Set out below is a list of statements to help you further apply basic principles of double entry accounting as they apply to cash sales, cash purchases, and credit sales. Drag the words 'Debit' and 'Credit' and drop them next to the statements to which you think they apply. When you are happy with your selection, click the 'Submit' button at the bottom of your screen to view your score and see feedback on your answers.

VAT ledger: the recording of VAT after issuing an invoice	Debit	Credit
Cash book: the receipt of cash (Net sum) following a sale of goods	Debit	Credit
Client ledger: the receipt of monies from the client following the issue of an invoice	Debit	Credit
Cash book: the receipt of VAT following a sale of goods for cash	Debit	Credit
The entry reducing a debit balance	Debit	Credit
Client ledger: recording the Net sum owed by the client	Debit	Credit
VAT ledger: the recording of VAT paid following the business's purchase of goods for cash	Debit	Credit
Cash book: the recording of VAT paid following the business's purchase of goods for cash	Debit	Credit

You should then undertake Exercise 7 which requires you to combine your learning to date by completing a number of ledgers to record cash sales, cash purchases, and credit sales. You will also be required to account for VAT on those transactions recorded.

The objective now is to combine learning to date and to account for VAT in a transaction involving cash sales, cash purchases, and credit sales.

Read the question below and the transactions that follow. In this exercise you are required to make all of the entries to correctly record the transactions linked to Shivani's business and you will be expected to include the date, corresponding ledger, input the correct debit or credit entry and calculate the correct balance required to correctly record each transaction.

When you are ready to start the exercise, click the 'Your ledgers' tab above or the 'Complete your ledgers' button at the bottom of your screen and make the necessary entries in the ledgers provided to record the transactions linked to Shivani's business. By way of example, and to help you start this exercise, the first entry has been made for you. When you are happy with the ledgers you have created, click 'Submit' at the bottom of your screen to see your feedback and score.

Don't forget, you can click 'Save' at any point if you want to come back to this exercise later.

Shivani made the following transactions in the course of her business in August. On 1 August she had £2,000 in her bank account. All invoices issued by Shivani are payable within 28 days.

- Aug 1   Shivani bought new tools for cash priced £100 plus £17.50 VAT.
- Aug 2   Shivani bought new stock for cash priced £200 plus £35 VAT.
- Aug 3   Shivani issued an invoice to Matthew for £60 plus £10.50 VAT.
- Aug 4   Shivani issued an invoice to Peter for £250 plus £43.75 VAT.
- Aug 5   Shivani paid her telephone bill of £150 plus £26.25 VAT.
- Aug 6   Shivani paid £10 plus £1.75 VAT cash for petrol.
- Aug 9   Shivani undertook some work for £90 plus £15.75 VAT for cash.
- Aug 9   Shivani issued an invoice for £75 plus £13.13 VAT to Alastair for fixing a leaking pipe.
- Aug 10   Shivani received a cheque for £70.50 from Matthew.

Finally, Exercise 8 requires you to answer a series of multiple-choice questions designed to test your understanding of the basic principles of double entry accounting applicable to cash sales, cash purchases, and credit sales.

This exercise sets out a number of multiple-choice questions to help you apply basic principles of double entry accounting as they apply to cash sales, cash purchases, and credit sales. Answer each of the questions in turn. When you are happy with your answers, click the 'Submit' button at the bottom of the screen to view your score and receive feedback on your answers.

Question 1
On 1 April Colette purchased a new laptop and paid in cash £750 plus £131.25 VAT. When making the entries, which of the following sequences is correct?

○ • Cash transaction, start with Cash book
• Credit Cash book with £750
• Go to Purchases (office equipment) ledger and credit with £750
• Return to Cash book and credit £131.25 VAT
• Go to VAT ledger and credit £131.25

○ • Cash transaction, start with Cash book
• Credit Cash book with £750
• Go to Purchases (office equipment) ledger and credit with £750
• Return to Cash book and debit £131.25 VAT
• Go to VAT ledger and debit £131.25

○ • Cash transaction, start with Cash book
• Debit Cash book with £750
• Go to Purchases (office equipment) ledger and credit with £750
• Return to Cash book and credit £131.25 VAT
• Go to VAT ledger and debit £131.25

○ • Cash transaction, start with Cash book
• Credit Cash book with £750
• Go to Purchases (office equipment) ledger and debit with £750
• Return to Cash book and credit £131.25 VAT
• Go to VAT ledger and debit £131.25

Question 2
On 3 April Colette sold six photographic prints, for £600 plus £105 VAT, to Christian for cash. When making the entries, which of the following sequences is correct?

○ • Cash transaction, start with Cash book
• Debit Cash book with £600
• Go to Sales ledger and credit with £600
• Return to Cash book and debit £105 VAT
• Go to VAT ledger and credit £105

Conclusion

So far, *LPC Accounts Online* has introduced you to the basic double entry book-keeping procedures. Whilst most law students may have an initial reluctance or fear of numbers, it is important that you appreciate that there is a logical approach to Solicitors' Accounts, which should become easier the more practice you undertake. As you progress through *LPC Accounts Online* we will also start to look at the application of the Solicitors' Account Rules 1998 and the dual ledger system of accounting, which should help you appreciate why it has been necessary for you to learn such basic book-keeping principles. Ultimately they will assist you in practice as you seek to qualify.

www.**oxford**interact.com

Section 2

Dual ledgers

Exercise map

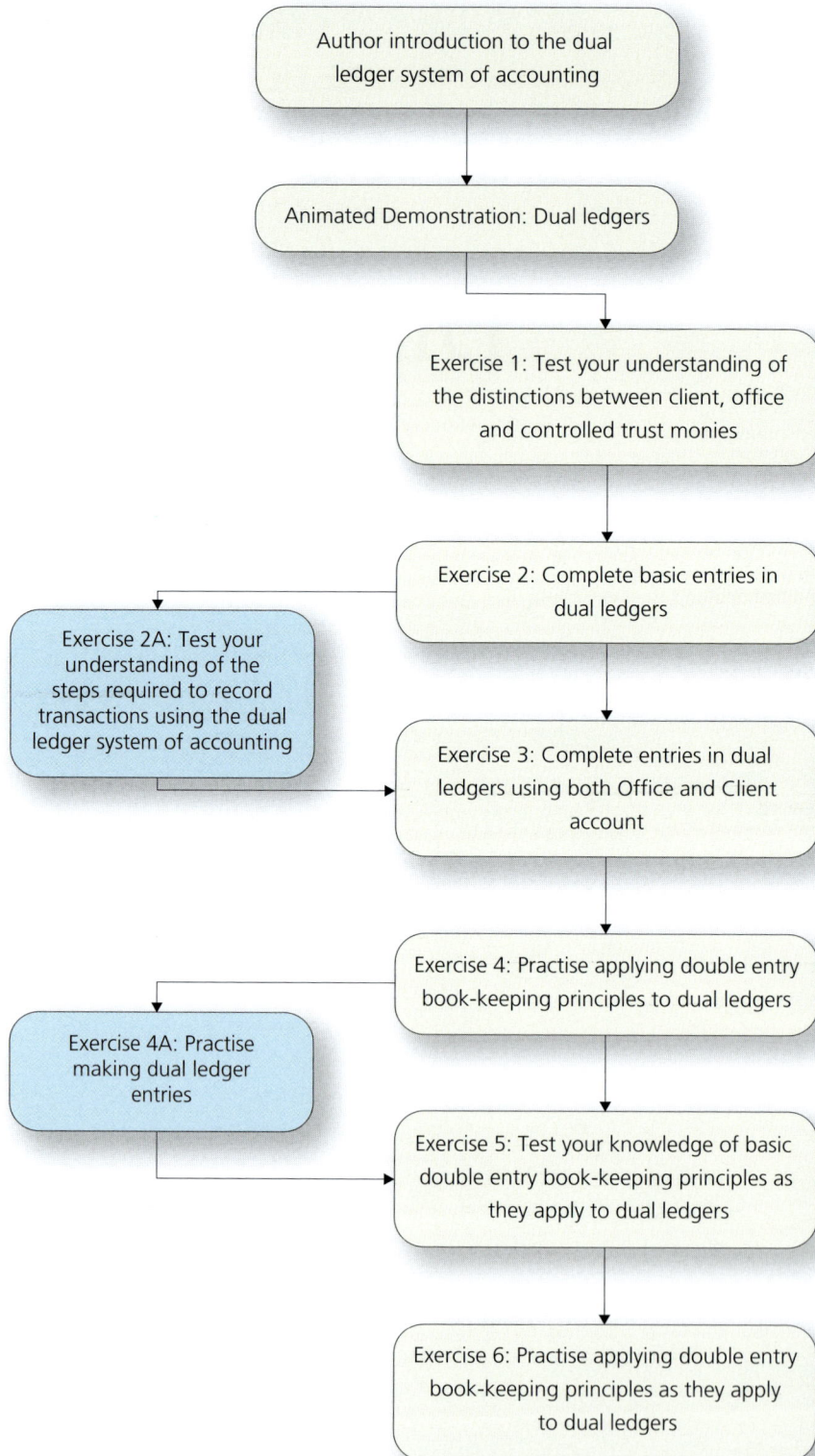

Author introduction to the dual ledger system of accounting

↓

Animated Demonstration: Dual ledgers

↓

Exercise 1: Test your understanding of the distinctions between client, office and controlled trust monies

↓

Exercise 2: Complete basic entries in dual ledgers

Exercise 2A: Test your understanding of the steps required to record transactions using the dual ledger system of accounting

Exercise 3: Complete entries in dual ledgers using both Office and Client account

↓

Exercise 4: Practise applying double entry book-keeping principles to dual ledgers

Exercise 4A: Practise making dual ledger entries

Exercise 5: Test your knowledge of basic double entry book-keeping principles as they apply to dual ledgers

↓

Exercise 6: Practise applying double entry book-keeping principles as they apply to dual ledgers

Introduction

In Section 1 of *LPC Accounts Online* we looked at the basic requirements of double entry book-keeping. We now need to turn our attention to book-keeping requirements that are more particular to solicitors.

Consequently, we will now start to examine and use the dual ledger system of book-keeping. Dual ledgers are ledgers that identify the two different bank accounts that must be operated by the solicitor's practice: the Office account and the Client account. The requirement to have two different types of bank account inevitably requires that different classifications of monies are only to be deposited within each. Therefore we will now also start to look at the Solicitors' Accounts Rules 1998 to help with this classification.

The requirement for using the dual ledger system and the manner in which it is used is outlined in the following section. However, for a detailed introduction and worked examples of the dual ledger system of accounting, watch the Animated Demonstration online before undertaking any of the accompanying exercises.

Cash book: Hawkins & Co.

Date	Detail	Office account			Client account		
		Dr (£)	Cr (£)	Bal (£)	Dr (£)	Cr (£)	Bal (£)

Client: Dr Richard Smart   Matter: Debt collection: Peter Phillips

Date	Detail	Office account			Client account		
		Dr (£)	Cr (£)	Bal (£)	Dr (£)	Cr (£)	Bal (£)

01:05 07:27

Dual ledgers

Why are solicitors required to use a dual ledger system for book-keeping? This is explained by looking at a number of fundamental principles of the Solicitors' Accounts Rules 1998 (SARs) set out in Rules 1 and 14 and also in Rule 32.

Solicitors' Accounts Rules 1998

Rule 1 – Principles

A *solicitor* must comply with the requirements of rule 1 of the Solicitors' Code of Conduct 2007, and in particular must:

. . . .

    (a) keep other people's money separate from money belonging to the *solicitor* or the practice;

So how can a solicitor's practice do this? This is easily achieved by having separate bank accounts: one for the solicitor's own money (the Office account) and, one for all third party money (the Client account).

Solicitors' Accounts Rules 1998

Rule 1 – Principles

A *solicitor* must comply with the requirements of rule 1 of the Solicitors' Code of Conduct 2007, and in particular must:

. . . .

   (b) keep other people's money safely in a *bank* or *building society* account identifiable as a *client account* (except when the rules specifically provide otherwise);

Solicitors' Accounts Rules 1998

Rule 14 – Client accounts

   (1) A *solicitor* who holds or receives *client money* must keep one or more *client accounts* . . .

   (2) A 'client account' is an account of a practice kept at a *bank* or *building society* for holding *client money* in accordance with the requirements of this part of the rules.

   (3) The client account(s) of:

   . . .

   and the name of the account must also include the word 'client'.

   . . .

In conjunction with Rule 1(a) and 1(b) and Rule 14 the Client account may only be used for holding *client money*; the Client account must be a bank or building society account, and the name of the account must clearly state that it is a Client account. Solicitors must maintain integrity and the trust of their clients, something that becomes much more important when the solicitor is holding money for, or on behalf of, a client. These overriding principles of the Solicitors' Accounts Rules 1998 seek to ensure that all practices maintain such levels of integrity.

Essential Principles

All terms that are *italicised* in the Solicitors' Accounts Rules 1998 are defined in Rule 2 – Interpretation.

As you will see from Rule 2, the SARs are to be interpreted by reference to the notes. The notes are set out below each of the individual rules of the SARs and provide considerable guidance on the application of the SARs; be sure to always read the notes as you read each rule.

Solicitors' Accounts Rules 1998

Rule 2 – Interpretation

(1) The notes form part of the rules and are mandatory.

Before we examine dual ledgers, there is one further rule that we need to consider:

Solicitors' Accounts Rules 1998

Rule 32 – Accounting records for client accounts, etc.

Account records which must be kept

(1) A *solicitor* must keep at all times accounting records properly written up to show the *solicitor's* dealings with:

    (a) *client money* received, held or paid by the *solicitor*; including *client money* held outside a *client account* under rule 16(1)(a) or rule 17(ca); and

    . . .

(2) All dealings with *client money* must be appropriately recorded:

    (a) in a client cash account or in a record of sums transferred from one client ledger account to another; and

    (b) on the client side of a separate client ledger account for each *client* (or other person, or *trust*).

No other entries may be made in these records.

Rule 32 of the SARs requires solicitors to identify clearly and keep separate money belonging to clients and money belonging to the practice. As we will see as we become more familiar with the SARs, to do otherwise would be a breach of the SARs.

So how do the requirements of Rules 1(a) and (b) and 32 of the SARs translate into a ledger? If we now look at the Cash book of Hawkins & Co., Solicitors, in Example 2.1, we will be able to see how the dual ledger system is constructed and works in practice. The Cash book and Client ledgers will all consist of two 'sides': the Office account and the Client account – each of which will be used for a particular purpose and which will be a separate bank account.

Example 2.1

> **Office account:** to record the activity of the business and any expenditure made on behalf of a client

Cash book: Hawkins & Co.

Date	Detail	Office account			Client account		
		Dr (£)	Cr (£)	Bal (£)	Dr (£)	Cr (£)	Bal (£)
Sept 1	Balance b/d			10,580.00Cr			180,500.00Dr

> **Client account:** only *client* money will be deposited into this account (with some exceptions). It will only be used when money held for the client is permitted to be used on that client's behalf

You will also see that both accounts have the familiar Debit (Dr) and Credit (Cr) columns. These will be used exactly as before. The only difference is that you must now decide which account you may use when you are seeking to deposit or withdraw money – this will be dependent on whether you have received, are allowed, or are intending, to use *client* or *office* money.

But before we look at what *client* and *office* money is, it is important to note the difference in the balances of both accounts.

The Cash book will show how much the practice is holding within each account. For example, the Cash book of Hawkins & Co., in Example 2.1 above shows a balance in the Office account of £10,580Cr. You should be able to recognize that a credit balance means that the practice has withdrawn more money than it has within the Office account, and consequently has gone into its overdraft facility, i.e. it is £10,580 overdrawn. It is perfectly acceptable for the Office account to have a credit balance, and in fact it is not an uncommon feature of business. Many practices may during the course of the financial year make use of their overdraft facility whilst they await payment from clients.

By contrast, the Client account has a balance of £180,500Dr. If the Office account credit balance means it is in overdraft, then obviously a debit balance means that the account has funds in it. In this case Hawkins & Co. is holding a total of £180,500 on behalf of its clients. It is now worth noting a further overriding principle set out in Rule 1.

> ### Solicitors' Accounts Rules 1998
>
> **Rule 1 – Principles**
>
> The following principles must be observed. A solicitor must:
>
> . . . .
>
>   (c) use each *client's* money for that *client's* matters only;

The importance of Rule 1(c) cannot be overstated. This Rule means that a solicitor may only withdraw money from the Client account if he/she is holding money for a particular client and is intending to use that client's own money on that client's matter. To withdraw money from the Client account for use for a client when no money is being held for that client means the solicitor has used another client's money.

Rule 1(c) has two consequences set out in the Essential Principles box below.

> ### Essential Principles
>
> Cash book: Client account must always have a debit (Dr) balance.
>
> Client ledger: Client account must always have a credit (Cr) or zero balance.
>
> Any other balance in either ledger means the practice will be in breach of the Solicitors' Accounts Rules 1998, Rule 1(c).

So let's now look at how a Client ledger is used under the dual ledger system. We will do this by looking at it together with the Cash book, which has slightly more entries. Both the Cash book and the Client ledger can be seen in Example 2.2.

Example 2.2

> Note the manner of referring to clients: Surname, Initial

Cash book: Hawkins & Co.

Date	Detail	Office account			Client account		
		Dr (£)	Cr (£)	Bal (£)	Dr (£)	Cr (£)	Bal (£)
Sept 1	Balance b/d			10,580.00Cr			180,500.00Dr
Sept 5	Yates, S.		100.00	10,680.00Cr			
Sept 8	Yates, S.		50.00	10,730.00Cr			
Sept 10	Yates, S.				2,500.00		183,000.00Dr

> Money received from the client on account of costs, client money (SAR 13(a), note (d)), therefore paid into Client account

> Office money used on behalf of Yates, S. as at the date of payment no client money is held for Yates, S.

Client: Yates, S.

Date	Detail	Office account			Client account		
		Dr (£)	Cr (£)	Bal (£)	Dr (£)	Cr (£)	Bal (£)
Sept 5	Cash: court fee	100.00		100.00Dr			
Sept 8	Cash: personal search	50.00		150.00Dr			
Sept 10	Cash: on account of costs					2,500.00	2,500.00Cr
Sept 12	Costs	1,500.00		1,650.00Dr			
Sept 12	VAT	262.50		1,912.50Dr			

> Total debt owed by Yates, S. includes both office money spent on her behalf, costs, and VAT

> Note Detail column: the Cash book and the purpose for which money spent or received are identified

In looking at Sarah Yates' Client ledger in Example 2.2, it is immediately evident that no client money is being held on her behalf. If it were, such monies would be identified in the Balance column of the Client account in the Client ledger – it is then important to ascertain the purpose for which the client money has been provided; this is a matter that we will cover in Section 3 below. As a consequence of not holding client money for Sarah, the two transactions made on her behalf on 5 and 8 September were made using the practice's own money from the Office account. The corresponding entries for these transactions are then recorded on Sarah's ledger in the Office account. This ensures that a clear distinction may be drawn between money spent using the practice's own office money and the money held (or maybe spent) on the client's behalf, and so ensures compliance with the SARs.

The following points are also worth noting:

- The normal rules of double entry book-keeping apply: each transaction has two components, i.e. a debit and a credit entry, and the balances have been added up according to the principles we have been using to date.

- The corresponding ledgers have also been identified in the Detail column, with more detail being included in the Client ledger – this serves a number of purposes:
  - It allows for the money which has been used to be identified, which will also be useful when preparing a bill of costs to send to the client.
  - It identifies the purpose for which the client may have provided money to the practice.
  - As we will see later in Section 3, it complies with certain requirements of the SARs to *clearly* and/or *appropriately* identify monies deposited into the Client account.

Monies: SAR 13

There is a difference between the types of money that we are now going to be using, as defined by Rule 13 of the SARs.

Solicitors' Accounts Rules 1998

Rule 13 – Categories of money

All money held or received in the course of practice falls into one or other of the following categories:

(a) 'client money' – money held or received for a *client* or as *trustee*, and all other money which is not *office money*; or

(b) 'office money' – money which belongs to the *solicitor* or the practice.

It is important that you also read the notes to Rule 13, as these provide considerable guidance on what is *client* and *office* money. Notes (i) and (xi) should be carefully read and their contents noted.

To help you differentiate between the categories of money, you should now consider undertaking Exercise 1 to gain a greater understanding of the different types of monies that we will be handling.

> Before we move on to learn how to work with dual ledgers, it is important that we first gain an understanding of the different types of monies that we will be working with. Set out below is a list of statements to test your understanding of the distinctions between client, office, and controlled trust monies — we will continually be referring to the Solicitors' Accounts Rules 1998 (SARs) classification of monies (SAR 13), and the definitions (SAR 2), and you are to start to use them in this exercise. The more familiar you become with the SARs, the easier Solicitors' Accounts will become. Once you have understood the types of monies that you are dealing with, you will then understand more about whether you will be depositing the money into a Client only account or an Office account.
>
> Drag the words 'Client money', and 'Office money' and drop them next to the statements to which you think they apply. When you are happy with your selection, click the 'Submit' button at the bottom of your screen to view your scores and see feedback on your answers.

Money received ready to complete the purchase of a property.	Client money / Office money
Money received on account of costs.	Client money / Office money
Money received in respect of fees due against an invoice.	Client money / Office money
Money received by the firm following the sale of trust investments, for which two of the firm's partners are co-trustees.	Client money / Office money
Money received in connection with advising a trust from a firm of accountants who are co-trustees of that trust.	Client money / Office money
Money received from a client following an oral agreement with a partner of the firm to undertake work for the client.	Client money / Office money

From now on, we will continually be referring to the Solicitors' Accounts Rules classification of monies and its definitions – the more familiar you become with the SARs, the easier *LPC Accounts Online* will become. Once you are familiar with the categories of monies, you will then be able to understand whether money is to be deposited into the Office account or the Client account.

Dual ledger entries

As we have briefly seen above, the same double entry principles that we have been using to date will continue to apply to dual ledgers, the only difference being that money will be withdrawn or deposited in either the Office or Client account of the ledger. Before we move on to the exercises on this topic, let's reaffirm our understanding of the principles applied in making the entries in the conduct of Sarah Yates' matter.

Let's look at two in particular: the entries made on 8 September the withdrawal of office money, and 10 September the deposit of client monies. Taking the withdrawal of office money first, review the entries that have been made in Example 2.3 and follow the sequence of entries set out below:

- Cash transaction, start with Cash book:
  — No client money being held on behalf of Yates, S., so office money must be used; entries must be made in Office account of Cash book;
  — Enter date and identify corresponding ledger, Yates, S.;
  — Money out = credit entry, £50;
  — Credit on a credit balance, makes a bigger credit balance.
- Corresponding entry, Client ledger:
  — No client money being held on behalf of Yates, S., so office money was used; corresponding entry must therefore be made in Office account of Client ledger;
  — Enter date and identify corresponding ledger, Cash, and purpose for which money was withdrawn i.e. personal search;
  — Money out/debt due to practice = debit entry, £50;
  — Debit on a debit balance, makes a bigger debit balance.

Now looking at the deposit of money received from the client on 10 September, for which the Client account must be used, the entries are as follows:

- Cash transaction, start with Cash book:
  — Money to be held on account of costs, SAR 13(a), note (i)(d), so entries to be made in Client account of Cash book;
  — Enter date and identify corresponding ledger, Yates, S.;
  — Money in = debit entry, £2,500;
  — Debit on a debit balance, makes a bigger debit balance.
- Corresponding entry, Client ledger:
  — Money to be held on account of costs, SAR 13(a), note (i)(d), so entry to be made in Client account of Client ledger;
  — Enter date and identify corresponding ledger, Cash, and purpose for which money was received, i.e. on account of costs;
  — Money in = credit entry, £2,500;
  — Credit on a zero balance, makes a credit balance.

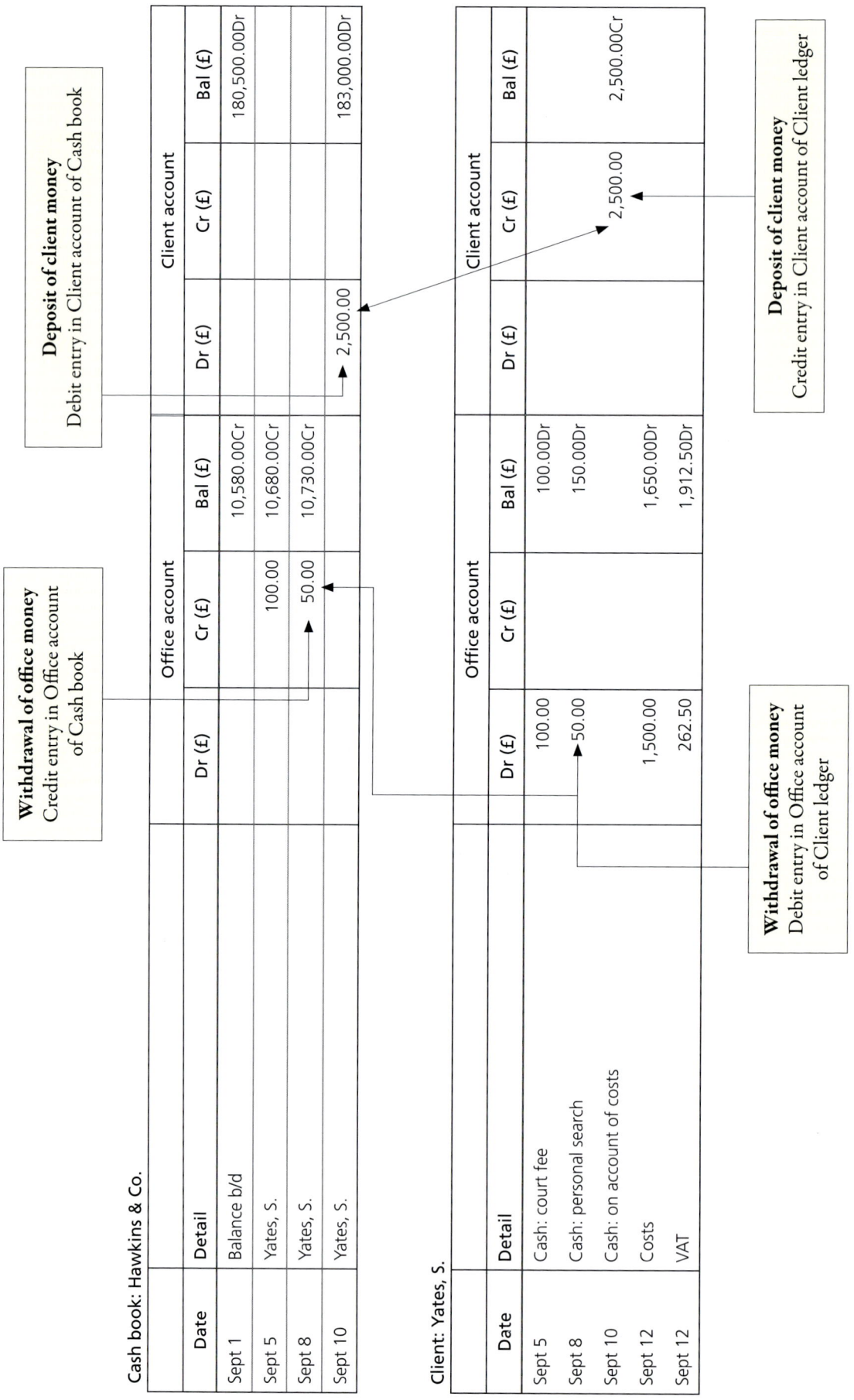

Example 2.3

Cash book: Hawkins & Co.

Date	Detail	Office account			Client account		
		Dr (£)	Cr (£)	Bal (£)	Dr (£)	Cr (£)	Bal (£)
Sept 1	Balance b/d			10,580.00Cr			180,500.00Dr
Sept 5	Yates, S.		100.00	10,680.00Cr			
Sept 8	Yates, S.		50.00	10,730.00Cr			
Sept 10	Yates, S.				2,500.00		183,000.00Dr

Withdrawal of office money
Credit entry in Office account of Cash book

Deposit of client money
Debit entry in Client account of Cash book

Client: Yates, S.

Date	Detail	Office account			Client account		
		Dr (£)	Cr (£)	Bal (£)	Dr (£)	Cr (£)	Bal (£)
Sept 5	Cash: court fee	100.00		100.00Dr			
Sept 8	Cash: personal search	50.00		150.00Dr			
Sept 10	Cash: on account of costs					2,500.00	2,500.00Cr
Sept 12	Costs	1,500.00		1,650.00Dr			
Sept 12	VAT	262.50		1,912.50Dr			

Withdrawal of office money
Debit entry in Office account of Client ledger

Deposit of client money
Credit entry in Client account of Client ledger

There are two further SARs that should now be noted:

Solicitors' Accounts Rules 1998

Rule 2 – Interpretation

(2) In the rules, unless the context otherwise requires:

. . .

    (z) 'without delay' means, in normal circumstances, either on the day of receipt or on the next working day; and

. . .

Rule 15 – Use of a client account

(1) *Client money* must *without delay* be paid into a *client account*, and must be held in a *client account*, except when the rules provide to the contrary (see rules 9,10,16,17,19, and 21).

As a consequence of Rule 15, interpreted by reference to Rule 2(2)(z), when Sarah sent Hawkins & Co. £2,500 to be held on account of costs, the practice was under an obligation to ensure that it was deposited *without delay*, having been identified as *client money*, into the Client account and accordingly credited in Sarah's ledger.

Now is an appropriate juncture for you to attempt Exercise 2 online. This exercise will introduce you to making entries in dual ledgers, using both Office and Client accounts for a number of clients. As you make the entries, ensure that you are identifying and categorising the money you are using by reference to the SARs, and not just making informed guesses – the more familiar you are with the categories of money, the easier you will find the use of dual ledgers. Also ensure that you follow the conventions used for recording dates, corresponding ledgers, and recording whether a balance is a debit or credit balance.

(i) In this exercise you will be introduced to the dual ledger system, showing Office and Client accounts and the making of simple entries for a number of clients. As you progress through this section you should seek to improve your understanding of the Solicitors' Accounts Rules 1998 (SARs), as many of the entries you will make will be based upon them and their interpretation.

Read the question below and the transactions that follow. When you are ready, click on the 'Your ledgers' tab above or the 'Complete your ledgers' button at the bottom of your screen to see the various ledgers in which you are required to record the transactions below by selecting the correct entry from the options available. For each transaction you should identify which ledger, and which side of the ledger, you are to use. You will also need to decide whether any receipt is office money or client money and, when a payment is made by you as a solicitor, whether you can use office or client money. Reference to SAR 13 may help you in this instance. When you are happy with the ledgers you have created, click 'Submit' at the bottom of your screen to see your feedback and score.

Don't forget, you can click 'Save' at any point if you want to come back to this exercise later.

(?) During October, you made the following entries. Record the entries by selecting the correct entry from the options available, taking care to identify which is client money and which is office money.

- Oct 4   Paid local search fee of £100 for George Williams.
- Oct 5   Received £500 on account of costs from Sarah Yates.
- Oct 6   Paid deposit of £5,000 on exchange of contracts for Cheryl Cheasley's new house purchase.
- Oct 7   Received £150 from Michael Morton to reimburse an expert's fee paid on his behalf last month.
- Oct 8   Received £4,000 from Jackwood Ltd to settle a debt due to your client Fast Food plc.
- Oct 11   Paid an expert's fee of £200 on behalf of Sarah Yates.

Save	Print		Complete your ledgers

Take care that you do not make the mistakes that are often made as this stage of *LPC Accounts Online*. These include depositing/withdrawing money from the wrong account, or when making the two entries, making one in the Client account and the other in the Office account. When making an entry you will only ever be making entries in one account (e.g. if a credit in the Office account of the Cash book, then a debit in the Office account of the Client ledger).

Recording credit transactions

Now that you have undertaken exercises in identifying categories of money and making basic double entries using the dual ledger system, let's now look at the recording of a credit transaction (i.e. the issuing of invoice) in dual ledgers.

Consider the basic principles of double entry book-keeping that we have applied so far to dual ledgers; the recording of credit transactions is no different. The only note of caution is that credit transactions (i.e. the issue of the invoice) will only ever be recorded in the Office account of the Client ledger – the practice will *never* take its costs directly out of the Client account, even if money is held on account of costs. Why is this? Rule 19, which we will look at in more detail in section 3 of *LPC Accounts Online*, dictates so.

If we look again at Sarah's ledger in Example 2.4, we will see that the practice's costs incurred in the conduct of her matter, and the VAT on those costs, are recorded in the Office account of the Client ledger. As before, the corresponding entries will be made in the Sales or Costs ledger and the VAT ledger. Only when Sarah settles her debt will the Cash book be used.

Example 2.4

Cash book: Hawkins & Co.

Date	Detail	Office account			Client account		
		Dr (£)	Cr (£)	Bal (£)	Dr (£)	Cr (£)	Bal (£)
Sept 1	Balance b/d			10,580.00Cr			180,500.00Dr
Sept 5	Yates, S.		100.00	10,680.00Cr			
Sept 8	Yates, S.		50.00	10,730.00Cr			
Sept 10	Yates, S.				2,500.00		183,000.00Dr

Client: Yates, S.

Date	Detail	Office account			Client account		
		Dr (£)	Cr (£)	Bal (£)	Dr (£)	Cr (£)	Bal (£)
Sept 5	Cash: court fee	100.00		100.00Dr			
Sept 8	Cash: personal search	50.00		150.00Dr			
Sept 10	Cash: on account of cost					2,500.00	2,500.00Cr
Sept 12	Costs	1,500.00		1,650.00Dr			
Sept 12	VAT	262.50		1,912.50Dr			

Costs and VAT on costs recorded in Office account of Client ledger.
Note: no entry will be made in the Cash book until the debt is paid by the client

Corresponding entry made in VAT ledger

Corresponding entry made in Costs ledger

Exercises 3 and 4 will now give you the opportunity to practise making double entries in dual ledgers to record both cash and credit transactions. Both exercises will also require you to consider whether you are able to use money that has been provided to you by clients for a particular purpose. To assist you in your deliberations, read Rule 22(1)(a) to see whether you are able to use such monies.

We will continue with a basic exercise relating to the dual ledger system, using both the Office and Client accounts. As you progress through this section you should seek to improve your understanding of the Solicitors' Accounts Rules 1998 (SARs), as many of the entries you will make will be based upon them and their interpretation.

Read the question below and the transactions that follow. When you are ready, click on the 'Your ledgers' tab above or the 'Complete your ledgers' button at the bottom of your screen to see the various ledgers in which you are required to record the transactions linked to the purchase of Ms McGuiness's flat by selecting the correct entry from the options available. For each transaction you should identify which ledger, and which side of the ledger, you are to use. You will also need to decide whether any receipt is office money or client money and, when a payment is made by you as a solicitor, whether you can use office or client money. Reference to SAR 13 and SAR 22 may help you in this instance. When you are happy with the ledgers you have created, click 'Submit' at the bottom of your screen to see your feedback and score.

Don't forget, you can click 'Save' at any point if you want to come back to this exercise later.

You are instructed by Ms McGuiness in connection with her flat purchase. You currently hold £12,000 as part of the deposit to be paid on exchange. Please record the following ledger entries by selecting the correct entry from the options available:

- June 1   Paid local land charges search fee of £200 to the relevant local council for a local search certificate.

- June 8   Paid for official copies of the registers of title to the flat, the fee being £12.

- June 10 Received Ms McGuiness's cheque for £20,000 to be used as part of the amount required for the deposit to be paid on exchange of contracts on the purchase of the flat.

- June 15 Exchanged contracts on behalf of Ms McGuiness for the purchase of the flat and paid the deposit of £32,000.

- June 19 Paid for Land Registry search certificate against flat; the fee for the search was £6.

- June 20 Sent Ms McGuiness invoice for £1,000 profit costs plus £175 VAT and disbursements paid for the purchase of flat.

Cash book: Hawkins & Co.

			Office account	
Date	Detail		Dr (£)	Cr (£)
Oct 1	Balance b/d			
Oct				

Client: Laurie Catchpole   **Matter: Sale of Unit 7D, Codling's Industrial Units, Wapping & purchase of 43 Royal Exchange**

			Office account	
Date	Detail		Dr (£)	Cr (£)

Once you have completed Exercises 3 and 4, undertake Exercises 5 and 6. Exercise 5 will test your understanding of the SARs that we have looked at and will require some careful reading of Rule 19, which we will then look at in more detail in section 3 of *LPC Accounts Online*.

This exercise sets out a number of multiple-choice questions to help you apply basic double entry accounting principles in the context of dual ledgers and consider the relevant Solicitors' Accounts Rules (SAR). Answer each of the questions in turn. When you are happy with your answers, click the 'Submit' button at the bottom of the screen to view your score and receive feedback on your answers.

Question 1
Which one of the following is not client money?

○ Stakeholder money.

○ Money to pay a solicitor's bill of costs.

○ A payment generally on account of costs.

○ A payment for Land Registry fees.

Question 2
Which one of the following is not office money?

○ Money to pay a solicitor's bill of costs.

○ A payment to reimburse the solicitor for a disbursement already paid.

○ Interest accrued on a general Client account.

○ A payment for unpaid professional disbursements.

Question 3
Tommy Jones sends a solicitor a cheque for £235 in satisfaction of the solicitor's bill for profit costs and VAT. Which one of the following statements is correct?

○ The cheque is client money and must be paid into the Client bank account without delay.

Exercise 6 is a longer exercise designed to test all of your knowledge to date, and which will require you to record a number of transactions on the dual ledgers provided.

Cash book: Hawkins & Co.

		Office account	
Date	Detail	Dr (£)	Cr (£)
July 2	Balance b/d		
July			

Conclusion

The introduction of dual ledgers should hopefully not be unduly complicated. They are ledgers that identify two different bank accounts: the Office account and the Client account. In essence they are a new form of ledger which has three extra columns included within it and which requires the application of a number of new rules. At this stage, we are primarily required to ascertain whether the money is to be paid into either of the two accounts. Once this has been decided, it is simply a matter of posting the double entry to the correct side of the ledgers.

The next section of *LPC Accounts Online* will introduce us to more of the SARs and their application.

Section 3

Solicitors' Accounts Rules 1998

Exercise map

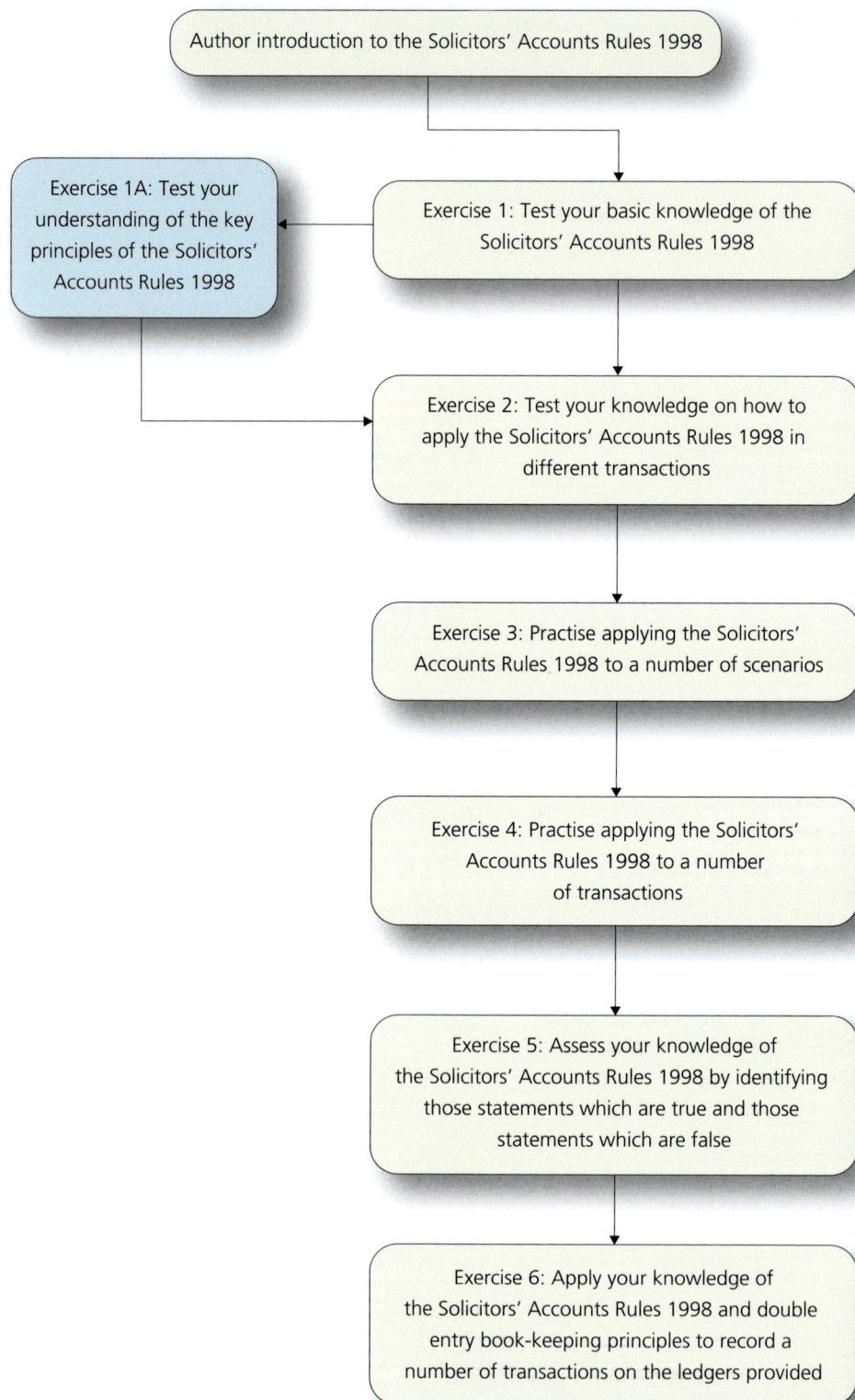

Author introduction to the Solicitors' Accounts Rules 1998

Exercise 1A: Test your understanding of the key principles of the Solicitors' Accounts Rules 1998

Exercise 1: Test your basic knowledge of the Solicitors' Accounts Rules 1998

Exercise 2: Test your knowledge on how to apply the Solicitors' Accounts Rules 1998 in different transactions

Exercise 3: Practise applying the Solicitors' Accounts Rules 1998 to a number of scenarios

Exercise 4: Practise applying the Solicitors' Accounts Rules 1998 to a number of transactions

Exercise 5: Assess your knowledge of the Solicitors' Accounts Rules 1998 by identifying those statements which are true and those statements which are false

Exercise 6: Apply your knowledge of the Solicitors' Accounts Rules 1998 and double entry book-keeping principles to record a number of transactions on the ledgers provided

Introduction

In section 2 of *LPC Accounts Online*, we started to look at, and use, the Solicitors' Accounts Rules 1998 (SARs). From this brief introduction, it will have been evident why solicitors are required to use the dual ledger system of double entry book-keeping, particularly given the need to categorise money that the practice receives and manages, and the requirements to keep such monies separate.

The SARs, created under s 32 Solicitors Act 1974, impose further restrictions on when money may be used by the practice and the requirement that it be *clearly* or *appropriately* identified when recorded on ledgers. It is these further rules that we will concentrate on in this section.

As you undertake the exercises associated with this section make sure that you read the SARs that have been identified for you. It is only by becoming familiar with the SARs that you will fully appreciate how and why you will make your entries.

Solicitors' Accounts Rules 1998

Whilst we have already briefly looked at the principles of the SARs, it is worth reminding ourselves of the key principles and how they apply.

Principles and compliance

The key principles are set out in Rule 1, which requires the solicitor to comply with the Solicitors' code of Conduct 2007, and thereby act with integrity and, in so doing, act in the client's best interest and maintain public trust in the solicitor's profession.

> ### Solicitors' Accounts Rules 1998
>
> **Rule 1 – Principles**
>
> A *solicitor* must comply with the requirements of rule 1 of the Solicitors' Code of Conduct 2007, and in particular must:
>
> . . .

In conjunction with Rule 32, Rule 1(a)–(c) and (e) establishes the requirement that solicitors' practice must operate an accounting system to keep client money separate. Such money must be kept in a separate bank account to money belonging to the practice. It is because of these rules that the dual ledger system must be used.

> ### Solicitors' Accounts Rules 1998
>
> **Rule 1 – Principles**
>
> . . .
>
> (a) keep other people's money separate from money belonging to the *solicitor* or the practice;
>
> (b) keep other people's money safely in a *bank* or *building society* account identifiable as a *client account* (except when the rules specifically provide otherwise);
>
> (c) use each *client's* money for that *client's* matters only;
>
> . . . .
>
> (e) establish and maintain proper accounting systems, and proper internal controls over those systems, to ensure compliance with the rules;

Rule 1(e) particularly requires the practice to establish internal controls to ensure compliance with the SARs – it is, however, all too frequent that the *Law Society Gazette* reports on individuals and practices that have failed to comply with the SARs. You will be in a position of trust, and it is important you maintain that trust with your clients when you handle their money. But to whom do the SARs apply?

As with all legislation you should always check that it applies to you. Rule 3 governs the geographical scope of the SARs, namely to any practice carried on from an office in England and Wales. Rule 4 states that the SARs apply to 'solicitors of the Supreme Court or registered European lawyers'. By reference to the notes (if we recall, Rule 2(1) states that the notes to the SARs form part of the rules and are mandatory), note (i) to Rule 4 states that 'all employees of a recognised body are directly subject to the rules'. For all purposes, you should be satisfied that this will include you, even while you are training to be a solicitor.

There are some exceptions to whom the SARs apply, and these are set out in Rule 5. However, for the purposes of *LPC Accounts Online* you are to assume that these exceptions will not apply to you – therefore we need to continue to understand the SARs.

Rule 6 goes further and requires the principals (i.e. partners or those being held out as partners) in a practice to ensure compliance with the SARs.

> ### Solicitors' Accounts Rules 1998
>
> **Rule 6 – Principals' responsibility for compliance**
>
> All the *principals* in a practice must ensure compliance with the rules by the *principals* themselves and by everyone employed in the practice. . . .

This requirement therefore places a collective obligation on all principals to ensure that the SARs are complied with and, as we will see, to remedy breaches. Ignorance of a misdemeanour will not be a defence for a principal given such stringent responsibility to comply with the SARs.

Duty to remedy breaches

What happens should there be a breach of the SARs? The extent to which principals are to be held collectively responsible is set out in Rule 7.

Solicitors' Accounts Rules 1998

Rule 7 – Duty to remedy breaches

(1) Any breach of the rules must be remedied promptly upon discovery. This includes the replacement of any money improperly withheld or withdrawn from a client account.

(2) In a private practice, the duty to remedy breaches rests not only on the person causing the breach, but also on all the *principals* in the practice. This duty extends to replacing missing *client money* from the *principals'* own resources, even if the money has been misappropriated by an employee or another *principal*, and whether or not a claim is subsequently made on the Solicitors' Indemnity or Compensation Funds or on the *firm's* insurance.

. . . .

Rule 7 therefore requires all breaches to be remedied as soon as they are discovered, even if this means that the principals must, from their own pockets, make good any funds missing from the Client account. What should be obvious is the paramount importance that the SARs place on ensuring that client money is safeguarded.

If you are fortunate enough to be invited to become a partner of a practice, consider carefully who it is that you are invited by and investigate carefully their compliance with the SARs – you would not want any nasty surprises after you had become a partner!

Categories of money

In section 2 you will already have looked at Rule 13, and the categorization of money held or received in the course of practice. We will not revisit this aspect of the SARs, other than to remind ourselves of the categories of money and that you will continually be referring to Rule 13 and its notes.

Solicitors' Accounts Rules 1998

Rule 13 – Categories of money

All money held or received in the course of practice falls into one or other of the following categories:

(a) 'client money' – money held or received for a *client*, and all other money which is not *office money*; or

(b) 'office money' – money which belongs to the *solicitor* or the practice.

Receipt of money from clients

The SARs are generally not concerned with the expenditure the practice will incur in its day-to-day running – other than the overriding principle that office money must be kept separate from client money. The SARs are focused on the protection and use of client money held or received by the practice, and it is these aspects which we now consider in the following section.

Use of a Client account

Whilst it may appear obvious, it is worth stating that a Client account is for *client money*. Subject to some notable exceptions under Rules 19 and 20, which we will look at below, this principle is affirmed in Rule 15.

Solicitors' Accounts Rules 1998

Rule 15 – Use of a client account

(1) *Client money* must *without delay* be paid into a *client account*, and must be held in a *client account*, except when the rules provide to the contrary (see rules 9,10,16,17, 19 and 21).

(2) Only *client money* may be paid into or held in a *client account*, except:

…

and except when the rules provide to the contrary (see note (iv) below).

(3) *Client money* must be returned to the *client* (or other person on whose behalf the money is held) promptly, as soon as there is no longer any proper reason to retain those funds. Payment received after the *solicitor* has already accounted to the *client*, for example by way of a refund, must be paid to the *client* promptly.

(4) A *solicitor* must promptly inform a *client* (or other person on whose behalf the money is held) in writing of the amount of any *client money* retained at the end of a matter (or the substantial conclusion of a matter), and the reason for that retention. The *solicitor* must inform the *client* (or other person) in writing at least once every twelve months thereafter of the amount of *client money* still held and the reason for the retention, for as long as the *solicitor* continues to hold that money.

…

As we have already seen, the primary obligation under Rule 15, interpreted by reference to Rule 2(2)(z), is that a practice is required to ensure that client money is deposited *without delay* into the Client account and accordingly credited in the Client ledger. This is a good example of one of the requirements that a practice must meet to ensure compliance with the SARs. Often a practice will require its post room to open the daily delivery of post and ensure that all cheques and banker's drafts are conveyed to the accounts department for processing and banking, rather than risk having unopened post lying in a recipient's in-tray who may be in a meeting or on holiday. Accordingly, practices can ensure all client money can be banked *without delay* in a general holding Client account and then credited to the correct Client account.

It is also worth noting the positive obligation upon a practice that Rule 15(3) and (4) imposes. Once the practice has no further reason to hold client money for a client, such monies must be returned promptly (Rule 15(3)). However, note (ix) to Rule 15 also reminds the practice that it is under a duty to act in the best interests of its clients and that it may need to take instructions as to whether the money should be returned or retained. In any event, should such client money be retained, Rule 15(4) requires the practice to keep the client informed on an annual basis that it is holding client money.

Receiving money from clients

It is Rule 19 on which we must now focus.

Solicitors' Accounts Rules 1998

Rule 19 – Receipt and transfer of costs

(1) A *solicitor* who receives money paid in full or in part settlement of the *solicitor's* bill (or other notification of *costs*) **must follow one of the following four options:**

 (a) **determine the composition of the payment** *without delay*, **and deal with the money accordingly:**

  (i) if the sum comprises *office money* only, it must be placed in an *office account*;

  (ii) if the sum comprises only *client money* (for example an unpaid *professional disbursement* – see rule 2(2)(s), and note (v) to rule 2), the entire sum must be placed in a *client account*;

  (iii) if the sum includes both *office money* and *client money* (such as unpaid *professional disbursements*; purchase money; or payments in advance for court fees, stamp duty, Land Registry registration fees or telegraphic transfer fess), the solicitor must follow rule 20 (receipt of mixed payments); **or**

 (b) **ascertain that the payment comprises only** *office money*, **and/or** *client money* **in the form of** *professional disbursements* **incurred but not yet paid, and deal with the payment as follows:**

  (i) place the entire sum in an *office account* at a *bank* or *building society* branch (or head office) in England and Wales; and

  (ii) by the end of the second working day following receipt, either pay any unpaid *professional disbursement*, or transfer a sum for its settlement to a *client account*; **or**

 (c) **pay the entire sum into a client account (regardless of its composition), and transfer any** *office* **money out of the** *client account* **within 14 days of receipt; or**

 (d) **on receipt of costs from the Legal Services Commission, follow the options in rule 21(1)(b).**

 . . .

Note: the emphasis in bold is as per the SARs and has not been added for effect.

Before we look at the effect of Rule 19 in more detail, we will eliminate two of its provisions for the purposes of *LPC Accounts Online*. Rule 19(1)(c) may in fact be what most practices follow to ensure that they comply with the requirements of Rule 15, but it is not a rule that we will employ during *LPC Accounts Online*. Rule 19(1)(d) will also be outside the scope of *LPC Accounts Online*.

It is Rule 19(1)(a) and (b) that we will now examine further and apply.

It is important to appreciate first that the practice has an obligation to determine the composition of the money it receives from a client (Rule 19(1)(a)). It must do so *without delay* (Rule 2(2)(z)), and then deal with the money in accordance with one of the three options set out under Rule 19(1)(a) or (b). Let's examine at each in turn.

Receipt of office money or client money only

Should you be in receipt of either *office money* or *client money* only, then such money should respectively be paid into either the *Office account* (Rule 19(1)(a)(i)) or the *Client account* (Rule 19(1)(a)(ii)).

To ensure compliance with Rule 19(1)(a)(i) and (ii), you will need to consider carefully Rule 13 and its notes to determine whether the money you have received is only *office money* or *client money*.

Receipt of both office money and client money

Clients will rarely differentiate between the categories of money that they are sending you, and a cheque from your client may comprise different categories of money. Upon receipt of such a cheque you need to determine its composition. Should you decide that the money is both *office money* and *client money*, then Rule 19(1)(a)(iii) requires that Rule 20 should be followed.

Solicitors' Accounts Rules 1998

Rule 20 – Receipt of mixed payments

(1) A 'mixed payment' is one which includes *client money* as well as *office money*.

(2) A *mixed payment* must either:

   (a) be split between a *client account* and *office account* as appropriate; or

   (b) be placed *without delay* in a *client account*.

(3) If the entire payment is placed in *client account*, all *office money* must be transferred out of the *client account* within 14 days of receipt.

. . .

By virtue of Rule 20, money that comprises both *office money* and *client money* is a *mixed payment*. As such, the money should be deposited in the Client account, in accordance with Rule 20(2)(b) – in practice, to split a cheque and so comply with Rule 20(2)(a) is an expense that a practice will rarely assume. Accordingly, Rule 20(2)(b) will always be followed on receipt of a *mixed payment*.

While it would appear that a deposit of a *mixed payment* in the Client account is in breach of Rule 15, which requires that only *client money* be paid in the Client account, note (iv) to Rule 15 provides that this is one of the exceptions to Rule 15.

However, two further rules must be complied with after Rule 20(2)(b) has been applied. First, the *office money* must be withdrawn from the Client account within 14 days of receipt of the *mixed payment* (Rule 20(3)). This 14 days gives the practice time to ensure that the money deposited has cleared, and that the practice does not then withdraw against a cheque that may not be honoured.

The second additional rule is contained in note (iv) to Rule 32.

Solicitors' Accounts Rules 1998

Rule 32 – Accounting records for client accounts, etc.

Notes

. . .

(iv) For the purpose of rule 32, money which has been paid into a client account under rule 19(1)(c) (receipt of costs), or under rule 20(2)(b) (mixed money), and for the time being remains in a client account, is to be treated as client money; it should be recorded on the client side of the client ledger account, but must be appropriately identified.

. . .

But what does 'appropriately identified' mean? In practice, it means that the portion of the money paid into the Client account that is office money must be identified. This is achieved by adding further explanatory detail in to the Detail column of the Client ledger. For example, if a client has sent a cheque for £81,121.33 which covers both the completion costs on a property purchase (which includes the outstanding amount required to complete, stamp duty land tax, and Land Registry fees, etc.), and the settlement of the practice's costs and VAT in conducting the matter of £8,301.33, the Detail column in the Client ledger should appear as in Example 3.1.

Example 3.1

Client: Yates, S.

Date	Detail	Office account	Client account
Date	Cash: balance to complete (£8,301.33 office money)		

The entry should:

- identify the corresponding ledger;
- state the purpose for which the money was received; and
- state how much office money has been deposited into the Client account, and accordingly be earmarked for withdrawal within 14 days of receipt.

To do otherwise would be a breach of the SARs.

Receipt of both office money and/or client money in the form of professional disbursement incurred but not yet paid

Rule 19(1)(b) raises one interesting anomaly within the SARs; it is the only time that *client money* may be paid into an Office account.

If it has been ascertained that money received from the client comprises both *office money* and *client money*, and the *client money* is only received for an unpaid *professional disbursement*, then it is possible to place all of the money into the *Office account* in accordance with Rule 19(1)(b)(i).

A professional disbursement is defined by Rule 2(2)(s).

Solicitors' Accounts Rules 1998

Rule 2 – Interpretation

(2) in the rules, unless the context otherwise requires:

. . .

(s) 'professional disbursement' means the fees of counsel or other lawyer, or of a professional or other agent or expert instructed by the *solicitor*.

As you are already aware, under note (i)(b) to Rule 13, money received for payment of an unpaid professional disbursement is *client money*.

The overriding condition for being permitted to pay *client money* into the Office account in these circumstances is that by the end of the second working day following receipt of the money, the unpaid *professional disbursement* must be paid, or the sum representing the unpaid *professional disbursement* must be transferred to a *Client account* (Rule 19(1)(b)(ii)).

So, whilst the money is permitted to be deposited in the Office account, in contrast to Rule 20(3) for the receipt of a mixed payment, there is no period of grace for the cheque to clear – again the paramount importance is the protection of *client money*, even if this means that office money is used for an interim period.

In addition to this requirement under Rule 19(1)(b)(ii), as you may have noted, the requirements for appropriately identifying the client money deposited into an Office account under note (iv) to Rule 32 apply. Accordingly, the Detail column would appear as in Example 3.2 below.

Example 3.2

Client: Yates, S.

Date	Detail	Office account	Client account
Date	Cash: costs (including client monies £3,000)		

Now is a suitable opportunity to attempt Exercises 1 and 2. Exercise 1 sets out a number of multiple-choice questions designed to test your understanding of the SARs.

ⓘ This exercise sets out a number of multiple-choice questions relating to the Solicitors' Accounts Rules 1998 (SAR). Taking time to select your answer, you should consider each in turn by reference to SAR 2, 7, 13, 15, 17, 19, 20, 24, and 32. When you are happy with your answers, click the 'Submit' button at the bottom of the screen to view your score and receive feedback on your answers.

⑦ **Question 1**
Which one of the following is *not* a mixed payment?

○ A sum received by your firm from your client for your firm's billed costs plus the balance of the money required to complete the purchase of his new home.

○ A sum paid by your firm on behalf of a client to the solicitor for the other party in court proceedings, amounting to £15,600, of which £12,100 represents the amount of the judgment awarded against your firm's client and the remaining £3,500 is the other party's costs.

○ A sum received by your firm for billed costs and unpaid counsel's fees.

○ A sum received by your firm, part of which is to reimburse a disbursement already incurred and the balance of which is money on account of costs.

⑦ **Question 2**
Which of the following statements is correct?

○ Trust money cannot be paid into a Client account.

○ Office money cannot be paid into a Client account to provide an initial balance when the account is opened at the bank.

○ Office money can be paid into a Client account to reimburse client money withdrawn in breach of the Solicitors' Accounts Rules 1998.

○ Controlled trust money cannot be paid into a Client account.

In Exercise 2 you will be required to consider the entries associated with one transaction, and identify the applicable SARs which must be followed to record each stage of the transaction to ensure that you do not breach the SARs.

Step	Activity: Receipt & Deposit of £3,172.50 from Archer, C.		Solicitors' Accounts Rule	
1.		▽		▽
2.		▽		▽
3.		▽		▽
4.		▽		▽
5.		▽		▽
6.		▽		▽
7.		▽		▽
8.		▽		▽
9.		▽		▽
10.		▽		▽

Back

Save	Print		If you are happy with your ledgers	Submit	Clear all

Withdrawing money from a Client account

Insofar as we have looked at compliance with the SARs and the use of *client money*, we have concentrated on the requirements for the determination and the deposit of *client money*.

However, it is not improbable that you will request money from your client in order to pay for disbursements that the client will need in the conduct of their matter, for example money on account of costs. As such it will be necessary to withdraw money from the Client account. This will require compliance with Rules 22 and 23.

Solicitors' Accounts Rules 1998

Rule 22 – Withdrawals from a client account

(1) *Client money* may only be withdrawn from a *client account* when it is:

    (a) properly required for a payment to or on behalf of the *client* (or other person on whose behalf the money is being held);

    (aa) properly required for a payment in the execution of a particular *trust*, including the purchase of an investment (other than money) in accordance with the *trustee's* powers;

    (b) properly required for a payment of a *disbursement* on behalf of the *client* or *trust*;

    . . . .

By virtue of Rule 22, *client money* may be withdrawn from a Client account provided it is required for a payment to or on behalf of the *client*. For example, client money may be withdrawn from a client account to pay your client the proceeds from a court settlement received in their favour or to pay, on your client's behalf, completion monies for the purchase of property.

It is also worth noting the provisions of Rule 22(2A) should the solicitor be in the position of holding not more than £50 in relation to any one individual client or trust matter. If so, provided certain conditions are fulfilled in relation to identifying and attempting to return the money to its rightful owner, such a sum may be withdrawn and paid to charity. The solicitor is required to comply with certain record-keeping requirements to evidence such attempts to return money and any subsequent withdrawals.

In addition to requiring a legitimate reason for the withdrawal of funds from the Client account, all such withdrawals will require a specific authority – a signed authority – from one of the four categories of individuals listed in Rule 23.

Solicitors' Accounts Rules 1998

Rule 23 – Method of authority for withdrawals from client account

(1) A withdrawal from a *client account* may be made only after a specific authority in respect of that withdrawal has been signed by at least one of the following:

  (a) a *solicitor* who holds a current practising certificate or a *registered European lawyer*;

  . . . .

For the purposes of *LPC Accounts Online*, we will only concern ourselves with the requirement that such authority be from a solicitor holding a current practising certificate. In practice, it is likely that firms will also impose their own additional requirements for the withdrawal of *client money*, normally the authority of a partner or other senior member of the fee-earning staff.

Now consider undertaking Exercises 3 and 4. Both exercises are similar to Exercise 2 and require you to consider the entries associated with a number of transactions and identify the applicable SARs to each activity associated with those transactions so as to ensure that you comply with the SARs.

This is a further exercise working through the application of the Solicitors' Accounts Rules 1998 (SAR). Before you start you may find it useful to read SAR 2(2), 13, 19, 20, 22, and 32, note (iv).

Read the question below. In this exercise you are required to identify the correct stages required, and the correct Solicitors' Accounts Rule which governs each stage, to deposit Emily Walton's cheque by selecting the correct option from those available. Remember, when you are making your selection you are to analyse the composition of the monies that you have received. As you do, you are to identify the relevant SAR with which you should be complying. To select your answers, click on the 'Your ledgers' tab above or the 'Complete your ledgers' button at the bottom of your screen. When you are happy with your selection, click 'Submit' at the bottom of your screen to see your feedback and score.

Don't forget, you can click 'Save' at any point if you want to come back to this exercise later.

You are instructed by Emily Walton, a design consultant, for whom you have been undertaking preliminary research relating to various design rights. She has now sent you a cheque for £3,000 to cover your recent invoice of £1,410 and a further £1,590 on account of costs generally. The invoice that you have sent included costs of £1,000 plus £175 VAT, an expert's fee of £200, plus £35 VAT already paid by you.

You are to deposit the cheque and undertake any further activity to comply with the SARs by selecting the correct answer from those available.

Save | Print | Complete your ledgers

Step	Activity: Receipt & Deposit of £3,000.00 from Walton, E.	Solicitors' Accounts Rule
1.		
2.		
3.		
4.		
5.		
6.		
7.		
8.		
9.		
10.		
11.		
12.		

Back

Step	Activity: Withdrawal, transfer, & return of client money to Graham & Boyd Ltd	Solicitors' Accounts Rule
1.	Balance to client may be withdrawn	
2.		SAR 22(1)(c)
3.		SAR 22(1)(a)
4.		SAR 22(1)(b)
5.		
6.		
7.		
8.		
9.		
10.		
11.		
12.		
13.		
14.		
15.		
16.		

Sum in lieu of interest

As the practice may on occasion hold client money for a period of time, the practice may be required to pay the client a sum in lieu of interest in accordance with Rule 24.

Solicitors' Accounts Rules 1998

Rule 24 – When interest must be paid

(1) When a *solicitor* holds money in a *separate designated client account* for a *client*, or for a person funding all or part of the *solicitor's fees*, the *solicitor* must account to the *client* or that person for all interest earned on the account.

(2) When a *solicitor* holds money in a *general client account* for a *client*, or for a person funding all or part of the *solicitor's fees* (or if money should have been held for a *client* or such other person in a *client account* but was not), the *solicitor* must account to the *client* or that person for a sum in lieu of interest calculated in accordance with rule 25.

(3) A *solicitor* is not required to pay a sum in lieu of interest under paragraph (2) above:

   (a) if the amount calculated is £20 or less;

   (b) (i) if the *solicitor* holds a sum of money not exceeding the amount shown in the left hand column below for a time not exceeding the period indicated in the right hand column:

Amount	Time
£1,000	8 weeks
£2,000	4 weeks
£10,000	2 weeks
£20,000	1 week

   (ii) if the *solicitor* holds a sum of money exceeding £20,000 for one week or less, unless it is fair and reasonable to account for a sum in lieu of interest having regard to all the circumstances;

   ...

   (f) if there is an agreement to contract out of the provisions of this rule under rule 27.

(4) If sums of money are held intermittently during the course of acting, and the sum in lieu of interest calculated under rule 25 for any period is £20 or less, a sum in lieu of interest should still be paid if it is fair and reasonable in the circumstances to aggregate the sums in respect of the individual periods.

The complicating factor with Rule 24 is the formula set out under Rule 24(3). Rather than stating that a sum in lieu of interest is due after a certain period, it states that a sum in lieu of interest does **not** have to be paid if the money held does not exceed the amount shown in the left-hand column for a period not exceeding that stated in the right-hand column – not straightforward! For example, if the practice held £8,000 on general Client account for a client for eight weeks, Rule 24(3)(b)(i) would tell you whether a sum in lieu of interest is to be paid. In this instance it would. If we look at the £10,000 row of the table contained in Rule 24(3)(b)(i) it can be determined that.

- the practice has held a sum not exceeding £10,000; BUT
- this sum not exceeding £10,000 has been held for a period exceeding two weeks.

However, by then using the £2,000 row:

- the practice has held a sum exceeding £2,000, therefore the four-week period does not apply; accordingly,
- the practice must account for a sum in lieu of interest.

As we progress through *LPC Accounts Online*, there will be opportunities to test your application of this rule.

The rate of interest to be applied is governed by Rule 25. However, a sum in lieu of interest does not have to be paid where the practice, in its terms of engagement with the client, has contracted out of the requirements to pay a sum in lieu of interest as permitted by Rule 27.

It is also worth noting that any interest that the practice earns on client money whilst it is deposited in the Client account is not, as one might otherwise expect, client money but is actually office money (Rule 13, note (xi)(b).) As such it should not be paid directly into the Client account, but into the practice's Office account. It is from the Office account that, should any sum in lieu of interest be due, the practice will credit the Client ledger.

Now attempt Exercise 5 online to test your understanding of the different SARs and their application.

To continue to help you learn the Solicitors' Accounts Rules 1998 (SARs), set out below are statements relating to the different mantras that you should always bear in mind. You need to identify whether the statements are true or false. When you have made your selection click the 'Submit' button at the bottom of your screen to view your score and receive feedback on your answers.

	True	False
A separate designated Client account is a deposit account for the holding of money for a single client.	○	○
It is not necessary to have two separate accounts for buyer and lender when acting on a house purchase.	○	○
If £200,000 is held in a separate designated Client account for a client, the solicitor must account for interest to the client on the money so held one week after the money is deposited in the designated Client account.	○	○
In the event that a client does not have sufficient funds, the SARs state that a client's money must not be used for another client.	○	○
A solicitor's bank calculates the actual amount of interest earned on the solicitor's general Client account over a three-month period to be £10,500. Such interest is client money.	○	○
Client money must never be paid into the Office account.	○	○

Acting for borrower and lender

When acting for a client who is purchasing a property, invariably the property will be purchased with the assistance of a mortgage advance from a bank, building society, or other financial institution.

As part of the conveyancing process, the mortgage advance will be forwarded directly to the practice, and not via the client. However, the mortgage advance is money belonging to the financial institution and not the client to whom it is being lent. Why is this?

By considering Rule 2(e) (definition of a client) and Rule 13(a) (definition of client money), the mortgage advance is:

- received in the course of practice; and
- held or received for a client (Rule 2(e)).

Therefore the mortgage advance is received on behalf of and held for the financial institution. This is because the client purchasing the property is not entitled to the mortgage advance until completion of the transaction. Until that time, the practice must continue to act for the financial institution and hold the money to its order – if the property purchase falls through, the financial institution will be entitled to request its return.

So, on receipt of the mortgage advance, if the financial institution is a client of the practice, does this then mean that a new Client ledger should be opened? It is Rule 32(6) that provides assistance on this point.

Solicitors' Accounts Rules 1998

Rule 32 – Accounting records for client accounts, etc.

Acting for both lender and borrower

(6) When acting for both lender and borrower on a mortgage advance, separate client ledger accounts for both *clients* need not be opened, provided that:
 (a) the funds belonging to each client are clearly identifiable; and
 (b) the lender is an institutional lender which provides mortgages on standard terms in the normal course of its activities.

Notes

. . .

(vii) 'Clearly identifiable' in rule 32(6) means that by looking at the ledger account the nature and owner of the mortgage advance are unambiguously stated. For example, if a mortgage advance of £100,000 is received from the ABC Building Society, the entry should be recorded as '£100,000, mortgage advance, ABC Building Society'. It is not enough to state that the money was received from the ABC Building Society without specifying the nature of the payment, or vice versa.

. . .

Provided that the financial institution lending the mortgage advance is:

- an institutional lender; and
- it offers mortgages on standard terms in the normal course of its activities,

the practice may record the receipt of the mortgage advance in the ledger of the client purchasing the property. The mortgage advance will be deposited and recorded as a credit entry in the Client account of the Client ledger.

As a consequence of Rule 32(6), the practice will then need to comply with note (vii) to Rule 32. This provides guidance on the minimum detail which must be included in the Detail column of the Client ledger for compliance with the requirement that funds belonging to each client are 'clearly identifiable'. An example of the detail required in the Detail column of the Client ledger can be seen in Example 3.3.

Example 3.3

Client: Yates, S.

Date	Detail	Office account	Client account
Date	Cash: mortgage advance (ABC Building Society)		

Records and regulatory intervention

Retention of records

The SARs also require that accounting records must be kept for prescribed periods. Under Rule 32(9) and (10) there are two retention periods: six years for documents and records required to be produced under Rule 32(1)–(8) and two years for all cheques and authorities to withdraw money from a Client account.

Production of records

If required to do so in writing by the Solicitors Regulation Authority under Rule 34, the practice must produce any of the documents referred to in Rule 34(1). The purpose of this requirement is to facilitate any investigation which the Solicitors Regulation Authority may be conducting. Those appointed to undertake such an investigation will be accountants appointed to investigate allegations or suspicions of irregularity.

Duty to deliver an accountant's report

Rule 35(1) requires *principals* to deliver an accountant's report if the practice holds or receives client money in the course of an accounting period. The report must cover the entire accounting period and be delivered within six months of the end of the accounting period. Rule 35(2) also permits the Solicitors' Regulation Authority to require a practice to deliver an accountant's report in circumstances other than those required by

Rule 35(1). Further, s 34 Solicitors Act 1974 states that a report must be submitted once every 12 months so a solicitor cannot reduce the regularity of producing an accountant's report by having an accounting period of a length greater than 12 months.

The accountant's powers and rights to report

Rule 38(1)(i) states that the engagement of an accountant by the practice must, within the letter of engagement, contain an express acceptance by the practice of the right of the accountant to report directly to the Solicitors Regulation Authority. Such referral may be done without prior reference to the practice should the accountant, during the course of carrying out work in preparation of his/her report, discover evidence of theft or fraud affecting client money, controlled trust money, etc., or other information which is likely to be of material significance in determining whether any solicitor and/or practice is a fit and proper person to hold client money or controlled trust money.

Refusal to produce documents required by the accountants

The only condition under which the practice may refuse to produce documents requested by an accountant is under Rule 45 and only if they are privileged from disclosure on the basis of the solicitor/client relationship.

Intervention by the Solicitors Regulation Authority

In the event that the Solicitors Regulation Authority deems it necessary, having undertaken an investigation into the practice, to intervene in the day-to-day running of the practice, the statutory basis for such intervention is under Schedule 1 Solicitors Act 1974 (and s 35).

Schedule 1 Solicitors Act 1974 permits the Solicitors Regulation Authority to intervene on one of three general grounds:

- default or misconduct (para 1(1)), including breach of the SARs (para 1(1)(c));
- the death of a sole practitioner (para 2);
- failure to give a proper explanation in response to a complaint to the Solicitors Regulation Authority of undue delay in connection with a client matter (para 3).

Should the Solicitors Regulation Authority deem it necessary to intervene, this may be achieved by another solicitor appointed by the Solicitors Regulation Authority taking control of the practice. On the rare occasion that such intervention occurs, it usually results in the practice being wound up (as most often intervention takes place on the death of a sole practitioner) after the clients' files have been checked and new solicitors found for them.

Conclusion

During this section of *LPC Accounts Online*, we have concentrated upon the main obligations and principles that govern the manner in which solicitors are required to conduct their practice, vis-à-vis their clients' money. Any deviation from the SARs, will mean that the records kept by the practice will be incorrect and may put at jeopardy the security of the clients' money. As we progress further, we will build upon our understanding and application of the SARs and will continue to refer to them in the exercises we undertake.

The final exercise of this section, Exercise 6, provides you with the chance to apply the SARs in the context of double entry book-keeping and dual ledgers. As you read through the list of entries you are required to make, identify the correct ledger by reference to the SARs and more importantly determine whether the entry is to be made in the Office or Client account of that ledger. As you make your entries, you should also ensure that you comply with the SARs requirement for the Detail column.

ⓘ This is a chance now to apply the Solicitors' Accounts Rules in the context of double entry book-keeping (well, more so than you have already!).

Read the question below and the transactions that follow. When you are ready, click on the 'Your ledgers' tab above or the 'Complete your ledgers' button at the bottom of your screen to see the various ledgers in which you are required to record the transactions linked to Boyle & Bird Partnership's sale and purchase of property. For each transaction you should identify which ledger, and which side of the ledger, to use. You will also need to decide whether any receipt is office money or client money and, when a payment is made by you as a solicitor, whether you can use office or client money. Reference to SARs 13, 19, 20, and 22 should help you. When you are happy with the ledgers you have created, click 'Submit' at the bottom of your screen to see your feedback and score.

Don't forget, you can click 'Save' at any point if you want to come back to this exercise later.

❓ Hawkins & Co. have been assisting Boyle & Bird Partnership in the purchase of a new plot of land it is seeking to develop for retirement homes. Boyle & Bird Partnership is selling one of its pre-existing plots of land, Plot 98 Eastway Drive, Clacton-on-Sea, for £275,000 and is purchasing a new property, 19 Second Avenue, Walton-on-the-Naze.

Boyle & Bird Partnership is purchasing 19 Second Avenue for £340,000 with the assistance of a mortgage advance of £282,500 from Home Counties Building Society. You are acting for the Home Counties Building Society in relation to the mortgage advance, which is to be received 10 days prior to completion.

On completion of the sale of Plot 98 Eastway Drive, the mortgage on that property is to be repaid to the lender, Barclays Bank plc. The outstanding amount is £210,000.

In your Cash book you are currently overdrawn by £15,529 and hold £412,365 in your Client account — you are to make these first entries.

Record the following transactions made on Boyle & Bird Partnership's file in the ledgers provided:

- Oct 4   Paid local land charges search fee of £250 to Walton-on-the-Naze Borough Council for local search on the purchase of 19 Second Avenue.

- Oct 4   Paid £12 for official copies of the register of title to Plot 98 Eastway Drive.

- Oct 4   Paid £39 for environmental search fee on the purchase of 19 Second Avenue.

- Oct 21   Received a cheque from Boyle & Bird Partnership for £6,500 to be used to pay the deposit on exchange of contracts for the purchase of 19 Second Avenue.

www.**oxford**interact.com

Section 4

Transfers and invoices

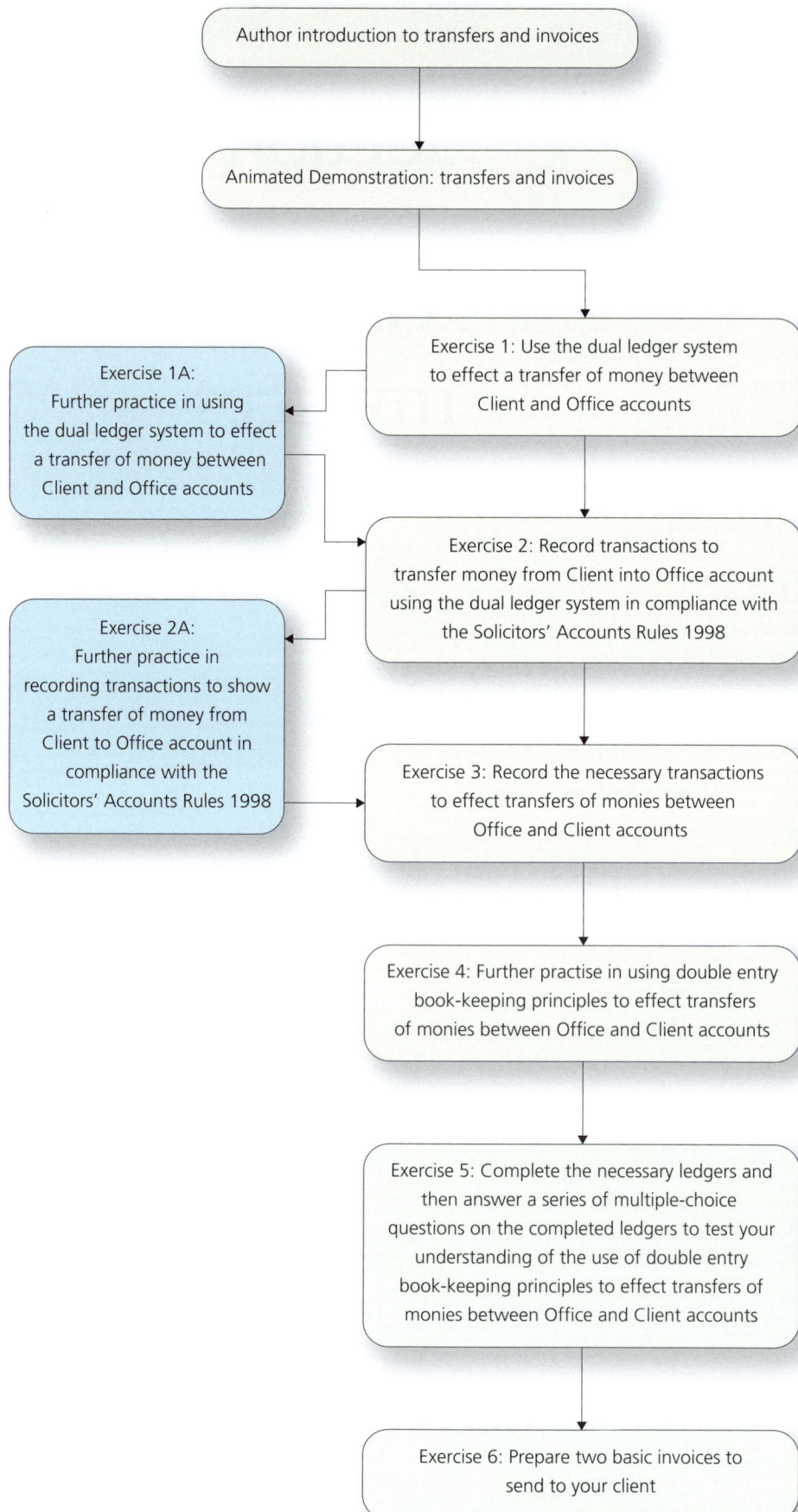

Exercise map

```
        ┌─────────────────────────────────────────┐
        │  Author introduction to transfers and     │
        │              invoices                      │
        └─────────────────────────────────────────┘
                          │
                          ▼
        ┌─────────────────────────────────────────┐
        │  Animated Demonstration: transfers and    │
        │              invoices                      │
        └─────────────────────────────────────────┘
```

Exercise 1A:
Further practice in using the dual ledger system to effect a transfer of money between Client and Office accounts

Exercise 1: Use the dual ledger system to effect a transfer of money between Client and Office accounts

Exercise 2A:
Further practice in recording transactions to show a transfer of money from Client to Office account in compliance with the Solicitors' Accounts Rules 1998

Exercise 2: Record transactions to transfer money from Client into Office account using the dual ledger system in compliance with the Solicitors' Accounts Rules 1998

Exercise 3: Record the necessary transactions to effect transfers of monies between Office and Client accounts

Exercise 4: Further practise in using double entry book-keeping principles to effect transfers of monies between Office and Client accounts

Exercise 5: Complete the necessary ledgers and then answer a series of multiple-choice questions on the completed ledgers to test your understanding of the use of double entry book-keeping principles to effect transfers of monies between Office and Client accounts

Exercise 6: Prepare two basic invoices to send to your client

Introduction

In earlier sections of *LPC Accounts Online* we have primarily concentrated on basic double entry book-keeping using dual ledgers, the receipt of monies, and determining the composition of monies and their deposit – focusing on the receipt of office and client money and mixed payments.

In Section 3 we looked in considerably more depth at applying the Solicitors' Accounts Rules 1998. In the context of dual ledgers, we now need to put our understanding and application of the SARs into practice.

In addition, and as we have already seen, there are circumstances in which office money may be deposited into the Client account under Rule 20(2). However, the only occasion on which client money may be deposited into the Office account is under Rule 19(1)(b). Further, it is not uncommon for solicitors, when being engaged by a new client, to require that funds be provided on account of future costs to ensure the practice is capable of being paid for its services. In this section we will look at how and when it is appropriate to transfer money from Client account to Office account.

For a detailed introduction and worked examples highlighting how to transfer money from Client to Office account, go online and watch the Animated Demonstration before attempting any of the exercises.

Cash book: Hawkins & Co.

		Office account			Client account		
Date	Detail	Dr (£)	Cr (£)	Bal (£)	Dr (£)	Cr (£)	Bal (£)
Oct 4	Balance b/d			50,000.00Cr			30,000.00Dr

Client: Dr Richard Smart   Matter: Debt collection: Peter Phillips

		Office account			Client account		
Date	Detail	Dr (£)	Cr (£)	Bal (£)	Dr (£)	Cr (£)	Bal (£)
Oct 1	Cash: on account of costs					500.00	500.00Cr
Oct 9	Cash: expert's fee	100.00		100.00Dr			
Oct 10	Costs	200.00		300.00Dr			
Oct 10	VAT	35.00		335.00Dr			

01:13 04:05

Transfers

The requirement for transfers

There are a number of reasons for transfers, some of which we looked at in the previous section. Two notable reasons are:

- Rule 20(3): Under Rule 20(3), following the deposit of a mixed payment into a Client account, the office money must be withdrawn within 14 days of its receipt.

- Rule 19(1)(b): If the practice receives money from a client that comprises both office and client money, and the client money is only for an unpaid professional disbursement, then Rule 19(1)(b) requires that the unpaid professional disbursement be paid within two days of receipt of the money.

In addition, one of the major reasons for a transfer from Client to Office account is for payment of a practice's costs. Many practices will require clients to provide monies on account of future costs incurred as a means of ensuring payment. Such money, under Rule 13, note (i)(d), is client money and is therefore deposited in the Client account.

Before going further, it is necessary to consider Rule 19(2)–(4).

Solicitors' Accounts Rules 1998

Rule 19 – Receipt and transfer of costs

. . .

(2) A *solicitor* who properly requires payment of his or her *fees* from money held for a *client* or *trust* in a *client account* must first give or send a bill of *costs*, or other written notification of the *costs* incurred, to the *client* or the paying party.

(3) Once the *solicitor* has complied with paragraph (2) above, the money earmarked for *costs* becomes *office money* and must be transferred out of the *client account* within 14 days.

(4) A payment on account of *costs* generally is *client money*, and must be held in a *client account* until the *solicitor* has complied with paragraph (2) above. (For an exception in the case of legal aid payments, see rule 21(1)(a).)

. . .

Rule 19(2) prevents a practice from withdrawing money unaccountably from a Client account to take for costs as and when it chooses – the client must receive an invoice before any money may be withdrawn by the practice from the Client account to pay for its services. As a consequence, all costs and VAT on costs should be recorded on the Office account side of the Client ledger.

Once the invoice has been sent to the client, the sum stated in the invoice must be transferred from Client to Office account within 14 days.

> **Essential Principles**
>
> The client must always be invoiced before any money held on account of costs generally may be withdrawn from the Client account.

It is also important to remind ourselves of the requirements of Rules 22 and 23. If we look further at Rule 22, we will see that there are a number of additional reasons for the withdrawal of client money from the Client account, such as payment towards a *disbursement* or reimbursement of money spent during the conduct of the client's matter.

Rule 22(3) permits the withdrawal of *office money* required under Rule 19(1)(c), (2) and (3) and Rule 20(2)(b) outlined above.

> **Solicitors' Accounts Rules 1998**
>
> **Rule 22 – Withdrawals from a client account**
>
> (1) *Client money* may only be withdrawn from a *client account* when it is:
>
> (a) properly required for a payment to or on behalf of the *client* (or other person on whose behalf the money is being held);
>
> (aa) properly required for a payment in the execution of a particular *trust,* including the purchase of an investment (other than money) in accordance with the *trustee's* powers;
>
> (b) properly required for payment of a *disbursement* on behalf of the *client* or *trust*;
>
> (c) properly required in full or partial reimbursement of money spent by the *solicitor* on behalf of the *client* or *trust*;
>
> . . .
>
> (3) *Office money* may only be withdrawn from a *client account* when it is:
>
> (a) money properly paid into the account to open or maintain it under rule 15(2)(a);
>
> (b) properly required for payment of the *solicitor's* costs under rule 19(2) and (3);
>
> (c) the whole or part of a payment into a *client account* under rule 19(1)(c);
>
> (d) part of a *mixed payment* placed in a *client account* under rule 20(2)(b); or
>
> (e) money which has been paid into a *client account* in breach of the rules (for example, interest wrongly credited to a *general client account*) – see paragraph (4) . . .

In addition to complying with Rule 22, the usual requirements under Rule 23 for having a specific authority also need to be complied with.

Solicitors' Accounts Rules 1998

Rule 23 – Method of and authority for withdrawals from client account

(1) A withdrawal from a *client account* may be made only after a specific authority in respect of that withdrawal has been signed by at least one of the following:

    (a) a solicitor who holds a current practising certificate or a *registered European lawyer*;

. . .

(3) A withdrawal from a *client account* in favour of the *solicitor* or the practice must be either by way of a cheque to the *solicitor* or practice, or by way of a transfer to the *office* account or to the *solicitor's* personal account. The withdrawal must not be made in cash.

It is worth noting that Rule 23(3) requires that a withdrawal from a Client account must be a transfer to the Office account or by cheque, not by cash – again the protection of the client's money is paramount.

Recording transfers

The recording of a transfer is relatively straightforward – four separate entries are required as follows:

- Withdraw money from Client account:
  - Client ledger: Client account: debit entry (money out);
  - Cash book: Client account: credit entry (money out).
- Deposit money into Office account:
  - Cash book: Office account: debit entry (money in);
  - Client ledger: Office account: credit entry (money in).

Example 4.1 highlights the two sets of double entries that are required to effect a transfer of money between Client and Office account.

Example 4.1

Cash book: Hawkins & Co.

Date	Detail	Office account			Client account		
		Dr (£)	Cr (£)	Bal (£)	Dr (£)	Cr (£)	Bal (£)
Sept 1	Balance b/d			10,580.00Cr			180,500.00Dr
Sept 5	Yates, S.		100.00	10,680.00Cr			
Sept 8	Yates, S.		50.00	10,730.00Cr			
Sept 10	Yates, S.				2,500.00		183,000.00Dr
Sept 20	Yates, S.: costs transfer					1,912.50	181,087.50Dr
Sept 20	Yates, S.: costs transfer	1,912.50		8,817.50Cr			

Entry 3: Deposit money received from Client account – debit entry (money in)

Entry 2: Withdraw money from Client account – credit entry (money out)

Client: Yates, S.

Date	Detail	Office account			Client account		
		Dr (£)	Cr (£)	Bal (£)	Dr (£)	Cr (£)	Bal (£)
Sept 5	Cash: court fee	100.00		100.00Dr			
Sept 8	Cash: personal search	50.00		150.00Dr			
Sept 10	Cash: on account of costs					2,500.00	2,500.00Cr
Sept 12	Costs	1,500.00		1,650.00Dr			
Sept 12	VAT	262.50		1,912.50Dr			
Sept 20	Cash: costs transfer				1,912.50		587.50Cr
Sept 20	Cash: costs transfer		1,912.50	0.00			

Entry 4: Deposit money received from Client account – credit entry (money in)

Entry 1: Withdraw money from Client account – debit entry (money out)

Now attempt Exercises 1 to 5 accompanying this section of *LPC Accounts Online*. These exercises concentrate upon double entry book-keeping using the dual ledger system and require you to make the appropriate entries in the ledgers provided to effect transfers of monies between Client and Office account in compliance with the SARs. As you undertake each exercise, you should ensure that you have fully considered the instructions and transactions you are required to record, and have identified the applicable SARs which you must comply with when you make each entry.

In this exercise we will remain with the dual ledger system, using both the Office and Client accounts to effect transfers between Client and Office account.

Read the question below and the transactions that follow. When you are ready, click on the 'Your ledgers' tab above or the 'Complete your ledgers' button at the bottom of your screen to see the various ledgers in which you are required to record the transactions below by selecting the correct entry from the options available. Remember, when withdrawing monies from the Client account and paying the firm by making a deposit into the Office account, a total of two double entries will be required: the first set withdrawing the monies from Client account, both from the Client ledger and then the Cash book, and the second set depositing the monies in the Cash book and then showing that the debt has been settled in the Client ledger. When you are happy with the ledgers you have created, click 'Submit' at the bottom of your screen to see your feedback and score.

Don't forget, you can click 'Save' at any point if you want to come back to this exercise later.

Record the following invoices and cost transfers made by Hawkins & Co. in the ledgers provided by selecting the correct entry from the options available:

- Sept 22   Iomega Sharp plc file: issued an invoice to client for £5,000 fees plus £875 VAT plus disbursements incurred.

- Sept 23   Roundstone plc file: issued an invoice to the client for £70,000 fees plus £12,250 VAT.

- Sept 23   Gakuin Ltd file: transferred £10,575 from Client account to Office to settle costs due.

- Sept 23   Hague Design Partnership file: transferred £942.50 from Client account to Office account to settle costs due.

- Oct 20   Received a cheque for £6,130 from Iomega Sharp plc.

- Oct 24   Received a cheque for £82,250 from Roundstone plc.

| Save | Print | | Complete your ledgers |

Cash book: Hawkins & Co.

Date	Detail	Office account Dr (£)	Office account Cr (£)	Office account Bal (£)
Aug 31	Balance b/d			75,000.00Cr
Aug 31				
Sept 3				
Sept 15				
Sept 27				
Sept 27				
Sept 27				
Sept 27				
Sept 27				
Sept 27				

Client: Moss, R.   Matter: Conveyancing—sale 'Kiss-me-Quick' souvenir shop at Clacton-on-Sea

Date	Detail	Office account Dr (£)	Office account Cr (£)	Office account Bal (£)
Aug 31				
Sept 3				
Sept 15				
Sept 16				
Sept 16				
Sept 27				

As we progress through this section of *LPC Accounts Online*, the more practice that you undertake in double entry and the application of the Solicitors' Accounts Rules, the easier it will become.

Read the question below and the transactions that follow. When you are ready to start the exercise, click on the 'Your ledgers' tab above or the 'Complete your ledger' button at the bottom of your screen to see the Cash book and personal ledger of the Devon Heritage Trust in which you are required to record the transactions linked to the Devon Heritage Trust's acquisition of the Zeenor site building.

For each transaction you should identify which ledger and, more importantly, which side of the ledger you are to use, i.e. whether any receipt is office money or client money and, when a payment is made by you as solicitor, whether you can use office or client money. Reference to SARs 13, 19, 20, 22, and 23 should help you. When you are happy with the ledgers you have created, click 'Submit' at the bottom of your screen to see your feedback and score.

Don't forget, you can click 'Save' at any point if you want to come back to this exercise later.

The Devon Heritage Trust have instructed you to act for them in respect of the acquisition of an old Devon tin mine site manager's grace and favour residence near Zeenor, Bideford. The Zeenor site building will cost £70,000, purchased with the assistance of a mortgage of £35,000 from HSBC plc and is to be part of a restoration programme with the assistance of lottery funding. You should record the following transactions in the Cash book and the personal ledger of the Devon Heritage Trust.

- Oct 1   Pay Bideford Borough Council £100 for local search certificate.

- Oct 1   Pay National Coal £24 for mining search certificate.

- Oct 1   Pay Devon County Council £14 for commons registration search certificate.

- Oct 9   Receive £7,000 from client for deposit to be paid on exchange of contracts.

- Oct 14   Pay £7,000 to Norman & Co., the solicitors for the seller, for the deposit of exchange of contracts, to be held by them as stakeholder.

- Oct 16   Pay £2 for bankruptcy search.

Cash book: Hawkins & Co.

		Office account		
Date	Detail	Dr (£)	Cr (£)	Bal (£)
Sept 6	Balance b/d			

This exercise is further practice both to help you with double entry book-keeping to effect transfers between Client and Office account, and to continue to consider the application of the Solicitors' Accounts Rules — reference to SARs 13, 19, 20, 22, and 23 should help you.

Read the question below and the transactions that follow. You are first required to record the transactions relating to Lucy Firim's sale and purchase of property in the Cash book and Ms Firim's personal ledger. For the purposes of this exercise you do not need to make entries in any other ledger. When you are ready to record these transactions click the 'Your ledgers' tab above or the 'Complete your ledgers' button at the bottom of your screen and make the necessary entries in the ledgers provided.

You are then required to answer a series of multiple-choice questions based on the accounts you have created. When you are happy with your selection, click 'Submit' at the bottom of your screen to see your feedback and to view your overall score for the exercise.

This exercise is substantially longer than previous exercises and you will need to ensure that you set aside sufficient time to spend on it — remember that you can click 'Save' at the bottom of your screen and return to this exercise at a later stage if you are unable to complete it in one attempt.

On behalf of Hawkins & Co. you have been assisting Lucy Firim in the sale of her photography studio, Studio 5a Canal Lane, Great Roding for £350,000 and the purchase of new premises for £495,000.

Ms Firim will be purchasing her new premises, 85 De'Friend Avenue, with the assistance of a mortgage advance of £285,000 from Writtle Building Society, to be received 10 days prior to completion. The firm acted for the building society in relation to the mortgage advance. When Studio 5a Canal Lane was sold the mortgage on that property, amounting to £200,000 and owed to HSBC plc, was repaid.

The following transactions were made on Ms Firim's file, and you should record each of the transactions in the Cash book and Ms Firim's ledger:

- April 4   Paid local land charges fee of £220 to Chelmsford Borough Council for local search certificate on the purchase of 85 De'Friend Avenue.

- April 4   Paid £8 for official copies of the register of title to Studio 5a Canal Lane.

- April 4   Paid £134.08 for environmental search fees on the purchase of 85 De'Friend Avenue.

- April 11   Received a cheque from Ms Firim for £14,500 to be used to pay the deposit on exchange of contracts for the purchase of 85 De'Friend Avenue.

Invoices

Each practice will adopt its own house style when preparing invoices (bill of costs). However, Rule 32(8) requires the following distinctions to be made.

Solicitors' Accounts Rules 1998

Rule 32 – Accounting records for client accounts, etc.

Bills and notifications of costs

(8) The *solicitor* must keep readily accessible a central record or file of copies of:

(a) all bills given or sent by the *solicitor*; and

(b) all other written notifications of *costs* given or sent by the *solicitor*;

in both cases distinguishing between *fees, disbursements* not yet paid at the date of the bill, and paid *disbursements*.

Accordingly, if we look at the invoice contained in Example 4.2 below which would represent the invoice sent to Sarah on 12 September, prior to the transfer of monies from Client account to Office account, the practice's costs have been distinguished from the disbursements. A further distinction has also been made in relation to whether certain disbursements attract VAT. This distinction will be explained in Section 7 of *LPC Accounts Online*.

Example 4.2

Disbursements: Those items paid for by the solicitor on behalf of a client for a service provided to the client. In this invoice, the disbursements do not attract VAT and have been identified as such. Those that do attract VAT would be identified as doing so and VAT would be added at the appropriate rate.

Provision of legal services: This represents the time costs of the solicitor, with VAT added separately. If there are any expenses (i.e. a payment made by the solicitor in order to provide legal services, which will attract VAT), these may either be shown separately or included in the solicitor's time costs.

Hawkins & Co.   INVOICE
Solicitors and Privy Agents
Great Clarenson Street
Oxford, OX2 4DR

Tel: 01865 998877
Fax: 01865 778899
eMail: account@Hawkins.co.uk

To: Ms Sarah Yates			
25 Vaughan Avenue	VAT number:	98 43298 843 92	
Richmond	Date:	12 September [year]	
London	Tax point:	12 September [year]	
	Invoice number:	42070	
Ongoing advice	Account no:	1287A4-005-1	

Description	Charge	VAT rate	VAT
Supply of legal services from 1 September [year]	1,500.00	17.5%	262.50
Add: **Disbursements not subject to VAT**			
Court fee	100.00		
Personal search	50.00		
	1,650.00		262.50
Add: Total VAT	262.50		
Total	1,912.50		

> Invoice total

Remittance advice	Invoice no:	42070
	A/c no:	1287A4-005-1
Ms Sarah Yates	Date:	12 September [year]
25 Vaughan Avenue		
Richmond		
London		
Ongoing advice	Amount:	£1,912.50

Total time costs and disbursements

Total VAT

Remittance advice: Provided for the client to enclose with payment, identifying the client, account file and matter reference number, the date of the invoice and invoiced amount.

Now attempt Exercise 6 which provides you with the opportunity to identify items that would be included in an invoice on the sale and purchase of a property. As you will see from the invoice contained in Example 4.2 the time costs of the solicitor are shown separately from the disbursements incurred during the course of the matter. Accordingly, when you undertake Exercise 6, you should take care to ensure that you identify the items separately. You will also be required to attribute disbursements incurred for the sale or purchase of a property correctly so that the entries you make accurately correspond to each activity.

Hawkins & Co. Solicitors and Privy Agents Great Clarenson Street Oxford, OX2 6DT Tel: 01865 998877 Fax: 01865 778899 eMail: account@Hawkins.co.uk		**INVOICE**	
To: Ms Lucy Firim Studio 5a Canal Lane Great Roding Essex Sale of Studio 5a Canal Lane, Great Roding, Essex	VAT number: Date: Tax point: Invoice number: Account no:	98 43298 843 92 1 May [year] 1 May [year] 42077 1287A4-005-1	
	Description	Charge	VAT Rate	VAT
	Supply of legal services from 4 April [year]		17.5%	
Add:	**Disbursements not subject to VAT**			
Add:	Total VAT			
	Total			

Conclusion

This section has briefly taken you through the SARs requirements and the provisions applicable to transferring money from the Client to Office account, as well as the basic preparation of invoices. From this point on, much of what you will be required to do will be the application of SARs to ever more in-depth exercises. The more practice you undertake the easier Solicitors' Accounts will become. However, if at any stage you have a query, do remember to take the time to ask your tutor for assistance with this topic.

Section 5

Stakeholder and interest

Exercise map

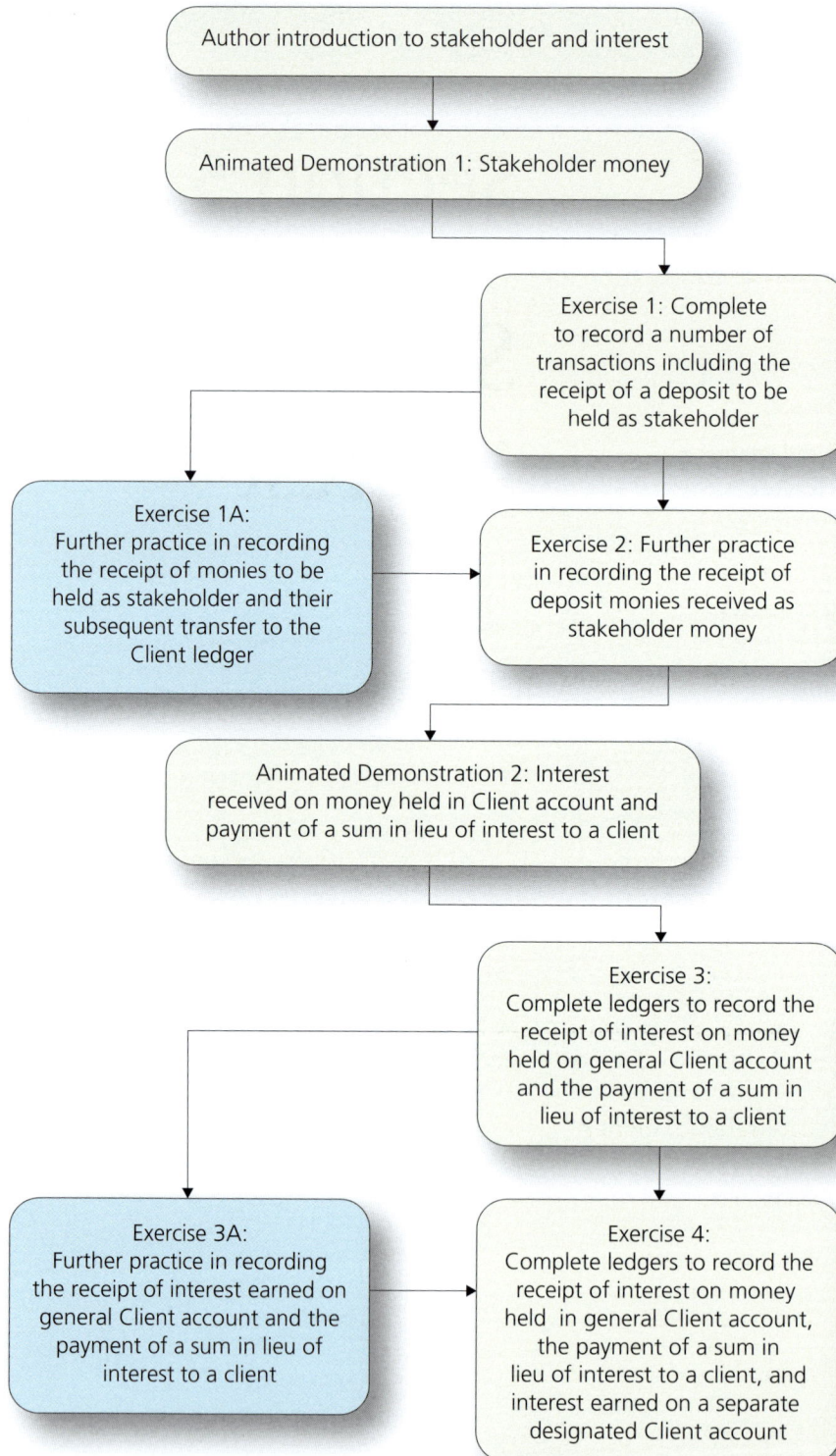

Author introduction to stakeholder and interest

Animated Demonstration 1: Stakeholder money

Exercise 1: Complete to record a number of transactions including the receipt of a deposit to be held as stakeholder

Exercise 1A: Further practice in recording the receipt of monies to be held as stakeholder and their subsequent transfer to the Client ledger

Exercise 2: Further practice in recording the receipt of deposit monies received as stakeholder money

Animated Demonstration 2: Interest received on money held in Client account and payment of a sum in lieu of interest to a client

Exercise 3: Complete ledgers to record the receipt of interest on money held on general Client account and the payment of a sum in lieu of interest to a client

Exercise 3A: Further practice in recording the receipt of interest earned on general Client account and the payment of a sum in lieu of interest to a client

Exercise 4: Complete ledgers to record the receipt of interest on money held in general Client account, the payment of a sum in lieu of interest to a client, and interest earned on a separate designated Client account

Introduction

In this section we will look at two separate topics: the receipt and holding of money as stakeholder money, and the receipt of interest and the payment of a sum in lieu of interest to clients.

In order to record these activities, we will be drawing upon some of the skills you have acquired from the previous section of *LPC Accounts Online*. For stakeholder money, this will require you to reallocate money held in the Client account between clients. In relation to making a payment of a sum in lieu of interest to a client, we will look at how you should withdraw money from the Office account and then deposit it into the Client account – the opposite of the transfers that you undertook in Section 4 of *LPC Accounts Online*.

Stakeholder money

Receipt of deposit monies

In property transactions, when a client's buyer pays the client's deposit on the exchange of contract, you, the solicitor, will receive that deposit either as:

- agent; or
- stakeholder.

In either case, and as we have already seen from our earlier reading of the Solicitors' Accounts Rules 1998, both forms of money are client money as defined in Rule 13.

Solicitors' Accounts Rules 1998

Rule 13 – Categories of money

All money held or received in the course of practice falls into one of the following categories:

(a) 'client money' – money held or received for a *client* or as *trustee*, and all other money which is not *office money*;

. . .

Notes

(i) 'Client money' includes money held or received:

. . .

(a) as agent, bailee, stakeholder, or as the donee of a power of attorney, or as a liquidator, trustee in bankruptcy, Court of Protection deputy or trustee of an occupational pension scheme;

. . .

On the receipt of sale deposit money paid on exchange and to be held as agent, the client can direct the solicitor on how to deal with that money. Most commonly, the client will seek to use the money as part of any deposit he or she is required to pay for their onward purchase. If you now consider some of the exercises that you have undertaken in earlier sections of *LPC Accounts Online*, you will remember that you have recorded such deposit money as client money in the Client account of the Client ledger. You will then have used this money as part of the deposit money paid by the client for their onward purchase.

Note also that the receipt of the sale deposit is always recorded as a credit entry in the Client ledger.

Receipt of stakeholder monies

In contrast to a sale deposit being paid by the buyer to be held by the seller's solicitor as agent, there may be times when the parties may agree that, for some reason, it is not appropriate for the seller to use that sale deposit such as when the seller's onward purchase is for a property overseas. However, the seller will still expect a deposit to be paid by the buyer.

It is in such circumstances that the deposit will be paid as stakeholder money. As such, it will not be held for the seller, but will be held jointly for the buyer and the seller, with the seller becoming entitled to that money when the sale has completed.

As you can see from reading Rule 13(a), note (i)(a), money received by the practice as stakeholder money is client money and as such must be paid into the Client account *without delay* (Rule 15(1)). However, as stakeholder money is to be held jointly for the buyer and seller, it cannot be credited to the seller's ledger but rather it will be recorded in a separate account, the 'Stakeholder account', and the Detail column will identify the matter for which it has been received. The manner in which this works can be seen in Example 5.1. On receipt of stakeholder money, as with all client money, a debit entry will be made in the Client account of the Cash book. However, the corresponding entry will not be made in the Client ledger but instead will be made in the Stakeholder ledger.

In a situation where the sale deposit is paid and held by the solicitor as agent, the client would ordinarily expect to use this deposit as part of his or her own onward deposit. However, as the client is not entitled to such money until completion, it is worth noting that in a stakeholder situation the client will be required to provide sufficient funds to finance the payment of his or her own deposit. You will see this when you undertake the accompanying exercises to this section online.

Transfer of stakeholder monies

It is only once the property sale has been completed that the client is entitled to the money paid as stakeholder money and held on the Stakeholder ledger. This will require a transfer from the Stakeholder ledger to the Client ledger.

As the stakeholder money was paid into the Client account upon receipt, there will be no need to withdraw that money from the Client account, but rather it will need to be reallocated between Client ledgers. Rule 30(1) permits this reallocation of monies held in the Client account.

Example 5.1

Cash book: Hawkins & Co.

Date	Detail	Office account			Client account		
		Dr (£)	Cr (£)	Bal (£)	Dr (£)	Cr (£)	Bal (£)
Sept 1	Balance b/d			10,508.00Cr			180,500.00Dr
Sept 5	Yates, S.		100.00	10,608.00Cr			
Sept 8	Yates, S.		50.00	10,658.00Cr			
Sept 20	Stakeholder				25,000.00		205,500.00Dr

Stakeholder money: received and identified as held in the Stakeholder account with the entry made in the Client account (debit entry)

Client: Stakeholder

Matter: Conveyancing deposits received

Date	Detail	Office account			Client account		
		Dr (£)	Cr (£)	Bal (£)	Dr (£)	Cr (£)	Bal (£)
Sept 1	Balance b/d						100,000.00Cr
Sept 20	Cash: Yates, S.					25,000.00	125,000.00Cr

Stakeholder money: corresponding credit entry in the Stakeholder account

Client: Yates, S

Matter: Conveyancing file

Date	Detail	Office account			Client account		
		Dr (£)	Cr (£)	Bal (£)	Dr (£)	Cr (£)	Bal (£)
Sept 5	Cash: court fee	100.00		100.00Dr			
Sept 8	Cash: personal search	50.00		150.00Dr			

Stakeholder money: paid into the Stakeholder account, but with acknowledgement of client for whom it is held

> ### Solicitors' Accounts Rules 1998
>
> **Rule 30 – Restrictions on transfers between clients**
>
> (1) A paper transfer of money held in a *general client account* from the ledger of one *client* to the ledger of another *client* may only be made if:
>
>   (a) it would have been permissible to withdraw that sum from the account under rule 22(1); and
>
>   (b) it would have been permissible to pay that sum into the account under rule 15;
>
> (but there is no requirement in the case of a paper transfer for the written authority of a solicitor, etc., under rule 23(1)).
>
> . . .

To effect such reallocation between Client ledgers, it is necessary to make a debit entry in the Stakeholder ledger with a corresponding credit entry in the Client ledger, an example of which can be seen in Example 5.2. Note also that, as this is only a reallocation of money held in the Client account, the balance in the Cash book's Client account does not alter.

It is also worth noting that under Rule 30, provided Rules 22(1) and 15 are applicable, no written authority, as normally required for any withdrawal from the Client account under Rule 23(1), is required.

Once the client has become entitled to and has received the stakeholder money, the solicitor will then be holding that money as agent and the client is free to direct the solicitor on how to use that money. Invariably, the client will then use that money as part of the money required to complete any purchase he or she is making.

> ### Essential Principles
>
> Receipt of money to be held as stakeholder money:
>
> - Cash book: debit entry, Client account;
> - Stakeholder ledger: credit entry, Client account.
>
> Transfer of stakeholder money:
>
> - Stakeholder ledger: debit entry, Client account;
> - Client ledger: credit entry, Client account.

Example 5.2

Cash book: Hawkins & Co.

Date	Detail	Office account			Client account		
		Dr (£)	Cr (£)	Bal (£)	Dr (£)	Cr (£)	Bal (£)
Sept 1	Balance b/d			10,508.00Cr			180,500.00Dr
Sept 5	Yates, S.		100.00	10,608.00Cr			
Sept 8	Yates, S.		50.00	10,658.00Cr			
Sept 20	Stakeholder				25,000.00		205,500.00Dr

Stakeholder money: note that as no money has been withdrawn from the Client account, the balance does not alter

Client: Stakeholder
Matter: Conveyancing deposits received

Date	Detail	Office account			Client account		
		Dr (£)	Cr (£)	Bal (£)	Dr (£)	Cr (£)	Bal (£)
Sept 1	Balance b/d						100,000.00Cr
Sept 20	Cash: Yates, S.					25,000.00	125,000.00Cr
Oct 1	Yates, S.				25,000.00		100,000.00Cr

Stakeholder money: when entitled, debit entry in the Stakeholder ledger

Client: Yates, S.
Matter: Conveyancing file

Date	Detail	Office account			Client account		
		Dr (£)	Cr (£)	Bal (£)	Dr (£)	Cr (£)	Bal (£)
Sept 5	Cash: court fee	100.00		100.00Dr			
Sept 8	Cash: personal search	50.00		150.00Dr			
Oct 1	Stakeholder					25,000.00	25,000.00Cr

Stakeholder money: when entitled, credit entry in the Client ledger

For a demonstration of the entries required to record the receipt and transfer of stakeholder money, watch Animated Demonstration 1 online before you undertake any of the accompanying exercises.

Cash book: Hawkins & Co.

Date	Detail	Office account Dr (£)	Cr (£)	Bal (£)	Client account Dr (£)	Cr (£)	Bal (£)
Sept 20	Balance b/d			35,000.00Dr			423,000.00Dr
Sept 20	Stakeholder				33,000.00		456,000.00Dr
Oct 1	North Recruitment Ltd				297,000.00		753,000.00Dr
Oct 4	Stakeholder				29,000.00		782,000.00Dr

Client: Stakeholder — **Matter: Conveyancing deposits received**

Date	Detail	Office account Dr (£)	Cr (£)	Bal (£)	Client account Dr (£)	Cr (£)	Bal (£)
Sept 20	Balance b/d			0.00			45,000.00Cr
Sept 20	Cash: North Recruitment Ltd					33,000.00	78,000.00Cr
Oct 1	North Recruitment Ltd				33,000.00		45,000.00Cr

Client: Singh, R. — **Matter: Conveyancing — sale and purchase of premises**

Date	Detail	Office account Dr (£)	Cr (£)	Bal (£)	Client account Dr (£)	Cr (£)	Bal (£)
Oct 4	Balance b/d			0.00			100,000.00Cr

05:46 07:32

Now attempt Exercises 1 and 2 which will provide you with the opportunity to practise recording the receipt of stakeholder money, and its subsequent transfer to, and use by, the client as part of an onward purchase.

This exercise is intended to test you on a number of the accounting principles and the Solicitors' Accounts Rules that you have been learning to date. In addition you will need to record correctly the receipt of a deposit to be held as a stakeholder.

Read the question below and the transactions that follow. In this exercise you are required to make the necessary ledger entries to record the transactions linked to the sale and purchase of Bruno Herbot's property. When you are ready to record these transactions in the appropriate ledgers, click on the 'Your ledgers' tab above or the 'Complete your ledgers' button at the bottom of your screen and make the necessary entries in the ledgers provided. When you are happy with the ledgers you have created, click 'Submit' at the bottom of your screen to see your feedback and score.

Don't forget, you can click 'Save' at any point if you want to come back to this exercise later.

Hawkins & Co. is acting for Bruno Herbots in respect of his sale of 15 St Katherine's Way, Harwich for £345,000 and his purchase of 12 Second Avenue, Frinton-on-Sea for £580,000. Mr Herbots did not have a mortgage on 15 St Katherine's Way, but will be buying 12 Second Avenue with the assistance of a mortgage of £100,000 from Nationwide Building Society. The firm was instructed by Nationwide Building Society to act on its behalf in relation to the mortgage.

Record the following transactions in the ledgers provided:

- Sept 1   Paid £4 for official copies from HM Land Registry.
- Sept 2   Paid £140 for local search from Tendering Borough Council on 12 Second Avenue.
- Sept 9   Received from the client the deposit of £58,000 to be paid on exchange of contract for the purchase of 12 Second Avenue.
- Sept 18   Exchanged contracts on the sale of 15 St Katherine's Way and received the deposit of £34,500, to be held by the practice as stakeholder.
- Sept 18   Exchanged contracts on the purchase of 12 Second Avenue and paid the deposit of £58,000 to the seller's solicitors.
- Sept 19   Issued invoice to client for sale of 15 St Katherine's Way (fees of £1,000 plus £175 VAT) and purchase of 12 Second Avenue (fees of £2,000 plus £350 VAT) and all disbursements incurred. The invoices were accompanied by a Completion Statement showing how much was required from the client in order to complete the transactions.

This exercise will again look at the receipt and transfer of money received by the practice as stakeholder money.

Read the exercise below and the transactions that follow. In this exercise you are required to make the necessary ledger entries to record each of the transactions linked to Griffin Ltd's sale and purchase of property. When you are ready to record these transactions in the appropriate ledgers, click on the 'Your ledgers' tab above or the 'Complete your ledgers' button at the bottom of your screen and make the necessary entries in the ledgers provided. When you are happy with the ledgers you have created, click 'Submit' at the bottom of your screen to see your feedback and score.

Don't forget, you can click 'Save' at any point if you want to come back to this exercise later.

Hawkins & Co. is acting for Griffin Ltd in the sale of its existing storage facility, Unit 15, Witham Industrial Estate, Essex, for £240,000 and the purchase of new facilities, 18 Navigation Road, Chelmsford, Essex, for £425,000. Unit 15 was bought with a loan from Abbey National of £200,000. Hawkins & Co. has also been instructed by HSBC plc to act on its behalf in relation to a mortgage advance on the new premises.

Record the following transactions in the ledgers provided:

- Aug 6   Paid local search fee of £100 on purchase.

- Aug 14   Received £42,500 from Griffin Ltd as the deposit for 18 Navigation Road on exchange of contracts.

- Sept 2   Contracts exchanged for the sale of Unit 15, and received a deposit of £24,000 to be held on the basis of stakeholder.

- Sept 2   Exchanged contracts for the purchase of 18 Navigation Road and paid the deposit of £42,500 to the solicitors acting for the sellers.

- Sept 12 Paid £6 for Land Registry search against title of 18 Navigation Road.

- Sept 12 Sent invoices to Griffin Ltd for the sale of Unit 15 (fees £2,000 plus £350 VAT) and for the purchase of 18 Navigation Road (fees £4,000 plus £700 VAT) and disbursements incurred. The invoices were accompanied by a Completion Statement showing how much was required from Griffin Ltd in order to complete the transactions.

Interest

The second topic to be covered in this section is that of interest, both in the context of interest received by the practice and the requirement to pay a sum in lieu of interest to a client.

If a practice is required to hold money on behalf of its clients, this money must be accruing interest. In fact, some practices will hold considerable sums of client money and, if it is carefully managed (and protected), it can be used as a supplementary means of earning revenue for the practice. As such, it becomes necessary to consider how the receipt of interest accrued on a Client account is handled by the practice.

Obviously, if the practice is holding a client's money, the client is not earning interest on that money. The Solicitors' Accounts Rules 1998, by requiring the practice to pay a sum in lieu of interest to clients in such circumstances, implicitly acknowledge this fact. We will look now at how a practice will pay a client a sum in lieu of interest and how, when a client's money is held in a separate designated Client bank account, interest accrued is recorded.

For a demonstration of how interest received by the practice is recorded and the requirement to pay a client a sum in lieu of interest, watch Animated Demonstration 2 online before you undertake any of the accompanying exercises.

Cash book: Hawkins & Co.

Date	Detail	Office account			Client account		
		Dr (£)	Cr (£)	Bal (£)	Dr (£)	Cr (£)	Bal (£)
June 1	Balance b/d			150,000.00Dr			400,000.00Dr
June 30	Interest Received	2,000.00		152,000.00Dr			

Client: Burns, A.   Matter: Personal injury litigation

Date	Detail	Office account			Client account		
		Dr (£)	Cr (£)	Bal (£)	Dr (£)	Cr (£)	Bal (£)
June 1	Balance b/d					6,500.00	6,500.00Cr

Interest Paid account ⬅

Date	Detail	Debit (£)	Credit (£)	Balance (£)
June 1	Balance b/d			3,000.00Dr

03:10 06:33

Receipt of interest on client money

Interest accrued on Client account monies is, by virtue of Rule 13(b), note (xi)(b), office money. As such it must be paid into the Office account, something that practices will ensure occurs as part of their arrangements with their bank or building society.

Solicitors' Accounts Rules 1998

Rule 13 – Categories of money

All money held or received in the course of practice falls into one or other of the following categories:

. . .

(b) 'office money' – money which belongs to the solicitor or the practice;

Notes

(xi) Office money includes:

. . .

(b) interest on general client accounts; the bank or building society should be instructed to credit such interest to the office account – but see also rule 15(2)(d); and

. . .

The recording of the receipt of interest by the practice is straightforward – it is the receipt of money into the practice. Accordingly, all that is required is a debit entry in the Office account of the Cash book with a corresponding credit entry in a ledger called 'Interest Received'. The Detail column in the Interest Received account will acknowledge the fact that the money relates to that accrued in the Client account. The entries made to record the receipt of interest by the practice can be seen in Example 5.3.

Essential Principles

Receipt of interest accrued on Client account:

- Cash book: debit entry, Office account;
- Interest Received account: credit entry.

Payment of a sum in lieu of interest

We have already looked at the requirement for the practice to pay a sum in lieu of interest to a client for money held on a general Client account as part of our examination of the Solicitors' Accounts Rules 1998 (see Section 3, 'Sum in lieu of interest' on page 72).

As we have seen, it is Rule 24 that governs when a sum in lieu of interest is to be paid, and the rate of such a sum in lieu of interest is set by Rule 25. The rate of interest must be calculated on the balance, or balances, held over the whole period for which cleared funds are held at a rate not less than (whichever is the higher of) the rate of interest payable on a separate designated Client account, or if placed on deposit on similar terms by a member of the business community, at the bank or building society where the money is held.

Assuming that the practice has not taken advantage of Rule 27 and contracted out of the requirement to pay a sum in lieu of interest, we now need to consider how to record the payment of a sum in lieu of interest to a client. You will need to employ the technique of transferring money from one account to another, as practised in Section 4 of *LPC Accounts Online* but in reverse. You will therefore be making two sets of double entries.

As the payment of a sum in lieu of interest is a payment by the practice, an appropriate sum will first be withdrawn from the Office account. It will then be deposited into the Client account and duly credited to the client who is to receive that payment. Once paid into the Client ledger, the Detail column will acknowledge that the payment is for interest on the Client account.

The corresponding entry for the withdrawal of money from the Office account will be made in a ledger called 'Interest Paid'. The Detail column in the Interest Paid account will acknowledge the fact that office money has been paid to a client by way of a payment of a sum in lieu of interest. The entries made to record the payment of a sum in lieu of interest can be seen in Example 5.4.

Example 5.3

Cash book: Hawkins & Co.

Date	Detail	Office account			Client account		
		Dr (£)	Cr (£)	Bal (£)	Dr (£)	Cr (£)	Bal (£)
Oct 31	Balance b/d			100,000.00Dr			200,000.00Dr
Nov 1	Interest Received	10,000.00		110,000.00Dr			

Interest accrued on Client account monies paid into the Office account, with a corresponding entry in the Interest Received account

Interest Received account

Date	Detail	Debit (£)	Credit (£)	Balance (£)
Oct 31	Balance b/d			80,000.00Cr
Nov 1	Cash: Client account interest		10,000.00	90,000.00Cr

Example 5.4

Cash book: Hawkins & Co.

Date	Detail	Office account			Client account		
		Dr (£)	Cr (£)	Bal (£)	Dr (£)	Cr (£)	Bal (£)
Nov 1	Balance b/d			100,000.00Dr			200,000.00Dr
Nov 2	Interest Paid		100.00	99,900.00Dr			
Nov 2	Yates, S.				100.00		200,100.00Dr

Entry 1: withdraw money from Office account

Entry 3: deposit the payment of a sum in lieu of interest into Client account

Client: Yates, S.

Date	Detail	Office account			Client account		
		Dr (£)	Cr (£)	Bal (£)	Dr (£)	Cr (£)	Bal (£)
Oct 1	Cash: on account of costs					10,000.00	10,000.00Cr
Nov 2	Cash: client account interest					100.00	10,100.00Cr

Entry 4: corresponding entry showing payment of a sum in lieu of interest and detailed as such in the Detail column

Interest Paid account

Date	Detail	Debit (£)	Credit (£)	Balance (£)
Nov 1	Balance b/d			80,000.00Cr
Nov 2	Cash: Yates, S.	100.00		79,900.00Cr

Entry 2: corresponding entry for the withdrawal of money from Office account, including reference of receiving client in the Detail column

Essential Principles

Payment of sum in lieu of interest:

- Withdraw money from Office account:
    - Cash book: Office account: credit entry (money out);
    - Interest Paid account: debit entry (money out).
- Deposit money into Client account and Client ledger:
    - Cash book: Client account: debit entry (money in);
    - Client ledger: Client account: credit entry (money in).

Now attempt Exercise 3 online and practise making the necessary entries to record the receipt of interest by the practice and the payment of a sum in lieu of interest to a client.

In this exercise you will be recording the receipt of interest on money held in a general Client account and the subsequent payment of a sum in lieu of interest to a client.

Read the question below and the transactions that follow. In this exercise you are required to make the necessary ledger entries to record the transactions below. When you are ready to record these transactions, click on the 'Your ledgers' tab above or the 'Complete your ledgers' button at the bottom of your screen and make the necessary entries in the ledgers provided. Remember when you record the receipt to pay it into the correct account and ensure that you make all the entries to record a payment of a sum in lieu of interest to a client by the practice on to the appropriate Client ledger. When you are happy with the ledgers you have created, click 'Submit' at the bottom of your screen to see your feedback and score.

Don't forget, you can click 'Save' at any point if you want to come back to this exercise later.

Hawkins & Co. are acting for various clients. As part of their terms of engagement with clients it is agreed that any payment of a sum in lieu of interest will be made on the first of the month, a day after they have received any interest on money held on Client account. Record the following transactions in the ledgers provided:

- Aug 31   Monthly interest of £1,380 is received on monies held on general Client account and is debited to the Office account.

- Sept 1   £25 is paid from Office account to Bruno Herbots by way of a sum in lieu of interest for money held on account of costs.

- Sept 10   Received from Haslemere Marina plc £12,500 on account of costs to be incurred in relation to planning advice associated with the St Katherine's Dock development.

- Sept 15   Issued invoice to Bruno Herbots for fees of £4,000 plus £700 VAT.

- Sept 25   Transferred all sums due to the firm from Bruno Herbots from Client account to Office account.

- Sept 30   Monthly interest of £1,545 is received on monies held on general Client account and debited to the Office account.

- Oct 1   £97.50 is paid from Office account to Haslemere Marina plc by way of a sum in lieu of interest for money held on account of costs.

Separate designated bank account

There may be instances when a client will request that his or her money is not deposited into the general Client account operated by the practice. As an alternative, a separate designated Client account may be opened and operated for that client only. It is Rule 14 that classifies such an account as a Client account.

> ### Solicitors' Accounts Rules 1998
>
> **Rule 14 – Client accounts**
>
> . . .
>
> (5) There are two types of client account:
>
>   (a) a 'separate designated client account', which is a deposit or share account for money relating to a single *client*, or other person or *trust* and which includes in its title, in addition to the requirements of rule 14(3) above, a reference to the identity of the *client* or *trust*; and
>
>   (b) a "general client account", which is any other *client account*.

Rule 24(1) requires that all interest accrued on any separate designated Client account must be paid to the client.

> ### Solicitors' Accounts Rules 1998
>
> **Rule 24 – When interest must be paid**
>
> (1) When a *solicitor* holds money in a separate designated client account for a *client*, or for a person funding all or part of the *solicitor's fees* or for a *trust*, the *solicitor* must account to the client or that person or *trust* for all interest earned on the account.
>
> . . .

The payment of interest on a separate designated Client account is straightforward to record, but it is worth first noting the content of Rule 32(3). It is this rule that requires the practice to maintain an account to record that money held in the separate designated Client account and to operate a Client ledger to record the activities undertaken in relation to that separate designated Client account. The use of the Client ledger will record the entries on the Client account side of the ledger, but this does not mean that the money is held in the practice's Client account, rather it is a means of providing the corresponding entries and ensuring that good standards of accounting with client money are maintained.

> **Solicitors' Accounts Rules 1998**
>
> **Rule 32 – Accounting records for client accounts, etc.**
>
> Accounting records which must be kept
>
> . . .
>
>   (3) If *separate designated client accounts* are used:
>
>   (a) a combined cash account must be kept in order to show the total amount held in *separate designated client accounts*; and
>
>   (b) a record of the amount held for each *client* (or other person, or *trust*) must be made either in a deposit column of a client ledger account, or on the client side of a client ledger account kept specifically for a *separate designated client account*, for each client (or other person, or *trust*).
>
> . . .

When interest has accrued on a separate designated Client account, the entries that are made are in the separate designated Client account ledger, as a debit entry, with a corresponding entry in a Client ledger. An example of these entries can be seen in Example 5.5.

It is important to note that when a separate designated Client account is operated, no entry will be made in the practice's Cash book. This is simply because the money is not held in the practice's general Client account, and the Cash book is therefore not required in this instance.

Having now looked at the separate designated Client account and how to record interest accrued, attempt Exercise 4 and practise recording the receipt of interest on money held in general Client account, the payment of a sum in lieu of interest to a client, and the payment of interest earned on a separate designated Client account.

ⓘ In this final exercise you will again be recording the receipt of interest on money held in general Client account, the payment of a sum in lieu of interest to the client, and interest earned on a separate designated Client account.

Read the question below and the transactions that follow. In this exercise you are required to make the necessary ledger entries to record the transactions below. When you are ready to record these transactions, click on the 'Your ledgers' tab above or the 'Complete your ledgers' button at the bottom of your screen and make the necessary entries in the ledgers provided. Remember, when you record the receipt, that you pay it into the correct account and ensure that you make all the entries to record a payment of a sum in lieu of interest to a client by the practice on to the appropriate Client ledger. When you are happy with the ledgers you have created, click 'Submit' at the bottom of your screen to see your feedback and score.

Don't forget, you can click 'Save' at any point if you want to come back to this exercise later.

❓ Hawkins & Co. are acting for various clients, one of whom it has been agreed that a separate designated Client bank account will be operated. Any interest earned on money held on Client account is notified on the last day of the month, the day after which any payment of a sum in lieu of interest will be made to clients. Record the following transactions in the ledgers provided:

- Nov 1   Helen Lane sends a cheque for £4,000 on account of costs generally in relation to advice that she is receiving in relation to a dispute with her employer.
- Nov 15   Subsequent to agreeing to do so, £45,000 is deposited into a separate designated Client bank account for Whitetech plc.
- Nov 30   The practice received notification that interest of £200 had been added to the separate designated Client bank account for Whitetech plc.
- Nov 30   Monthly interest of £2,560 is received on monies held on general Client account and are debited to the Office account.
- Dec 1   £20 is paid from Office account to Helen Lane by way of a sum in lieu of interest for money held on account of costs.

Example 5.5

Yates, S.: Separate designated Client account

Date	Detail	Debit (£)	Credit (£)	Balance (£)
Dec 1	Client account: Whitetech plc separate designated Client account	20,000.00		20,000.00Dr
Jan 2	Client account: Whitetech plc separate designated Client account (interest)	200.00		20,200.00Dr

Debit entry to show receipt of interest accrued on money held in a separate designated Client account

Client: Yates, S.: Separate designated Client account

Date	Detail	Office account			Client account		
		Dr (£)	Cr (£)	Bal (£)	Dr (£)	Cr (£)	Bal (£)
Dec 1	Whitetech plc: separate designated Client account					20,000.00	20,000.00Cr
Jan 2	Whitetech plc: separate designated Client account (interest)					200.00	20,200.00Cr

Corresponding entry to show interest received in separate designated Client account

Conclusion

In this section, we have considered two separate topics: first, the recording of stakeholder money upon receipt and its subsequent transfer to the client upon completion; and, second, the receipt of interest and the recording of a payment of a sum in lieu of interest to a client. While the exercises accompanying this section primarily concentrate on stakeholder money in the context of conveyancing on sales, money may also be held by a solicitor as stakeholder money in other types of transaction such as business sales in which the same principles apply. Finally, in relation to interest, it can be a matter of contention between client and practice as to the rate of interest paid or whether a sum is to be paid in lieu. It is therefore important in practice to be able to determine how much interest should be paid and when any payment made should be recorded in the appropriate ledgers.

Section 6

Completion Statements

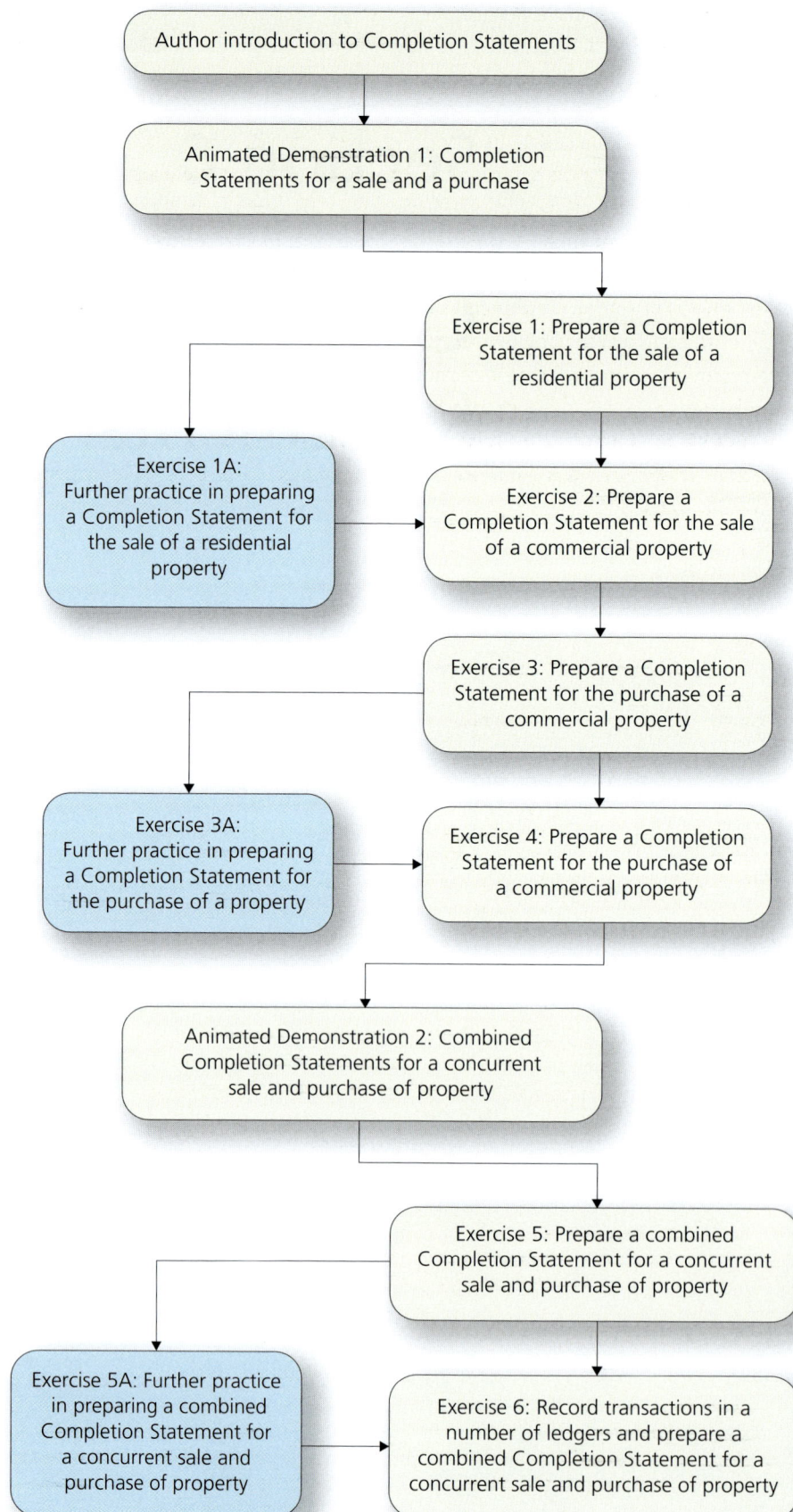

Exercise map

Author introduction to Completion Statements

Animated Demonstration 1: Completion Statements for a sale and a purchase

Exercise 1: Prepare a Completion Statement for the sale of a residential property

Exercise 1A: Further practice in preparing a Completion Statement for the sale of a residential property

Exercise 2: Prepare a Completion Statement for the sale of a commercial property

Exercise 3: Prepare a Completion Statement for the purchase of a commercial property

Exercise 3A: Further practice in preparing a Completion Statement for the purchase of a property

Exercise 4: Prepare a Completion Statement for the purchase of a commercial property

Animated Demonstration 2: Combined Completion Statements for a concurrent sale and purchase of property

Exercise 5: Prepare a combined Completion Statement for a concurrent sale and purchase of property

Exercise 5A: Further practice in preparing a combined Completion Statement for a concurrent sale and purchase of property

Exercise 6: Record transactions in a number of ledgers and prepare a combined Completion Statement for a concurrent sale and purchase of property

Introduction

You may have observed from the exercises you have been undertaking that, when the client is nearing the completion of their property purchase, he or she conveniently provides the precise funds to cover the monies required to complete, to pay stamp duty land tax and Land Registry fees, and to cover the costs of the practice.

It will not be by chance that the client will send you the precise funds. Rather it will be after you have prepared a statement of account setting out what the client will need to provide so that the property transaction may proceed to completion. It will be your role to prepare and send to the client such a Completion Statement. In this section we will look at the preparation of Completion Statements for the sale and then the purchase of properties, before moving on to consider a combined Completion Statement in a situation when the client is both selling and purchasing property.

The accompanying exercises to this section will require you to prepare Completion Statements relating to some of the exercises which you may have undertaken in previous sections. Before you begin the exercises, read the section below and watch Animated Demonstrations 1 which provides guidance on how to prepare Completion Statements for both a sale and a purchase.

Completion Statement
Suffolk Plumbing Supplies Ltd
Sale of Unit 10 Bilton Road, Ipswich

Sale price		690,000.00
Less Mortgage redemption (HSBC plc)		350,000.00
		340,000.00
Less		
Our costs (as per bill attached)	2,500.00	
Estate agent's fee	15,000.00	17,500.00
Balance due to you (£):		322,500.00

01:16 05:28

Completion Statements: Sale

When the client is selling a property, the aim of the Completion Statement is to show how much, by way of proceeds of sale, they will receive upon completion. As a result the Completion Statement for a sale will, from the sale price, be a series of deductions.

As we can see from the Completion Statement prepared for Sarah Yates in Example 6.1, from the sale price of £250,000 the first item to be deducted relates to any charges associated with the property, in this case an outstanding mortgage of £120,000. From the resulting figure of £130,000, being the initial proceeds of sale, the cost of selling the property must be taken into account. For a sale these will include your fees, any expenses and disbursements that you may have incurred as part of the property sale, and estate agency fees. From Example 6.1, we can see that in Sarah's case, it will have cost a total of £8,750 to sell the property, and once this is deducted from the £130,000 she will receive £121,250 as the proceeds of the sale of her property.

Example 6.1

Completion Statement
Sarah Yates
Sale of 20 First Avenue, Frinton-on-Sea

Sale price		250,000.00
Less: mortgage redemption (Nationwide Building Society)		120,000.00
		130,000.00
Less:		
Our costs (as per bill attached)	2,500.00	
Estate agent's fee	6,250.00	8,750.00
Balance due to you (£):		121,250.00

It must be noted that in practice any number of house styles may be adopted, and it will be for you to ensure that you prepare Completion Statements, and other documents, that conform to that house style. However, for the purposes of *LPC Accounts Online*, the detail that would otherwise be set out in an invoice will not be set out in the Completion Statement. When Completion Statements are prepared, an invoice will normally also be prepared at the same time and both documents will be sent to the client together. Consequently, it will only be the total value of the invoice that will be included in the Completion Statement.

Essential Principles

Completion Statements: Sale

■ State sale price

— deduct: charges against the property;

— deduct: costs of transaction.

On *LPC Accounts Online* as you complete your Completion Statement for a sale when deducting any mortgage that is being redeemed against the property, state this as 'mortgage redemption [name of mortgage provider]'. An example of this is set out on Example 6.1. Note also the title style of the heading of the Completion Statement. As you can see, from Example 6.1 the document is first headed with 'Completion Statement', with the name of the client and the property to which it relates included directly beneath. You should follow this style when completing the exercises in this section of *LPC Accounts Online*.

Once you have watched Animated Demonstration 1, undertake Exercises 1 and 2 and practise preparing Completion Statements for the sale of both a residential and a commercial property. The information that you will need for their preparation may be drawn from the Client ledgers and additional information provided.

ⓘ This first exercise will look at a basic Completion Statement for a residential sale.

Read the question below and consider the information provided to you in the Client ledger. Based on this information you are to prepare a Completion Statement for Richard Moss to illustrate how much will be due to him following completion. When you are ready to create the Completion Statement, click the 'Your ledgers' tab above or the 'Complete your ledgers' button at the bottom of your screen and make the necessary entries in the Completion Statement provided. Once you are happy with the Completion Statement you have created click 'Submit' to see your feedback and score.

Don't forget, you can click 'Save' at any point if you want to come back to this exercise later.

❓ Hawkins & Co. acted for Richard Moss who sold his 'Kiss-me-Quick' souvenir shop at Clacton-on-Sea for £78,000. The property is mortgaged to Writtle Building Society for £30,000, which was repaid with the proceeds of sales. Upon completion of the sale, the firm will send Richard a cheque for the amount of the proceeds of sale after deduction of all expenses.

Use the information recorded on the Client ledger below to create Richard's Completion Statement. Remember, when you are preparing the Completion Statement to ensure that it is logically prepared and easy for your client to understand.

Client: Moss, R.   **Matter: Conveyancing—sale 'Kiss-me-Quick' souvenir shop, Clacton-on-Sea**

Date	Detail	Office account Dr (£)	Office account Cr (£)	Office account Bal (£)	Client account Dr (£)	Client account Cr (£)	Client account Bal (£)
Aug 31	Cash: deeds fee	25.00		25.00Dr			
Sept 3	Cash: official copies	12.00		37.00Dr			
Sept 15	Cash: deposit on sale					7,800.00	7,800.00Cr
Sept 16	Costs	600.00		637.00Dr			
Sept 16	VAT on costs	105.00		742.00Dr			
Sept 27	Cash: completion money					70,200.00	78,000.00Cr
Sept 27	Cash: mortgage redemption				30,000.00		48,000.00Cr
Sept 27	Cash: costs transfer				742.00		47,258.00Cr
Sept 27	Cash: costs transfer		742.00	0.00			
Sept 27	Cash: estate agent's fees				1,950.00		45,308.00Cr
Sept 27	Cash: balance to client				45,308.00		0.00

Completion statement

Back

Save | Print | If you are happy with your ledgers | Submit | Clear all

Completion Statements: Purchase

In contrast to a Completion Statement for a sale, a Completion Statement for a purchase will need to state clearly what is required from the client in order that the practice has sufficient funds to complete the property purchase successfully.

In relation to a Completion Statement for a purchase, once all contributions have been deducted from the purchase price, it will then be necessary to add the costs of the transactions and all post-completion disbursements that the client must pay in order to complete.

For example, if we look at the Completion Statement prepared for Sarah in Example 6.2 below, we can see that, from the purchase price of £350,000, a mortgage of £200,000 will be advanced towards the purchase. In addition, the 10 per cent deposit of £35,000 already paid by Sarah at exchange of contracts will be deducted and, consequently, this will mean that there is currently a shortfall of funds towards the purchase price of £115,000. However, to this shortfall, the costs of purchasing the property must be added to ensure that there are sufficient funds to pay your costs, the expenses and disbursements associated with a property purchase, and the stamp duty land tax and Land Registry fees due on the property to be paid at completion. As a result, in Example 6.2 we can see that a further £12,720 needs to be provided. These costs, added to the shortfall towards the purchase price, mean that prior to completion Sarah must provide a total of £127,720.

Example 6.2

Completion Statement
Sarah Yates
Purchase of 45 Upper Fourth Lane, Frinton-on-Sea

Purchase price		350,000.00
Less:		
Mortgage advance (Barclays Bank plc)	200,000.00	
Deposit paid by you	35,000.00	235,000.00
		115,000.00
Add:		
Our costs (as per bill attached)	2,000.00	
Stamp duty land tax	10,500.00	
Land Registry fees	220.00	12,720.00
Balance required from to you to complete (£):		127,720.00

It is important to note that if the Completion Statement is incorrectly prepared, and insufficient funds are requested from the client, the practice will have to make the decision either to delay completion, and so potentially hold up the entire chain of property transactions, or seek to make up the difference while the shortfall in funds is requested from the client. Either is an undesirable outcome and may also have a consequential impact on how the client has budgeted for his or her purchase and could, in the most extreme case, possibly affect the decision to proceed.

Essential Principles

Completion Statements: Purchase

- State purchase price
  — deduct:
    - mortgage advance; and
    - deposit contributed by the client
  — add:
    + costs of transaction;
    + post-completion disbursements.

In *LPC Accounts Online* when identifying any mortgage contribution that the client will be receiving towards the property in the Purchase Completion Statement use the following format: 'mortgage advance [name of mortgage provider]' An example of this is set out in Example 6.2 above.

Exercises 3 and 4 provide you with the opportunity to prepare Completion Statements for a purchase. Again, when you are preparing these statements, the information that you require can be drawn from the Client ledgers and additional information provided.

ⓘ This is the first exercise to look at Completion Statements for a purchase, in the context of commercial property.

Read the question below and consider the information provided in the Client ledger. Based on this information you are to prepare a Completion Statement for the Devon Heritage Trust. When you are ready to create the Completion Statement click the 'Your ledgers' tab above or the 'Complete your ledgers' button at the bottom of your screen and make the necessary entries in the Completion Statement provided. When you are happy with the Completion Statement you have created click 'Submit' to see your feedback and score.

Don't forget, you can click 'Save' at any point if you want to come back to this exercise later.

❓ Hawkins & Co. act for the Devon Heritage Trust who are purchasing an old Devon tin mine site manager's grace and favour residence near Zeenor, Bideford. The Zeenor site building will cost £70,000, purchased with the assistance of a mortgage of £35,000 from HSBC plc and is to be part of a restoration programme; it is to be restored with the assistance of lottery funding.

Use the information recorded on the Client ledger below to prepare the Completion Statement. Remember, when you are preparing the Completion Statement to ensure that it is logically prepared and easy for your client to understand.

Client: Devon Heritage Trust   **Matter: Purchase of Zeenor site building**

Date	Detail	Office account Dr (£)	Office account Cr (£)	Office account Bal (£)	Client account Dr (£)	Client account Cr (£)	Client account Bal (£)
Oct 1	Cash: local search	100.00		100.00Dr			
Oct 1	Cash: mining search	24.00		124.00Dr			
Oct 1	Cash: commons registration search	14.00		138.00Dr			
Oct 9	Cash: deposit from client					7,000.00	7,000.00Cr
Oct 14	Cash: deposit paid on purchase				7,000.00		0.00
Oct 16	Cash: bankruptcy search	2.00		140.00Dr			
Oct 17	Costs	500.00		640.00Dr			
Oct 17	VAT on costs	87.50		727.50Dr			
Oct 20	Cash: balance to complete (£727.50 office money)					28,787.50	28,787.50Cr
Oct 24	Cash: mortgage advance (HSBC plc)					35,000.00	63,787.50Cr
Oct 25	Cash: balance paid to complete				63,000.00		787.50Cr
Oct 25	Cash: Land Registry fee				60.00		727.50Cr
Oct 27	Cash: costs transfer				727.50		0.00
Oct 27	Cash: costs transfer		727.50	0.00			

	I	

Back

Save   Print   If you are happy with your ledgers   Submit   Clear all

Drawing against uncleared funds

A further consideration as to the timing of a Completion Statement on a purchase is that it will need to be prepared in good time to permit the receipt of cleared funds from the client prior to completion. If cleared funds are not received, the practice will have to consider whether to proceed. Rule 1(c) of the Solicitors' Accounts Rules 1998 poses problems for a practice that seeks to use uncleared funds for a client matter only to find that the cheque is dishonoured. The same can be said of electronic transfers of money; there will still be a need to wait for the transfer to complete before one can be sure that the funds have been cleared.

Solicitors' Accounts Rules 1998

Rule 1 – Principles

A *solicitor* must comply with the requirement of rule 1 of the Solicitors' Code of Conduct 2007, and in particular must:

. . .

   (c) use each *client's* money for that *client's* matters only;

. . .

Consequently, if the practice is waiting for funds to be cleared, and money is withdrawn from the Client account to complete the transaction, this may mean that another client's money is being used while clearance is awaited. The Solicitors' Accounts Rules 1998 appear to condone this approach, not explicitly, but by implication through the wording of

Rule 22, notes (v) and (vi) and paragraph 4.3 of Appendix 3; consideration must be given to the risk assessment policy operated by the practice.

Solicitors' Accounts Rules 1998

Rule 22 – Withdrawals from a client account

...

Drawing against uncleared cheques

(v) A solicitor should use discretion in drawing against a cheque received from or on behalf of a client before it has been cleared. If the cheque is not met, other clients' money will have been used to make the payment in breach of the rules. See rule 7 (duty to remedy breaches). A solicitor may be able to avoid a breach of the rules by instructing the bank or building society to charge all unpaid credits to the solicitor's office or personal account.

Non-receipt of telegraphic transfer

(vi) If a solicitor acting for a client withdraws money from a general client account on the strength of information that a telegraphic transfer is on its way, but the telegraphic transfer does not arrive, the solicitor will have used other clients' money in breach of the rules. See also rule 7 (duty to remedy breaches).

...

Solicitors' Accounts Rules 1998

Appendix 3

SRA Guidelines – Accounting Procedures and Systems

...

4.3 The firm should have a system for checking the balances on client ledger accounts to ensure no debit balances occur. Where payments are to be made other than out of cleared funds, clear policies and procedures must be in place to ensure that adequate risk assessment is applied.

N.B. If incoming payments are ultimately dishonoured, a debit balance will arise, in breach of the rules, and full replacement of the shortfall will be required under rule 7. See also rule 22, notes (v) and (vi).

...

The consequences for a practice, and the fee earner who permits a payment out of the Client account against an uncleared cheque which is subsequently dishonoured, will be a breach of Rule 1(d) (see Rule 22, notes (v) and (vi)). Further, both the Principals in the practice and the fee-earner responsible will have a duty to remedy the breach (Rule 7), which will mean replacing any missing client money from the Principals' own resources. Without question, the practice will look to the fee-earner to indemnify the Principals, although any prudent practice will not permit a non-partner to sign or authorise withdrawals from the Client account in such circumstances.

Completion statements: Combined sale and purchase

So far we have only considered separate transactions relating first to the sale of a property and second to the purchase of a property. Obviously, once on the property ladder most clients, when moving from one property to another, will seek to undertake the sale and purchase transactions concurrently. As a result it will be necessary to prepare a combined sale and purchase Completion Statement.

Having undertaken a number of exercises in preparing separate Completion Statements, you will now need to combine these. The aim is to provide the client with a statement that shows, once proceeds of sale have been used by way of contribution towards the purchase, what the shortfall is that the client must provide. Whilst this may appear straightforward, there are a number of matters of which you should be aware.

From the Completion Statement set out in Example 6.3, we can see that Sarah is undertaking a sale and purchase concurrently. The first part of the Completion Statement will be for the sale. As you can see there is no difference from that set out in Example 6.1 on page 112. The difference arises when we start to look at the purchase.

Let's assume that the deposit of £25,000 received from Sarah's buyer has been used as part of the deposit that she has paid for her onward purchase. Whilst the seller of the property Sarah is buying will have received a deposit of £35,000 representing 10 per cent of the sale price, because Sarah has used the deposit she received herself, she only needs to contribute a further £10,000 to make up the difference towards that deposit. Sarah has used some of the proceeds from her sale early.

As a result, when the monies required for the purchase are calculated, it appears that, compared to when Sarah was undertaking a purchase only, more is required in order to complete the purchase aspect of the combined transaction. However, once the proceeds of sale and the shortfall on purchase have been calculated separately, a further calculation is required to work out the difference. This requires the inclusion of a summary statement to show the balance needed to complete both transactions once all the proceeds of the sale have been used as a contribution towards the purchase. In Sarah's case, we can see from Example 6.3 that a further sum of £31,470 is required to complete both transactions. For further guidance on the calculation of the summary statement, watch Animated Demonstration two Online.

Accordingly, when preparing a combined Completion Statement, care should be taken to ensure that when identifying the contributions toward the purchase price only the sum sent to you by the client is used, and that there is not any early use of the proceeds of sale, i.e. any deposit from the buyer.

Example 6.3

Completion Statement
Sarah Yates
Sale of 20 First Avenue, Frinton-on-Sea and
Purchase of 45 Upper Fourth Lane, Frinton-on-Sea

Sale of 20 First Avenue, Frinton-on-Sea

Sale price		250,000.00
Less: Mortgage redemption (Nationwide Building Society)		120,000.00
		130,000.00
Less:		
Our costs (as per bill attached)	2,500.00	
Estate agent's fee	6,250.00	8,750.00
Balance available from the sale:		121,250.00

Purchase of 45 Upper Fourth Lane, Frinton-on-Sea

Purchase price		350,000.00
Less:		
Mortgage advance (Barclays Bank plc)	200,000.00	
Deposit paid by you:	10,000.00	210,000.00
		140,000.00
Add:		
Our costs (as per the bill attached)	2,000.00	
Stamp duty land tax	10,500.00	
Land Registry fees	220.00	12,720.00
Balance required to complete purchase:		152,720.00

Summary

Balance required to complete purchase:		152,720.00
Less: Balance available from the sale:		121,250.00
Balance required to complete both transactions (£):		31,470.00

Essential Principles

Combined Completion Statements:

Sale:

- State sale price
  - — deduct: charges against the property
  - — deduct: costs of transaction.

Purchase:

- State purchase price
  - — deduct:
    - – mortgage advance; and
    - – deposit contributed by the client.
  - — add:
    - + costs of transaction;
    - + post-completion disbursements.

Summary statement:

- Balance required to complete purchase
- *Less* balance available from the sale.

If you have not done so already, watch Animated Demonstration 2 online for further information on how to prepare combined Completion Statements and the potential pitfalls to watch out for.

Completion Statement
Helen Lane
Sale of 27 The Gables, Winchester & Purchase of 14 Lawn Lane, Swindon

Sale of 27 The Gables

Sale price		275,000.00
Less Mortgage redemption (Nationwide Building Society)		210,000.00
		65,000.00
Less		
Our costs (as per the bill attached)	482.00	
Estate agent's fee	4,700.00	5,182.00
Balance available from the sale:		59,818.00

Purchase of 14 Lawn Lane, Swindon

Purchase price		340,000.00
Less		
Mortgage advance (Abbey National)	282,500.00	
Deposit contribution from you	6,500.00	289,000.00
		51,000.00
Add		
Our costs (as per the bill attached)	1,002.00	
Stamp duty land tax	10,200.00	
Land Registry fees	220.00	11,422.00
Balance required to complete purchase:		62,422.00

01:01 05:21

Once you have watched Animated Demonstration 2, attempt Exercise 5 and practise preparing a combined Completion Statement for a sale and a purchase.

Sale of Flat, 12 Mountgrove Road		
Purchase of White Pillars, Essex.		

The final exercise of this section, Exercise 6, will require you first to record a number of transactions relating to the sale and purchase of a property in the ledgers provided. You will then be required to prepare a combined Completion Statement using the information recorded in the ledgers you have created. This exercise is longer than others you may have undertaken so make sure you leave yourself plenty of time in which to undertake this exercise.

This is the final exercise relating to Completion Statements.

Read the question below and the transactions that follow. In this exercise you are required to record the transactions relating to Louise Morse's sale and purchase of property in the Cash book and personal ledger of Ms Morse. You should then prepare a combined Completion Statement to send to your client in order for them to send you the appropriate funds required to complete the purchase.

When you are ready to record these transactions and prepare the combined Completion Statement click the 'Your ledgers' tab above or the 'Complete your ledgers' button at the bottom of your screen and make the necessary entries in the ledgers and Completion Statement provided. When you are happy with the ledgers and combined Completion Statement you have created click 'Submit' to see your feedback and score.

Don't forget, you can click 'Save' at any point if you want to come back to this exercise later.

Hawkins & Co. act for Louise Morse on the sale of her property, 23 Upper Street, London, for £260,000 and the purchase of Rosewood Cottage, Cambridge for L395,000.

Ms Morse will be purchasing Rosewood Cottage with the assistance of a mortgage advance of £300,000 from HSBC plc, to be received two days prior to completion. Hawkins & Co. will also act for HSBC plc in relation to the mortgage advance. On completion of the sale of 23 Upper Street the mortgage on that property, amounting to £165,000 and owed to Coutts Bank, is to be repaid.

The following transactions were completed by the firm on Ms Morse's file:

- Oct 3   Paid local land charges fee of £250 for local search on the purchase of Rosewood Cottage.

- Oct 3   Paid £39 for water and drainage search on the purchase of Rosewood Cottage.

- Oct 3   Paid £49 for environmental survey on the purchase of Rosewood Cottage.

- Oct 3   Paid £12 for official copies of the register of title to 23 Upper Street.

- Oct 19   Received £13,500 from Ms Morse, to be used towards the deposit on the purchase of Rosewood Cottage.

- Oct 24   Exchanged contracts on the sale of 23 Upper Street and received £26,000 deposit from the buyer's solicitor.

- Oct 24   Exchanged contracts on the purchase of Rosewood Cottage and paid the deposit of £39,500 to the seller's solicitors.

Conclusion

The importance of preparing accurate Completion Statements cannot be understated. An inaccuracy may mean that you request too much from your client and give good cause for your client to question your abilities. Alternatively, if too little is requested, this will not only cause problems for your client but may also result in a series of property transactions being delayed.

Section 7

VAT on expenses and disbursements

Exercise map

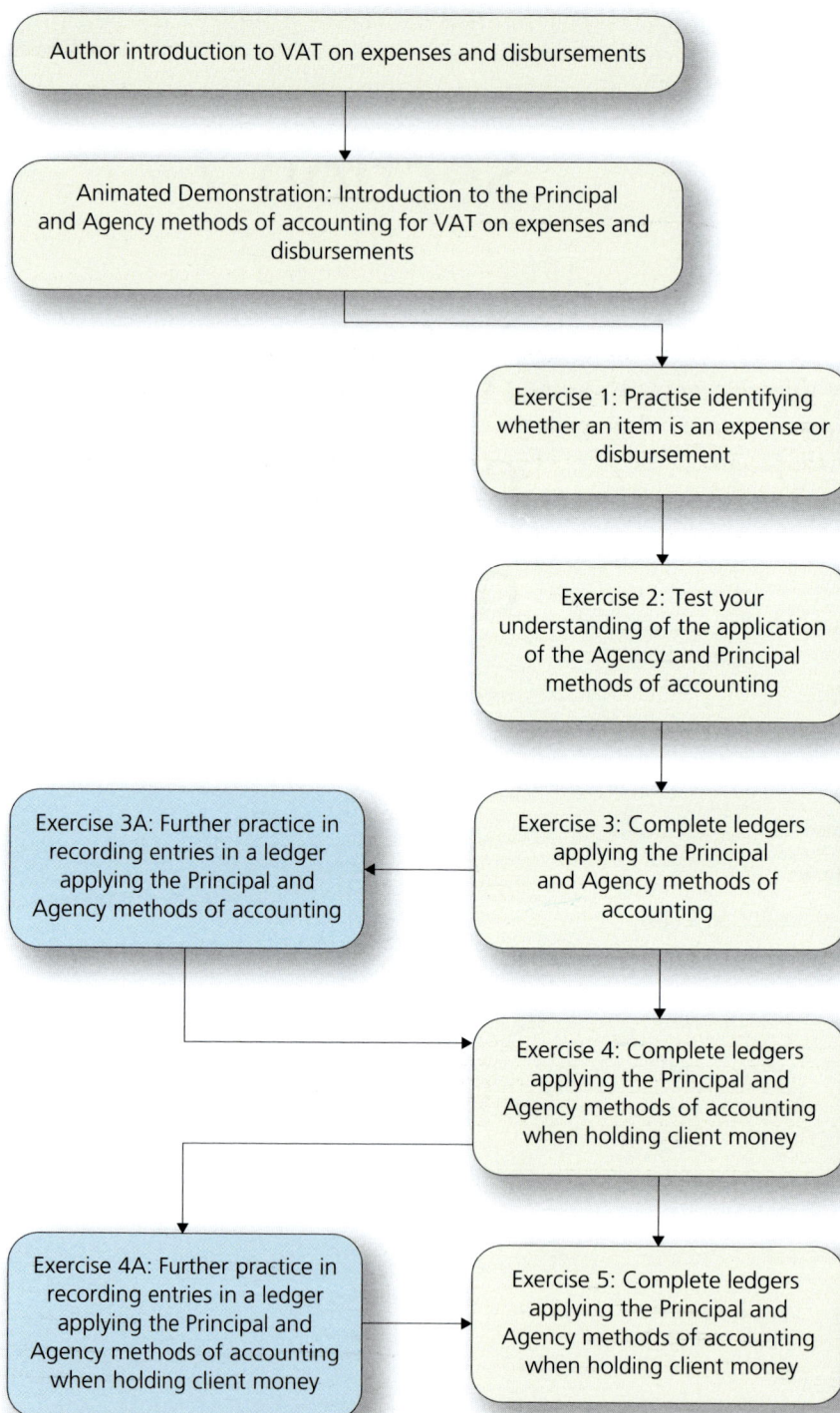

Author introduction to VAT on expenses and disbursements

↓

Animated Demonstration: Introduction to the Principal and Agency methods of accounting for VAT on expenses and disbursements

↓

Exercise 1: Practise identifying whether an item is an expense or disbursement

↓

Exercise 2: Test your understanding of the application of the Agency and Principal methods of accounting

↓

Exercise 3A: Further practice in recording entries in a ledger applying the Principal and Agency methods of accounting ← Exercise 3: Complete ledgers applying the Principal and Agency methods of accounting

↓

Exercise 4: Complete ledgers applying the Principal and Agency methods of accounting when holding client money

↓

Exercise 4A: Further practice in recording entries in a ledger applying the Principal and Agency methods of accounting when holding client money → Exercise 5: Complete ledgers applying the Principal and Agency methods of accounting when holding client money

Introduction

In this section we will look at VAT on out-of-pocket expenses incurred by a practice during the provision of legal services to a client, including how this is recorded and subsequently invoiced to the client. To do so, we will first look at the differences between expenses and disbursements. This will be followed by looking at how two methods of accounting, the Principal and Agency methods, are used to record such items.

So far during *LPC Accounts Online* no VAT has been charged upon those items that you have been recording on Client ledgers when incurred by the practice. However, there will be times when the practice will incur items that are subject to VAT and you will be required to record the net sum and VAT separately – to refresh yourself as to how to record the net sum and VAT see 'Accounting for VAT' in Section 1 on page 26. We now need to consider how this will work in the context of the dual ledger system and ensure that when the practice pays for an item during the provision of legal services to a client any VAT that is charged to the practice at the point of purchase or invoice is recovered from the client, or charged at the standard rate of VAT. For a detailed explanation and worked examples highlighting how to account for VAT, go online and watch the Animated Demonstration.

Cash book: Hawkins & Co.

Date	Detail	Office account Dr (£)	Cr (£)	Bal (£)	Client account Dr (£)	Cr (£)	Bal (£)
Sept 1	Balance b/d			200,000.00Dr			65,000.00Dr

Client: Davies, D.   Matter: Contract litigation

Date	Detail	Office account Dr (£)	Cr (£)	Bal (£)	Client account Dr (£)	Cr (£)	Bal (£)

Client: Moss, R.   Matter: Contract litigation

Date	Detail	Office account Dr (£)	Cr (£)	Bal (£)	Client account Dr (£)	Cr (£)	Bal (£)

01/01 10:00

Expenses and disbursements

Expenses

An expense is simply a payment made by a solicitor in the course of a client's matter to enable the solicitor to provide a legal service to the client.

In addition to an hourly rate charged by the solicitor in advising a client (which is set at a rate to account for the overheads of the practice), any additional item that a solicitor has to incur to be able to provide a legal service and advise a client is an expense. For example, for the solicitor to attend a meeting with a client the cost incurred in getting to that meeting is an expense – i.e. the solicitor would not be able to provide the service of advising the client at the meeting without incurring the expense of travelling.

> ### Essential Principles
>
> **Expense**
>
> A payment made by a solicitor required to be incurred in the provision of legal services.

Disbursements

By contrast, a disbursement is a payment made by a solicitor on behalf of a client for a service or product supplied to the client.

For example, a court fee that must be paid by the client in order for him or her to use the facilities of the court is a disbursement. Remember, it is not the solicitor that goes to court; it is the client that is in need of the court services in order to obtain a legal resolution to a dispute – the client has come to you, the solicitor, to seek your assistance and expertise. If the client had not come to you, the client would still be required to pay the court fee so as to make use of the court service.

> ### Essential Principles
>
> **Disbursement**
>
> A payment made by a solicitor on behalf of a client for a service provided to the client.

Now is a suitable opportunity to undertake Exercise 1 to test whether you are able to distinguish items of expense and disbursement.

(i) This exercise is designed to assist you in identifying whether an item incurred during a client's matter is an expense or a disbursement. Drag the words 'Expense' and 'Disbursement' and drop them next to the statements to which you think they apply. When you are happy with your selection, click the 'Submit' button at the bottom of your screen to view your scores and see feedback on your answers.

(?) Office copy entries

                                             Expense   Disbursement

(?) Personal search fee to Companies House

                                             Expense   Disbursement

(?) Train fare to travel to conference with counsel

                                             Expense   Disbursement

(?) Environmental search

                                             Expense   Disbursement

(?) Telegraphic transfer fee

                                             Expense   Disbursement

(?) Expert's report

                                             Expense   Disbursement

(?) Bankruptcy search

                                             Expense   Disbursement

(?) Water & Drainage search

                                             Expense   Disbursement

The significance of distinguishing expenses and disbursements

Distinguishing expenses and disbursements is important, as one of two methods of accounting will be applied to the manner in which they are recorded on the ledgers and then recharged to the client.

- Expenses:

  When recording the payment of an expense and its recharge to the client the *Principal* method of accounting must be used.

- Disbursements:

  When recording the payment of a disbursement and its recharge to the client, if the invoice is addressed to:

  — the practice, the *Principal* method of accounting must be used;

  — the client or there is no VAT invoice, the *Agency* method of accounting must be used.

The Principal method of accounting

As we have noted above, the Principal method of accounting must be used and applied to the recording of:

- expenses; and
- disbursements, where the VAT invoice is addressed to the practice.

Under the Principal method of accounting it is the solicitor who is deemed to have received the service, even in the case of a disbursement (as the invoice is addressed to the practice), and it is the solicitor who is therefore required to pay for the item. As a consequence, when the Principal method of accounting applies, office money will always be used to pay for the item of expense or disbursement.

We now need to consider how we are going to record the payment for an item of expense or disbursement. When VAT is charged, we must ensure that the net value of the item and the VAT are recorded separately. For example, if we look at Example 7.1, we can see the Cash book, the Client ledger for Sarah Yates, and the VAT ledger. Let's assume that the practice has paid for the photocopying of duplicate bundles prior to a court hearing and was charged £100 plus £17.50 for VAT.

When making the necessary entries for this expense, the net value of £100 will first be recorded as a credit entry in the Office account of the Cash book with a corresponding debit entry in the Office account of the Client ledger. The VAT will then be recorded as a credit entry in the Office account of the Cash book, with its corresponding debit entry in the VAT ledger.

But if the VAT is recorded in the VAT ledger, how does the practice ensure that it is then able to recover the VAT paid for the item of expense or disbursement? To include a further entry in the Client ledger is not possible as there is no possible means for making a corresponding entry anywhere. Consequently, and as you can see in Example 7.1, a 'memo' has been included in the Detail column of the Client ledger to indicate that VAT was charged on the purchase of this item and that when the client is invoiced VAT is to be reclaimed.

Essential Principles

Principal method of accounting:

- Cash book (Office account):
  - net sum = credit entry
  - VAT = credit entry.
- Client ledger (Office account):
  - net sum = debit entry (and memo to record net to charge/recover VAT at standard rate).
- VAT ledger:
  - VAT = debit entry.

Reclaiming and charging VAT

When the practice invoices the client for an expense and/or disbursement, the practice *must charge* the client VAT, even if the practice was not charged VAT at the point of purchase – such as for rail travel, which is zero-rated for the purposes of VAT.

Example 7.1

Cash book: Hawkins & Co.

Date	Detail	Office account			Client account		
		Dr (£)	Cr (£)	Bal (£)	Dr (£)	Cr (£)	Bal (£)
Oct 1	Balance b/d			10,508.00Cr			180,500.00Dr
Oct 5	Yates, S.		100.00	10,608.00Cr			
Oct 5	VAT		17.50	10,625.50Cr			

Client: Yates, S.

Date	Detail	Office account			Client account		
		Dr (£)	Cr (£)	Bal (£)	Dr (£)	Cr (£)	Bal (£)
Oct 5	Cash: photocopying (memo: VAT £17.50)	100.00		100.00Dr			

VAT (HM Revenue & Customs)

Date	Detail	Debit (£)	Credit (£)	Balance (£)
Oct 1	Balance b/d			1,200.00Cr
Oct 5	Cash		17.50	1,182.50Cr

Entry 1: record the net value of the expense or disbursement

Entry 3: record the VAT charged on the expense or disbursement

Client ledger detail:
'Cash: photocopying (memo: VAT £17.50)'

Entry 2: corresponding entry in the Client ledger for the net value of the expense or disbursement

Entry 4: corresponding entry in the VAT ledger for the VAT charged on the expense or disbursement

It is the practice that is deemed to have made the supply of legal services to the client, and this will include any necessary expenses and/or disbursements incurred by the practice – all of which are subject to VAT at the standard rate. Accordingly, when the practice invoices the client, if VAT is charged at the point of purchase or payment of an invoice, then this must be recovered from the client or, if no VAT was paid, the client must be charged VAT on the item.

> ### Essential Principles
>
> Principal method of accounting:
>
> ■ Invoicing client: charge (recover) VAT even if you did not pay input VAT.

If we now look at Sarah's ledger in Example 7.2, we can see that a number of further items of expenses and disbursements have been incurred, and the Principal method of accounting has been applied. When Sarah is then subsequently invoiced, after the costs and the VAT on costs have been recorded, a further entry must be made to ensure that all VAT paid on items of expense and disbursement is then recovered, or if none was paid, that it is charged. The corresponding entry for this further item of VAT is made in the VAT ledger.

The Agency method of accounting

By contrast, the Agency method of accounting is only to be used for disbursements when the invoice is addressed to the client, including disbursements for which no VAT invoice will be issued (such as for court fees).

Under the Agency method of accounting the practice is deemed to make the payment to the supplier on behalf of the client, and if there is a VAT invoice addressed to the client, it is for the client to recover the VAT on the invoice. Consequently, under the Agency method of accounting the practice will record and pay the gross sum only, and when invoicing the client, will seek only to recover this gross sum. No entry will be made in the VAT ledger as VAT is the client's concern, not the practice's.

We can see how this works by looking at the Cash book and Sarah's ledger in Example 7.3. Let's assume that the practice has received an invoice addressed to Sarah from an expert for £1,000 plus £175 VAT, and that the invoice was paid by the practice. The entries required are a credit entry in the Office account of the Cash book with a corresponding debit entry in the Office account of the Client ledger, recording the gross sum in each. And, when Sarah is subsequently invoiced, only the gross sum is to be recovered.

Example 7.2

Client: Yates, S.

Date	Detail	Office account			Client account		
		Dr (£)	Cr (£)	Bal (£)	Dr (£)	Cr (£)	Bal (£)
Oct 5	Cash: photocopying (memo: VAT £17.50)	100.00		100.00Dr			
Oct 10	Cash: train fare (memo: VAT £21.00)	120.00		220.00Dr			
Oct 20	Cash: expert fee (memo: VAT £175.00)	1,000.00		1,220.00Dr			
Nov 1	Costs	2,000.00		3,220.00Dr			
Nov 1	VAT on costs	350.00		3,570.00Dr			
Nov 1	VAT on expenses & disbursements	213.50		3,783.50Dr			

> When invoicing the client, after recording the costs and the VAT on costs, add all 'memos' together and include a further figure for VAT to recover, or charge, on expenses and disbursements incurred by the practice

VAT (HM Revenue & Customs)

Date	Detail	Debit (£)	Credit (£)	Balance (£)
Oct 1	Balance b/d			1,200.00Cr
Oct 5	Cash	17.50		1,182.50Cr
Oct 20	Cash	175.00		1,007.50Cr
Nov 1	Yates, S.		350.00	1,357.50Cr
Nov 1	Yates, S.		213.50	1,571.00Cr

> Corresponding entry for VAT to be charged or recovered on expenses or disbursements incurred

Example 7.3

Cash book: Hawkins & Co.

Date	Detail	Office account			Client account		
		Dr (£)	Cr (£)	Bal (£)	Dr (£)	Cr (£)	Bal (£)
Nov 1	Balance b/d			10,500.00Cr			180,500.00Dr
Nov 5	Yates, S.		1,175.00	11,675.00Cr			

Agency disbursement: withdraw only the gross sum from the Cash book and make a corresponding debit entry in the Client ledger

Client: Yates, S.

Date	Detail	Office account			Client account		
		Dr (£)	Cr (£)	Bal (£)	Dr (£)	Cr (£)	Bal (£)
Nov 5	Cash: expert fee	1,175.00		1,175.00Dr			
Nov 10	Costs	2,000.00		3,175.00Dr			
Nov 10	VAT on costs	350.00		3,525.00Dr			

Essential Principles

Agency method of accounting:

- Invoicing client: recover gross sum only.

Only when an expense or disbursement is addressed to the practice will a further entry be made to record that the client is being invoiced VAT at the standard rate on those items.

Now attempt Exercise 2 to see whether you can identify when and how to apply the Principal and Agency methods of accounting for VAT in respect of expenses and disbursements.

This exercise is designed to help you identify how to apply the Agency and Principal methods of accounting for VAT in respect of expenses and disbursements. Set out below are statements relating to how expenses and disbursements are to be recorded in the Client ledger. You need to identify which statements are true and which are false. When you have made your selection click the 'submit' button at the bottom of your screen to view your score and receive feedback on your answers.

	True	False
You incurred travel costs getting to a meeting with your client; the train fare you purchased is zero-rated for the purposes of VAT. When you record this item of expense in the Client ledger, you will apply the Principal method of accounting and charge VAT when invoicing the client.	○	○
In acting for your client in a litigation matter, you pay court fees of £400, which is exempted from VAT. When you record this item of expense in the Client ledger, you will apply the Agency method of accounting and will not charge VAT when invoicing the client.	○	○
You receive an invoice from an expert witness engaged on behalf of the client's matter; the invoice is addressed to the client. When recording the payment of this invoice you apply the Agency method of accounting and pay the net amount and VAT separately.	○	○
You are acting for a client for whom you are holding money on account of costs generally in the Client account. You incur travel expenses. You must use office money to pay for the expense.	○	○
You receive counsel's invoice addressed to the practice. Accordingly you will apply the Principal method of accounting. When recording the payment of this invoice you make two entries, one in the Cash book to record the payment of the gross amount and a corresponding entry in the Client ledger for the gross amount.	○	○

Once you have completed Exercise 2, undertake Exercise 3 which will require you to apply the Principal and Agency methods of accounting whilst making entries on a number of Client ledgers. Don't forget, when you are making entries applying the Principal method of accounting, to include a 'memo' in the Detail column of the Client ledger.

This first dual ledger exercise relating to VAT will require you to determine whether an item is an expense or a disbursement.

Read the question below and the transactions that follow. When you are ready, click on the 'Your ledgers' tab above or the 'Complete your ledger' button at the bottom of your screen to see the various ledgers in which you are required to record the transactions linked to Beach Huts Ltd and Boyle & Bird Partnership. For each transaction you will be expected to apply the appropriate accounting method, either the Agency or Principal method of accounting. When you are happy with the ledgers you have created, click 'Submit' at the bottom of your screen to see your feedback and score.

Don't forget, you can click 'Save' at any point if you want to come back to an exercise later.

Hawkins & Co. are acting for various clients on different matters, and have incurred a number of expenses and disbursements during the course of those matters. Record the following transactions in the ledgers provided:

- May 3   Beach Huts Ltd file: paid £146 (zero-rated for VAT) train fare to travel to site meeting with expert.

- May 6   Beach Huts Ltd file: paid an expert's fee of £1,000 plus £175 VAT. The expert's invoice was addressed to the practice.

- May 14   Boyle & Bird Partnership file: received expert's invoice addressed to the practice and paid fees of £2,500 plus £437.50 VAT.

- May 15   Boyle & Bird Partnership file: paid £26 plus £4.55 VAT for photocopying expenses.

- May 15   Boyle & Bird Partnership file: paid £300 (VAT exempt) for court fee paid on issue of proceedings on behalf of the client.

- May 15   Beach Huts Ltd file: received expert's invoice addressed to the client and paid £600 on behalf of the client.

- May 18   Boyle & Bird Partnership file: paid £55 (zero-rated for VAT) train fare for conference with counsel.

Money on account of costs

Quite simply, when the practice is holding money on account of costs for a client, such money may then be used for the payment of a disbursement that is addressed to the client, i.e. an Agency disbursement.

Essential Principles

Agency method of accounting:

- Cash book:

  — gross sum = credit entry

    Client account if holding client money, otherwise Office account if not holding client money.

- Client ledger:

  — gross sum = debit entry

    Client account if holding client money, otherwise Office account if *not* holding client money.

Client money must never be used for payment of an expense or a disbursement addressed to the practice. Only once the client has been invoiced may the practice seek to transfer money held on account of costs from the Client account to the Office account (see SAR 19(2) and (3)).

Counsel's fees

The final item to consider is the payment of counsel's fees. Counsel will always invoice the practice and never the client directly. As counsel's fees are regarded as a disbursement, and the invoices are addressed to the practice, the Principal method of accounting will be used as outlined above – see 'The Principal method of accounting' at page 127.

However, under HM Revenue & Customs rules there is a dispensation in respect of counsel's fees. These rules permit, when client money on account of costs generally is held by the practice, client money to be used to pay for counsel's fees directly from the Client account. Accordingly, when client money is held, the Agency method of accounting will be used to pay counsel's fees.

It is worth noting that it is not incorrect for the practice to pay counsel's fees from the Office account in any event, even if client money is held. However, it is more prudent to use the client's money whenever possible. It is this Agency method of accounting when client money is held that *LPC Accounts Online* will adopt in respect of counsel's fee.

> **Essential Principles**
>
> Counsel's fees:
> - Holding client money on account of costs:
>   — Agency method of accounting.
> - No client money:
>   — Principal method of accounting.

Having looked at the use of client money and the dispensation in relation to counsel's fees, attempt Exercises 4 and 5. These exercises will again require you to apply the Principal and Agency methods of accounting for expenses and disbursements, but where possible you should seek to use client money. Before you start the exercises, identify those entries for which you may use client money. Again, when you can only apply the Principal method of accounting, be sure to include the 'memo' in the Detail column of the Client ledger.

In this exercise we will look again at how to apply the Agency and Principal methods of accounting for expenses and disbursements, but, where possible, you should use Client money to pay for such items.

Read the question below and the transactions that follow. When you are ready click on the 'Your ledgers' tab above or the 'Complete your ledgers' button at the bottom of your screen to see the various ledgers in which you are required to record the various transactions linked to Beach Huts Ltd and Boyle & Bird Partnership. Remember, in this exercise, where it is possible and correct to do so, you should make the entries using client money. When you are happy with the ledgers you have created, click 'Submit' at the bottom of your screen to see your feedback and score.

Don't forget, you can click 'Save' at any point if you want to come back to this exercise later.

Hawkins & Co. are acting for various clients on different matters, and have incurred a number of expenses and disbursements during the course of those matters. Record the following transactions in the ledgers provided:

- May 1   Boyle & Bird Partnership file: received and banked the client's cheque for £6,500 on account of costs generally.

- May 1   Beach Huts Ltd file: received and banked the client's cheque for £5,000 on account of costs generally.

- May 3   Beach Huts Ltd file: paid £146 (zero-rated for VAT) train fare to travel to site meeting with expert.

- May 6   Beach Huts Ltd file: paid counsel's fee of £1,000 plus £175 VAT. Counsel's invoice was addressed to the practice.

- May 14 Boyle & Bird Partnership file: received expert's invoice addressed to the client and paid fees of £2,500 plus £437.50 VAT.

- May 15 Boyle & Bird Partnership file: paid £26 plus £4.55 VAT for photocopying expenses.

- May 15 Boyle & Bird Partnership file: paid £300 (VAT exempt) for court fee paid on issue of proceedings on behalf of the client.

- May 15 Beach Huts Ltd file: received expert's invoice addressed to the client and paid £600 on behalf of the client.

Cash book: Hawkins & Co.

Date	Detail	Office account		
		Dr (£)	Cr (£)	Bal (£)
Aug 12	Balance b/d			1,500.00Dr

Client: Walton, E.　　　　**Matter: Design infringement litigation**

Date	Detail	Office account		
		Dr (£)	Cr (£)	Bal (£)

Conclusion

Once you have completed the exercises accompanying this section, you will have fully applied the Principal and Agency methods of accounting for expenses and disbursements, having first distinguished each. The application of these rules of accounting will ensure that the practice is capable of recording all payments of VAT and that it then recovers those payments or, as appropriate, charges VAT at the standard rate as part of the overall provision of legal services. It also means that the practice is able to pay for items directly from the Client account, rather than having continually to use office money.

www.**oxford**interact.com

Section 8

Abatements and bad debts

Exercise map

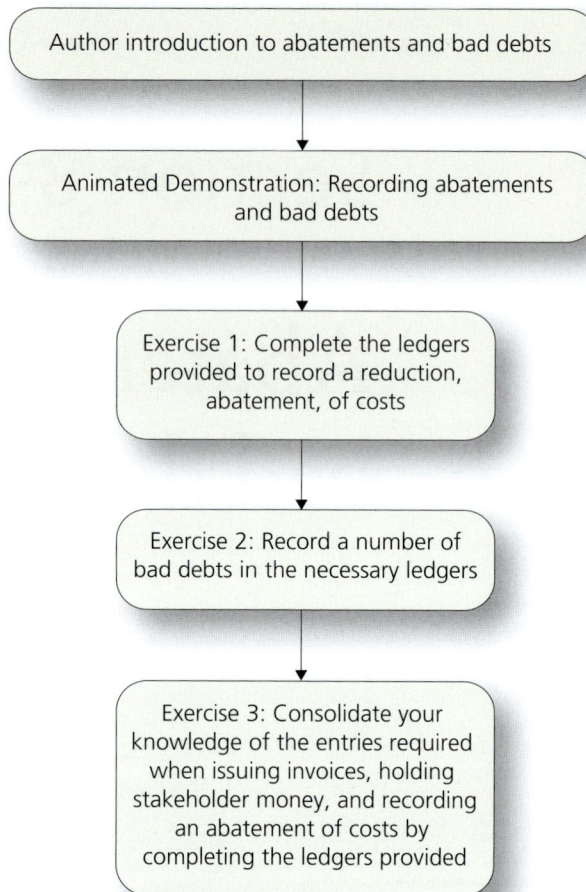

```
┌─────────────────────────────────────────────┐
│  Author introduction to abatements and bad   │
│                    debts                      │
└─────────────────────────────────────────────┘
                      │
                      ▼
┌─────────────────────────────────────────────┐
│  Animated Demonstration: Recording abatements │
│               and bad debts                    │
└─────────────────────────────────────────────┘
                      │
                      ▼
        ┌─────────────────────────────┐
        │  Exercise 1: Complete the ledgers │
        │  provided to record a reduction,  │
        │     abatement, of costs           │
        └─────────────────────────────┘
                      │
                      ▼
        ┌─────────────────────────────┐
        │  Exercise 2: Record a number of │
        │  bad debts in the necessary ledgers │
        └─────────────────────────────┘
                      │
                      ▼
        ┌─────────────────────────────┐
        │  Exercise 3: Consolidate your     │
        │  knowledge of the entries required │
        │  when issuing invoices, holding   │
        │  stakeholder money, and recording │
        │  an abatement of costs by         │
        │  completing the ledgers provided  │
        └─────────────────────────────┘
```

Introduction

We have now reached the final section of Solicitors' Accounts in *LPC Accounts Online*. In getting to this stage we have progressed through the basic principles of double entry book-keeping, to looking at and using the dual ledger system of accounting. We have also sought to apply extensively the Solicitors' Accounts Rules 1998.

In this final section we will look at how the practice will make the necessary accounting entries to reflect a reduction in a client's invoice or the need to write off debt owed by a client as bad. If a client disagrees with the sum stated on an invoice, they may seek to reduce the invoice. This is the issue of abatement that we will look at first. We will then turn to the final issue and address how to deal with the unfortunate reality that not all clients pay their invoices, and the subsequent need to write off the debt owed by such clients as bad.

As you work your way through this section undertake the exercises provided online. However, before you attempt any exercises, go online and watch the Animated Demonstration which illustrates how abatements and bad debts are recorded.

Client: Johnson, H.		Matter: Employment dispute					
		Office account			Client account		
Date	Detail	Dr (£)	Cr (£)	Bal (£)	Dr (£)	Cr (£)	Bal (£)
Jan 7	Cash: expert's fee (memo: VAT £70.00)	400.00		400.00Dr			
Mar 5	Cash: counsel's fee (memo: VAT £105)	600.00		1,000.00Dr			
Mar 17	Cash: court fee	150.00		1,150.00Dr			
Sept 9	Costs	6,000.00		7,150.00Dr			
Sept 9	VAT on costs	1,050.00		8,200.00Dr			
Sept 9	VAT on disbursements	175.00		8,375.00Dr			

Sales & Costs account

Date	Detail	Debit (£)	Credit (£)	Balance (£)
Sept 1	Balance b/d			13,250.00Cr
Sept 9	Johnson, H.		6,000.00	19,250.00Cr

VAT (HM Revenue & Customs)

Date	Detail	Debit (£)	Credit (£)	Balance (£)
Sept 1	Balance b/d			10,200.00Cr
Sept 9	Johnson, H.		1,050.00	11,250.00Cr
Sept 9	Johnson, H.		175.00	11,425.00Cr

Bad debts

Date	Detail	Debit (£)	Credit (£)	Balance (£)
Sept 1	Balance b/d			18,980.00Dr

01:16 05:13

Abatements

The legal profession is no different from any other business activity in that there will be times when clients are not happy with the invoices they receive. There may be any number of reasons why, after discussing the matter with the client, the practice may agree to reduce, or abate, the costs of providing a service to a client. The need for such agreement on the part of the practice may arise if the client considers the service below the standard expected, regards the invoice as excessive, or identifies an error in the invoice. Whatever the reason for agreeing to reduce the costs, the practice will issue a credit note to the client to reflect the fact that a lesser sum is now due. It is this reduced sum that the practice will seek to recover.

When this abatement of costs occurs, it will need to be reflected on the Client ledger to show a reduction in the costs and a corresponding reduction in VAT. Under HM Revenue & Customs rules a proportionate reduction in VAT charged on the invoice is permitted.

Accordingly, when making the entries to record a reduction in a client's invoice, it will be necessary first to show the reduction in the costs charged against the Client ledger and then a proportionate reduction in VAT. If we look at Example 8.1 which show the ledgers for Sarah Yates, we can see that, as at 10 September, once costs of £1,000 plus VAT of £175 have been added to her ledger and she has been invoiced, she owes £8,175.

If we then assume that it has been agreed with Sarah to reduce the costs invoiced by £500, a credit entry will be made in the Client ledger to show this reduction (and to reflect the issuing of a credit note), with a corresponding debit entry being made in the Sales & Costs ledger. The next entry to be made will be to reduce the VAT by a proportionate sum. In this example, as the costs are being reduced by £500, VAT on this sum at the standard rate is £87.50. It is this £87.50 that is entered into the Client ledger and the corresponding entry is entered into the VAT ledger.

Example 8.1

Client: Yates, S.

Date	Detail	Office account Dr (£)	Office account Cr (£)	Bal (£)	Client account Dr (£)	Client account Cr (£)	Bal (£)
Sept 10	Balance b/d			7,000.00Dr			
Sept 10	VAT on costs	1,000.00		8,000.00Dr			
Sept 10	VAT on disbursements	175.00		8,175.00Dr			
Oct 29	Costs: abatement		500.00	7,675.00Dr			
Oct 29	VAT: abatement		87.50	7,587.50Dr			

Entry 1: credit entry to reflect the agreed reduction in costs

Entry 3: credit entry to reflect proportionate reduction in VAT on costs

Sales & Costs account

Date	Detail	Debit (£)	Credit (£)	Balance (£)
Sept 1	Balance b/d			13,250.00Cr
Sept 10	Yates, S.		6,000.00	19,250.00Cr
Oct 29	Yates, S.	500.00		18,750.00Cr

Entry 2: debit entry to reflect both the agreed reduction in costs and costs charged by the practice

VAT (HM Revenue & Customs)

Date	Detail	Debit (£)	Credit (£)	Balance (£)
Sept 1	Balance b/d			10,200.00Cr
Sept 10	Yates, S.		175.00	10,375.00Cr
Oct 29	Yates, S.	87.50		10,287.50Cr

Entry 4: debit entry to reflect both the proportionate reduction in VAT on costs and VAT to be collected by the practice

It is worth noting that where VAT has been charged on expenses and disbursements, unless it has been agreed to remove any such item from the invoice, there is no reduction on VAT charged on such items. This is further explained in the Animated Demonstration online, which you should now watch if you have not done so already.

Essential Principles

Abatement of costs:

■ Reduction in costs:
— Client ledger: credit entry, Office account;
— Sales & Costs ledger: debit entry.

■ Proportionate reduction in VAT on costs:
— Client ledger: credit entry, Office account;
— VAT ledger: debit entry.

You should now attempt Exercise 1 and practise recording the abatement of costs against a client's invoice.

ⓘ This first exercise will concentrate on the entries required to reflect a reduction in the solicitor's invoice. Any number of reasons may require a reduction of the solicitor's costs, and when such a reduction is agreed a credit note will be issued.

Read the question below and the transactions that follow. In this exercise you are required to make the entries necessary to reflect a reduction in the client's invoice. When you are ready, click the 'Your ledgers' tab above or the 'Complete your ledgers' button at the bottom of your screen and make the entries required in the ledgers provided to reduce the invoices linked to both Helen Lane and Ellingworth Contracting Ltd. When you are happy with the ledgers you have created, click 'Submit' at the bottom of your screen to see your feedback and score.

Don't forget, you can click 'Save' at any point if you want to come back to this exercise later.

❓ Hawkins & Co. have recently agreed to reduce its invoices for Helen Lane and Ellingworth Contracting Ltd. Record the following transactions in the appropriate ledgers provided:

- Nov 5 Issued invoice to Helen Lane in relation to age discrimination advice for £1,200 plus £210 VAT.
- Nov 12 Issued invoice to Ellingworth Contracting Ltd to cover costs and expenses incurred in relation to planning advice for £18,000 plus £3,150 VAT.
- Nov 30 Following a telephone conversation with Helen Lane, it has been agreed to reduce her invoice by £200 plus VAT.
- Dec 13 The firm agrees to reduce its costs on its invoice to Ellingworth Contracting Ltd to £17,000 plus VAT.

Save | Print | Complete your ledgers

Bad debts

It is a harsh, but commercial, reality that some debts will never be paid for any number of reasons. As with all businesses, a law practice will, at the end of each accounting period, review the debts owed to it and ask itself whether these debts will be paid. Those debts identified as unlikely to be recovered will be written off.

When a practice decides to write a debt off, the accounts must be adjusted to reflect correctly that the client's debt has been written off and that, as a business, the acumulated bad debts of the business over the year have increased.

The recording of bad debts is straightforward and will only require an entry in the Client ledger and the Bad debts ledger. If we look at Example 8.2 and assume that the outstanding debt owed by Sarah, even after an abatement of costs, is unlikely to be paid to the practice, and that the practice has decided to write the debt off as bad, we must make a credit entry of £7,587.50, being the outstanding balance, in the Client ledger. The corresponding entry should then be made in the Bad debts ledger, as can be seen in Example 8.2.

Essential Principles

Bad debts:

- Client ledger: credit entry, Office account;
- Bad debts ledger: debit entry.

Now attempt Exercise 2 to practise how to record the need to write off a number of debts by the practice.

This exercise will now look at how to record bad debts. It is an inevitable fact of business that not all customers will pay their debts, and this also applies to solicitors' clients.

Read the question below and the transactions that follow. In this exercise you are required to make the entries necessary to reflect the writing off of debts owed to the firm. When you are ready, click the 'Your ledgers' tab above or the 'Complete your ledgers' button at the bottom of your screen and make the necessary entries in the ledgers provided to record debts that the practice has had to write off as non-recoverable. When you are happy with the ledgers you have created, click 'Submit' at the bottom of your screen to see your feedback and score.

Don't forget, you can click 'Save' at any point if you want to come back to this exercise later.

Hawkins & Co. have reached their year end, 31 January, and are currently reviewing their various ledgers in readiness to prepare their year end financial statements. A number of ledgers require updating to reflect invoices that have been issued and debts that the practice has had to write off as non-recoverable. Record the following transactions in the appropriate ledgers provided:

- Dec 15   Issued invoice to Phillip Wickendon following the preparation of his will for £275.00 plus £48.13 VAT.

- Dec 16   Issued invoice to Eleanor Round in relation to a debt recovery action undertaken to cover costs and expenses incurred for £400.00 plus £70.00 VAT.

- Jan 31   It has been agreed that the following client debts are unlikely to be unrecoverable and should therefore be written off as bad:
  - Helen Lane;
  - Ellingworth Contracting Ltd;
  - Phillip Wickendon;
  - Eleanor Round.

Save   Print   Complete your ledgers

Example 8.2

Client: Yates, S.

Office account / Client account

Date	Detail	Dr (£)	Cr (£)	Bal (£)	Dr (£)	Cr (£)	Bal (£)
Sept 10	Balance b/d			7,000.00Dr			
Sept 10	VAT on costs	1,000.00		8,000.00Dr			
Sept 10	VAT on disbursements	175.00		8,175.00Dr			
Oct 29	Costs: abatement		500.00	7,675.00Dr			
Oct 29	VAT: abatement		87.50	7,587.50Dr			
Dec 31	Bad debts		7,587.50	0.00			

Entry 1: credit entry to clear the balance (debt) owed by the client

Bad debts

Date	Detail	Debit (£)	Credit (£)	Balance (£)
Oct 31	Balance b/d			80,000.00Dr
Nov 1	Yates, S.	7,587.50		87,587.50Dr

Entry 2: debit entry to record that debt associated with a client has been written off

Once you have completed Exercise 2, move on to complete Exercise 3, the final exercise in this section of *LPC Accounts Online*. This exercise is designed to help you consolidate your learning to date and test your knowledge and understanding of a number of accounting principles.

This final exercise in this section of *LPC Accounts Online* is designed to help you consolidate your learning and to test your knowledge and understanding of a number of accounting principles.

Read the question below and the transactions that follow. When you are ready, click the 'Your ledgers' tab above or the 'Complete your ledgers' button at the bottom of your screen to see the various ledgers in which you are required to make the necessary entries to record the transactions linked to the sale of Mandy Sherman's property. When you are happy with the ledgers you have created, click 'Submit' at the bottom of your screen to see your feedback and score.

Don't forget, you can click 'Save' at any point if you want to come back to this exercise later.

Hawkins & Co. acts for Mandy Sherman on the sale of her property, The Long House, London, for £850,000. On completion of the sale, the mortgage on that property, amounting to £450,000 and owed to St James' Place Bank, is to be repaid.

The following transactions were completed by the firm on Ms Sherman's file. Record each transaction in the appropriate ledgers provided:

- Nov 11 Paid £12 to HM Land Registry for official copies.

- Nov 12 Cheque for £12 received from Ms Sherman to cover the cost of official copies.

- Nov 19 Deposit of £85,000 is received on exchange of contracts to be held by the practice as stakeholder.

- Nov 20 Issued bill to Ms Sherman for the sale of The Long House for £4,000 plus £700 VAT and any disbursements and expenses. Ms Sherman has also been sent a Completion Statement showing how much she will receive upon completion.

- Nov 22 Ms Sherman called to discuss the invoice and highlighted that it is higher than anticipated; the practice agrees to reduce its costs by £500 plus VAT. The Completion Statement previously prepared is adjusted and resent to Ms Sherman.

- Dec 5   The balance on the sale of £765,000 is received from purchaser's solicitors.

Conclusion

This was the final section of *LPC Accounts Online* relating to Solicitors' Accounts. You should now have developed an understanding of, and should be confident with, the application of double entry book-keeping principles. You should also be aware of your professional body's accounts rules as they apply to the dual ledger system of accounting and ensure that you are complying with these rules when recording transactions on the ledgers. You have also considered the need to pay your clients a sum in lieu of interest when you are undertaking work for them which requires you to hold their money, and have an awareness of the correct application of the rules relating to VAT so that you charge and recover the correct money from your clients. This final topic of abatement and bad debts finishes the Solicitors' Accounts course.

www.**oxford**interact.com

Introduction

Part 2

Business Accounts

Section 9

Preparation of financial Statements

Exercise map

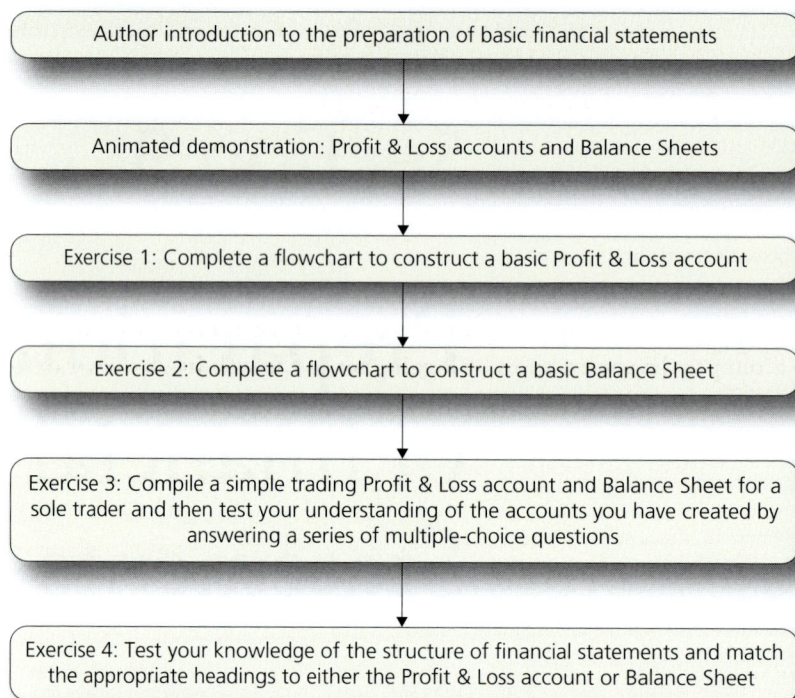

Author introduction to the preparation of basic financial statements

↓

Animated demonstration: Profit & Loss accounts and Balance Sheets

↓

Exercise 1: Complete a flowchart to construct a basic Profit & Loss account

↓

Exercise 2: Complete a flowchart to construct a basic Balance Sheet

↓

Exercise 3: Compile a simple trading Profit & Loss account and Balance Sheet for a sole trader and then test your understanding of the accounts you have created by answering a series of multiple-choice questions

↓

Exercise 4: Test your knowledge of the structure of financial statements and match the appropriate headings to either the Profit & Loss account or Balance Sheet

Introduction

During Part 2 of *LPC Accounts Online* you will be introduced to Profit & Loss accounts and Balance Sheets; financial statements that all businesses prepare at the end of their financial year. In particular we will look at and examine the financial statements for different business entities, including sole traders, partnerships and companies. It is only by examining the financial statements for each of these different business entities that you will gain a level of understanding that will assist you in analysing the financial statements to which we will apply various assessment ratios in Section 13 of *LPC Accounts Online*.

It is important to understand early that the more practice you undertake in the analysis and construction of financial statements, the easier you will find Business Accounts. To aid you in this purpose at various stages throughout the sections that follow you will be directed to attempt relevant exercises by logging on to the website at <www.oxfordinter-act.com/lpcaccounts>.

Why Business Accounts?

Why is it that you, as an aspiring lawyer, are required to gain an understanding and knowledge of financial statements?

Whilst it will be most unlikely that you will prepare financial statements for your clients' businesses, you will need to understand the information presented to you. In whatever area of practice you train and qualify into, you will be required to draw upon a vast area of personal experience and knowledge to be able to fully advise your clients. Although you may assume that the need to understand financial statements is restricted to a business context, other practice areas will also require a working knowledge of the construction and composition of financial statements. For example if you are conducting litigation, involved in property transactions, or even in a family practice you will often be required to understand business accounts in order to progress a client's matter. It will be rare that you will not come across financial statements; at the very least, you will be required to understand the advice you are receiving from other professionals who may be interpreting financial statements for you. It is by having this understanding that you will be able to help your client achieve their aims, be that the financial ramifications of entering into a business transaction or analysing the accounts belonging to another party so that you can identify assets to pursue in a litigation claim.

But why will your clients be preparing financial statements in the first place? This may seem obvious, but it is only by understanding why clients do something will that you will be able to fully advise them. Clients, by maintaining financial accounts (such as those which you may already have encountered in your study of Solicitors' Accounts) are recording the business' dealings, showing how the business is making and spending money during the course of a financial year, normally 12 months. It is from these records that financial statements are prepared, and so aid in the regular monitoring of the business' financial performance and its accountability to its proprietors. It is only by this process of regular review that your client's management will know if they are being successful in making money to pay the business' debts as they fall due and pay the proprietors, be they a sole trader, partner or shareholder, a return on their investment. These regular reviews also help the business' management formulate appropriate strategic decisions to push the business forward and help secure its future. Put simply, financial statements represent a summary of all of a business' dealings during a defined period extracted from records of every type of business transaction.

Who prepares financial statements?

From the day-to-day business records maintained by the business, accountants will collate and present, in accordance with industry standards, two key financial statements:

- Profit & Loss accounts, and

- Balance Sheets.

We will look at these financial statements in more detail below. However, further reports may also be prepared for internal purposes to drill down the high level of information presented to permit, for example, analysis of the performance of certain departments, business sectors, products or services supplied to or by the business.

Depending on the business entity concerned, it is also the accountant who will assist in identifying possible tax reliefs and exemptions that the business can adopt, thereby efficiently using the assets it has at its disposal and reducing the burden of tax for both the business and its proprietors. As a lawyer, you may be called upon to help implement such tax efficient schemes, either as part of a larger commercial transaction or as part of estate planning for an individual client; only by having an understanding of the accounts of a business will you be able to do so. Further, it will not just be the business and its advisers who will have an interest in financial statements; other external parties such as HM Revenue & Customs will take an active interest in the performance of a business to ensure that both the business' and proprietors' tax liability are correctly calculated.

Accounting Standards

As we will see when we move on to consider Company Accounts (see Section 12), certain accounting standards are set by statute. The Companies Act 2006 requires companies to present their accounts so as to give a '*true and fair view of the state of affairs of the company*' (emphasis added). However, the Companies Act 2006 is not the only source of accounting regulation and standards. The accountancy profession imposes standards so that financial statements are prepared on a uniform basis, applying agreed and accepted conventions to allow valid comparison of accounts prepared on a uniform basis – and in the global economy, many are internationally recognised standards, and so permit comparison of similar businesses in different jurisdictions.

The original big six UK accountancy firms were the driving force behind the standardisation of financial accounting and reporting. In the early 1990's the Accounting Standards Board's (ASB) inception and its adoption of existing standards meant that the developing standards gained statutory force. The ASB issued accounting standards are known as Financial Reporting Standards (FRSs). It is these standards that will be applied during

LPC Accounts Online, and we will look at them in more detail in Section 12. It is also such standards that qualified auditors will seek to ensure are correctly applied – a requirement that certain entities such as companies must ensure occurs regularly.

Auditors will not only be engaged in ensuring the application of accounting standards, but will often be engaged as an independent external party to help the management appraise the business. When financial audits are undertaken on a business, the duty owed is to the company members (i.e. the shareholders), and therefore the management of a business will often request audits as a means of confirming the reports they present to shareholders.

Preparation of financial statements

Let's now move on to the preparation of basic financial statements. We will first look at their structure and composition and then move on to consider the requirement to make adjustments to ensure their accuracy. Businesses at the close of an accounting period will prepare two financial reports:

- Profit & Loss account: a summary indicating how revenue generated by the business has, after operating expenses have been deducted, transformed into either a net profit or loss. The Profit & Loss account will often be expressed in terms of a 12 months period.

- Balance Sheet: a summary of the business' assets and liabilities as at a determined date, normally the last day of the accounting period.

Note at this early stage the distinction made between the two financial statements in that one identifies and includes the business' operating expenses (Profit & Loss account), whilst the other identifies the business' assets and existing and forthcoming liabilities (Balance Sheet). It is these two financial statements that we will seek to understand as you progress through your Business Accounts course and *LPC Accounts Online*.

One source of information used in the construction of financial statements is the trial balance. The trial balance is financial information relating to the business drawn from individual ledgers relating to each item of expense, revenue or asset - you will not be expected in *LPG Accounts Online* to extract this information from the ledgers themselves, but for some exercises such information will be provided to you as notes to the trial balances requiring you to make adjustments and so take account of facts that would not otherwise appear in the ledgers.

As you progress through the exercises, the construction and the need to make adjustments prior to the compilation of financial statements will become clearer. Let's now look at each of the two financial statements.

The Profit & Loss account

The first account that we will be looking at is the Profit & Loss account - it is from this that the Balance Sheet can be finalised. The Profit & Loss account will be prepared at the end of an accounting period to inform the management how much net profit or loss was made in that period. As the accounting period will normally be one year, the Profit & Loss account will accordingly be headed with the period to which it relates.

Classification of items & construction

The business will calculate its Net Profit or Loss by subtracting its operating expenses from any income generated from the sales made by the business. For the purposes of examining the structure of a Profit & Loss account we will be using Gerald's business accounts which are set out in Example 9.1.

Example 9.1

Gerald Boyle
Trading and Profit & Loss account for the year ending 31 September 2010

	£	£
Sales		22,000
less Cost of sales		
Opening stock	6,500	
add Purchases of stock	22,300	
	28,800	
less Closing stock	(10,000)	(18,800)
Gross Profit		3,200
less **Expenses**		
Administration	1,000	
Rent	400	
Telephone	140	
Utilities	220	
Wages	780	(2,540)
Net Profit		660

Top Line — brackets Sales through Gross Profit.

Bottom Line — brackets less Expenses through Net Profit.

The basic structure that you can see in Gerald's Profit & Loss account will, subject to some differences, be used throughout the following sections of *LPC Accounts Online*.

As you can see from Example 9.1 Gerald's Profit & Loss account has been set out to show first the total sales (or revenue) collected by his business, and then the Gross Profit – this is often referred to as the 'Top Line' as it appears at the top of the Profit & Loss account.

From the Gross Profit, the operating expenses of the business will be deducted to calculate the business' Net Profit – and since it forms the last line of the Profit & Loss account it is often referred to as the 'Bottom Line'; a phrase that you will often hear investors talking about when they enquire about the viability of a business.

Now let's divide the Profit & Loss account on this Top and Bottom line basis and look at each component in turn. If we look at Example 9.2, we will first consider how Gross Profit is calculated.

Having calculated Gross Profit, the indirect expenses of the business will need to be deducted to calculate Net Profit. The term indirect expenses refers to those business operating expenses that will be incurred even if the business does not buy or sell any goods, such as rent, wages or rates. Using the Gross Profit figure already calculated, Gerald will then deduct his expenses. This deduction is set out in Example 9.3.

Example 9.2

Heading: as the Profit & Loss account is a summary of the business' revenue and operating expenses showing either a Net Profit or Loss for a 12 month period, its title will be expressed as 'Trading and Profit & Loss account for the year ending…'.

Gerald Boyle
Trading and Profit & Loss Account for the year ending 31 September 2010

	£	£
Sales		22,000
less Cost of sales		
Opening stock	6,500	
add Purchases of stock	22,300	
	28,800	
less Closing stock	(10,000)	(18,800)
Gross Profit		3,200

Sales (the 'Top Line'): From the business' day-to-day activities, how much money has it generated? In this instance, Gerald has generated £22,000.

Note, the Sales figure will not include any sale (or disposal) of any asset (such as a shop) as this is not how income is generated by the business – such a sale will only be the conversion of one asset into another, i.e. property to cash cash, and therefore will be shown on the Balance Sheet as a Current Asset (cash) and not in the Profit & Loss account.

Gross Profit: Once the Sales figure is known, a separate calculation will be undertaken 'on sheet' to deduct the cost of goods sold by the business and so calculate Gross Profit. As a result, purchases of stock will be added to the opening stock held by the business at the start of the financial year. This figure then represents the total stock purchased or acquired during the financial year. The closing stock (i.e. the amount left at the end of the financial year) is then deducted. This figure now represents the cost of goods sold, and is deducted from Sales to determine Gross Profit.

As a result of having identified the total Sales for Gerald's business, from which the costs of goods sold and the business operating expenses have been deducted, the Net Profit is determined. In this instance, Gerald has made a modest profit of £660.

Essential Principles

Net Profit = (Gross Profit – Expenses)

Example 9.3

> **Expenses:** All those items of expense incurred by the business so it was able to operate and generate an income during the accounting period will be identified. In this instance, Gerald incurred expenses for administration, rent, telephone, utilities and wages.
>
> The Profit & Loss account will only include expenses applicable for the relevant year - so, items of expenses which have been paid and relate to the following year (pre-payments) will not be included, but those expenses which have not yet been paid by the business (and which arewhich are not therefore recorded in the ledgers) and relate to the year in question will be included (accruals). These latter items will require adjustments, which we will look at in more detail from page XX.

Gross Profit		3,200
less **Expenses**		
Administration	1,000	
Rent	400	
Telephone	140	
Utilities	220	
Wages	780	(2,540)
Net Profit		660

> **Net Profit (the 'Bottom Line'):** Once all operating business expenses for the accounting period have been identified and totalled, these will then be deducted from the Gross Profit figure and will give the business' Net Profit or Loss.

As we progress through the various business entities, we will gradually build on our understanding of the construction and various components of the Profit & Loss account. It will then be possible to see how the Net Profit figure (and others) influences the Balance Sheet.

The Balance Sheet

The Balance Sheet provides a snapshot of the overall business' value and relative wealth. It lists the assets and liabilities of the business, for one day only, i.e. the last day of the accounting period.

At the end of the accounting period, the business will close its income and expense ledgers and will transfer the balances to the Profit & Loss account to calculate Net Profit. The remaining ledgers will represent assets and liabilities which will remain open and their values will be listed on the Balance Sheet – their value will be carried forward from the end of one accounting year into the next.

Classification of items & construction

The Balance Sheet is so called because there are two balancing components. These represent how the business is using (employing) the capital investment that the proprietors have injected into the business in order that it can generate revenue and a profit (the top half), and secondly what the business owes to its proprietors (the bottom half). Every Balance Sheet needs to balance in this way. Let's now look at Gerald's Balance Sheet set out in Example 9.4.

Example 9.4

Gerald Boyle Balance Sheet as at 31 September 2010			
	£	£	£
Employment of Capital			
Fixed Assets			
Plant and machinery			16,000
Premises			18,000
			34,000
Current Assets			
Stock	10,000		
Trade debtors	12,260		
Cash at Bank	5,200	27,460	
less **Liabilities**			
Bank overdraft	2,000		
Creditors	14,800	(16,800)	10,660
Net Assets			**44,660**
Capital Employed			
Capital			40,000
Retained Profit to 31 September 2010			4,660
			44,660

Top Half / Bottom Half

As we did with the Profit & Loss account, we will look at each component in turn, separating the two halves, first looking at the Employment of Capital and then the Capital Employed section:

- **Employment of Capital:** The 'top half' of the Balance Sheet shows how money invested by and owed to the proprietor has been used and is shown as a 'Net Assets' figure. As you can see from Gerald's Balance Sheet, set out in Example 9.5, his investment has been used to buy various assets, both fixed and current. However offsetting this value, there are also debts (liabilities) owed to third parties.

Example 9.5

Heading: as the Balance Sheet is a summary of the business' assets and liabilities as at a determined date, normally the last day of the accounting period, its title will be expressed as 'Balance Sheet as at…'.

Fixed Assets: items of capital, such as plant and machinery or premises, bought and used by the business as part of its day-to-day business activities rather than for sale.

Although there are various conventions, LPC Accounts Online will always list these items alphabetically.

Gerald Boyle
Balance Sheet as at 31 September 2010

	£	£	£
Employment of Capital			
Fixed Assets			
Plant and machinery			16,000
Premises			18,000
			34,000
Current Assets			
Stock	10,000		
Trade debtors	12,260		
Cash at Bank	5,200	27,460	
less Liabilities			
Bank overdraft	2,000		
Creditors	14,800	(16,800)	10,660
Net Assets			44,660

Total Fixed Assets

Total Current Assets

Total Current Liabilities

Current Assets: These are assets that continually fluctuate (e.g. stock will be constantly changing as it is used and replenished) in value during the course of the year. They are listed according to their relative liquidity (i.e. the hardest to convert to cash is listed first).

Current Liabilities: Those items of debt due for repayment by the business within 12 months, such as bank overdrafts, taxation or creditors.
LPC Accounts Online will always list Current Liabilities alphabetically.

Total Current Assets *less* Current Liabilities

Net Assets: the total value of the business calculated as: Fixed Assets + (Current Assets - Current Liabilities)

In relation to the liabilities of the business, it is worth noting at this stage that anything repayable 12 months or more from the date of the Balance Sheet is a long term liability. Anything repayable within 12 months is a Current Liability. In this instance, you will note that Gerald has a bank overdraft, a short-term facility provided by banks which is capable of repayment on demand, and so classified as a Current Liability. Longer term loans and mortgages will be long term liabilities. This distinction between current and long-term liabilities is particularly important when we look at company Balance Sheets in Section 12 - something that is required by the Companies Act 2006 and prescribed by the Financial Reporting Standards.

Essential Principles

Net Assets = Fixed Assets + (Current Assets – Current Liabilities)

- **Capital Employed:** The 'bottom half' of the Balance Sheet shows the amount the business owes the proprietor and will include the initial capital invested and used by the business upon its creation and any profits it has retained. This is illustrated in Example 9.6.

Example 9.6

Balance: note that the 'bottom half' of the Balance Sheet has the same total as the **Employment of Capital** section showing that all the proprietors funds have accordingly been accounted for as being employed by the business.

Capital Employed			
Capital			40,000
Retained Profit to 31 September 2010			4,660
			44,660

Capital Employed: in Gerald's business we can see that he has £40,000 of **capital,** representing his initial and subsequent capital investment, and that the business has **retained profit** of £4,660, representing profit made to date but not withdrawn from the business by Gerald.

Compared to partnerships and companies, as a sole trader, Gerald will only have under the Capital Employed section sums representing Capital and Retained profits. In the case of a partnership the Capital Employed section will also identify the partners' own capital and their individual current accounts (see Section 11). For companies, the Capital Employed section will also show sums representing its share capital, any premium paid on its shares, reserves and Accumulated Retained Profit (see Section 12 for further detail).

Essential Principles

Once both halves have been calculated, they should balance (i.e. be the same):
Employment of Capital = Capital Employed

For further information on the basic structure and construction of both the Profit & Loss account and Balance Sheet go online and watch the Animated Demonstration.

Once you have viewed the Animated Demonstration, attempt Exercises 1 and 2 and identify the structure of each financial statement for yourself.

Capital Employed: Retained Profits

As we have already seen, under the Capital Employed section of the Balance Sheet, one of the items that may represent the proprietors' funds in the business, and so be employed by the business, is any profit that may have been retained. Whilst the expectation may be that the proprietors withdraw from the business any profits it makes as one of the benefits of investing, this will not always happen – it may be that the business wants to expand, and one of the obvious sources of finance will be to use the profits that the business has made to date.

ⓘ We have already seen how a basic Profit & Loss account and Balance Sheet should look. In this exercise you are required to identify the correct order in which the various headings should appear in a basic Profit & Loss account. Complete the flowchart below by placing the various headings in the correct order by selecting the correct option from those available. The first and final steps are completed for you. When you are happy with your flowchart, click 'Submit' at the bottom of your screen to see your feedback and score.

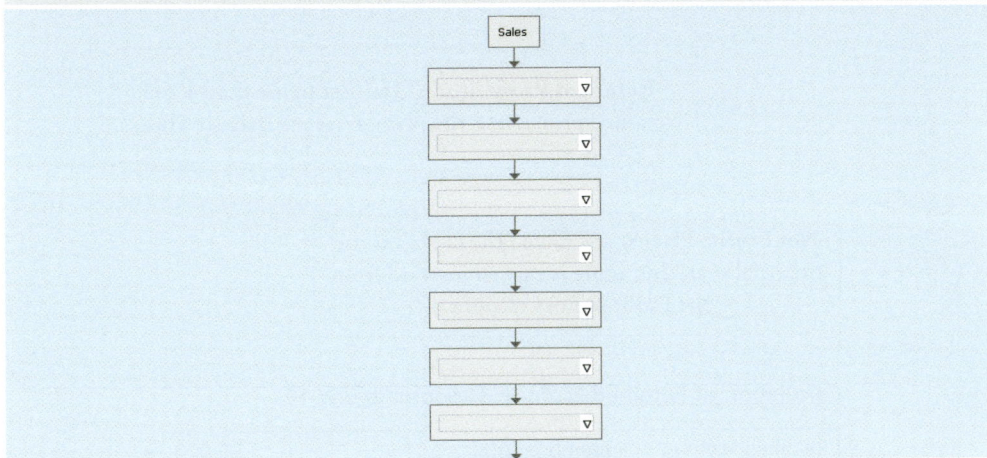

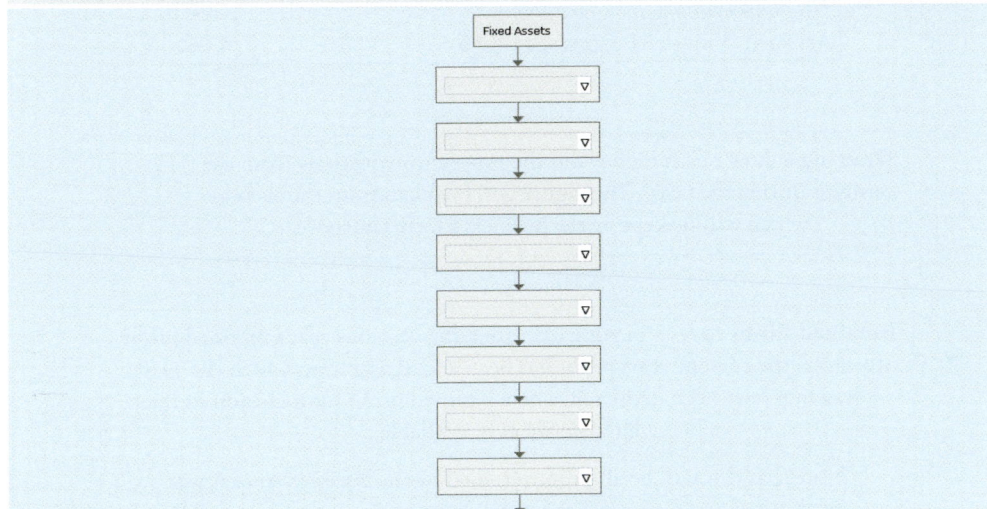

```
                    ┌──────────┐
                    │  Sales   │
                    └────┬─────┘
                         │
         ┌───────────────────────────────▽┐
         └─────────────────────────────────┘
                         │
         ┌───────────────────────────────▽┐
         └─────────────────────────────────┘
                         │
         ┌───────────────────────────────▽┐
         └─────────────────────────────────┘
                         │
         ┌───────────────────────────────▽┐
         └─────────────────────────────────┘
                         │
         ┌───────────────────────────────▽┐
         └─────────────────────────────────┘
                         │
         ┌───────────────────────────────▽┐
         └─────────────────────────────────┘
                         │
         ┌───────────────────────────────▽┐
         └─────────────────────────────────┘
                         │
```

ⓘ We have already seen how a basic Profit & Loss account and Balance Sheet should look. In this exercise you are required to identify the correct order in which the various headings should appear in a basic Balance Sheet. Complete the flowchart below by placing the various headings in the correct order by selecting the correct option from those available. The first and final steps are completed for you. When you are happy with your flowchart, click 'Submit' at the bottom of your screen to see your feedback and score.

```
                    ┌─────────────┐
                    │ Fixed Assets│
                    └──────┬──────┘
                           │
         ┌─────────────────────────────▽┐
         └───────────────────────────────┘
                           │
         ┌─────────────────────────────▽┐
         └───────────────────────────────┘
                           │
         ┌─────────────────────────────▽┐
         └───────────────────────────────┘
                           │
         ┌─────────────────────────────▽┐
         └───────────────────────────────┘
                           │
         ┌─────────────────────────────▽┐
         └───────────────────────────────┘
                           │
         ┌─────────────────────────────▽┐
         └───────────────────────────────┘
                           │
         ┌─────────────────────────────▽┐
         └───────────────────────────────┘
                           │
         ┌─────────────────────────────▽┐
         └───────────────────────────────┘
                           │
```

As a consequence, at the end of each accounting period, it is necessary to review and update the amount that the business has retained of its profit. This will then accurately reflect that amount retained by the business 'as at' the date of the Balance Sheet.

This calculation is not included in, nor is it part of, the Balance Sheet. Rather it is calculated separately to show how much retained profit is being held by the business. Example 9.7 illustrates the calculation used to determine Gerald's retained profit which, as we saw in Example 9.6 above, you will note amounts to £4,660.

Essential Principles

Retained Profit for the current year = (Retained Profit from previous year + Net Profit) – Drawings

Example 9.7

Retained Profit at . . . : The first figure used is the retained profit from the previous year's Balance Sheet.

Net Profit: Having calculated the profit for the financial year, this figure is carried forward from the Profit & Loss account.

Calculation of Retained Profit to 31 September 2010

Retained Profit at 1 September 2009	36,000
add Net Profit for the year	660
	36,660
less Drawings	32,000
Retained Profit to 31 September 2010	4,660

Drawings: how much money did the proprietor withdraw from the business during the year? This figure will be taken from the account which will be kept by the business for this purpose.

Retained Profit to . . . : Having identified the previous year's retained profit, to which the current years profit has been added and from which the year's drawings have been deducted, a new retained profit for inclusion in the Balance Sheet is available.

Note that this will be all profit retained by the business since it was established and represents the component of the proprietors funds in the business.

Now that we have looked through the basic construction of the Profit & Loss account and the Balance Sheet, and have considered the further calculation required to determine Retained Profit, you should attempt Exercise 3 and use the information provided to practise compiling your own basic financial statements.

As you undertake Exercise 3, note that when a sum is required to be calculated within a financial statement, the items that form part of that sum are placed in the left-hand column and the answers in the right. This is illustrated in Example 9.8.

For example and as you can see from Example 9.8, to determine Net Assets, you need to add total Fixed Assets to the sum of Current Assets *less* Current Liabilities. All the items for Current Assets and Current Liabilities have been listed in the left-hand column, with their totals then placed to the right of the last item. The difference between Current Assets and Current Liabilities is again placed to the right directly below the item (i.e. total Fixed Assets) that it will be added to.

James Rendall
Trading and Profit & Loss account for the year ending 31 March 2010

Sales
Opening stock
Purchases of Stock

Example 9.8

Gerald Boyle Balance Sheet as at 31 September 2010			
	£	£	£
Employment of Capital			
Fixed Assets			
Plant and machinery			16,000
Premises			18,000
			34,000
Current Assets			
Stock	10,000		
Trade debtors	12,260		
Cash at Bank	5,200	27,460	
less **Liabilities**			
Bank overdraft	2,000		
Creditors	14,800	(16,800)	10,660
Net Assets			44,660
Capital Employed			
Capital			40,000
Retained Profit to 31 September 2010			4,660
			44,660

rent Assets he sum of ne business' sets listed cording to eir relative iquidity

Total abilities is sum of all e business' lities listed lphabetical order

The total for each calculation for the sum of the items listed in the left-hand column is placed to the right of the last item. Note that the totals for both calculations are placed in the same column

Once total Liabilities have been deducted from total Current Assets, the resulting sum is placed in the right-hand column directly below total Fixed Assets. It will then be added to Fixed Assets to determine Net Assets

In relation to the use of brackets, brackets indicate if an item is either a loss or is to be deducted/subtracted from an item.

Remember when preparing the Profit & Loss account, you need to show Gross Profit and Net Profit separately. Also, think carefully about each figure to go into the Balance Sheet and where it should go – is it an asset or a liability? Is it a Current Asset or a Fixed Asset? If it is a liability, but not a current liability where should it go?

Once you have completed Exercise 3, undertake Exercise 4 to check your understanding of the structure and composition of both the Profit & Loss account and Balance Sheet by correctly identifying the financial statement in which each heading or item should appear.

(?) Net Assets	Profit & Loss	Balance Sheet
(?) Fixed Assets	Profit & Loss	Balance Sheet
(?) Opening stock	Profit & Loss	Balance Sheet
(?) Cash at Bank	Profit & Loss	Balance Sheet
(?) Premises	Profit & Loss	Balance Sheet
(?) Gross Profit	Profit & Loss	Balance Sheet
(?) Debtors	Profit & Loss	Balance Sheet
(?) Wages	Profit & Loss	Balance Sheet
(?) Sales	Profit & Loss	Balance Sheet
(?) Current Assets	Profit & Loss	Balance Sheet
(?) Capital	Profit & Loss	Balance Sheet
(?) Net Profit	Profit & Loss	Balance Sheet
(?) Current Liabilities	Profit & Loss	Balance Sheet

Conclusion

We have now progressed a considerable way towards understanding some of the basic principles that apply to the construction of financial statements. In the following sections of *LPC Accounts Online* we will continually draw upon these principles and use them to consider the structure and composition of the financial statements of different business entities, in particular, sole traders, partnerships and companies.

www.**oxford**interact.com

Section 10

Sole trader accounts

Exercise map

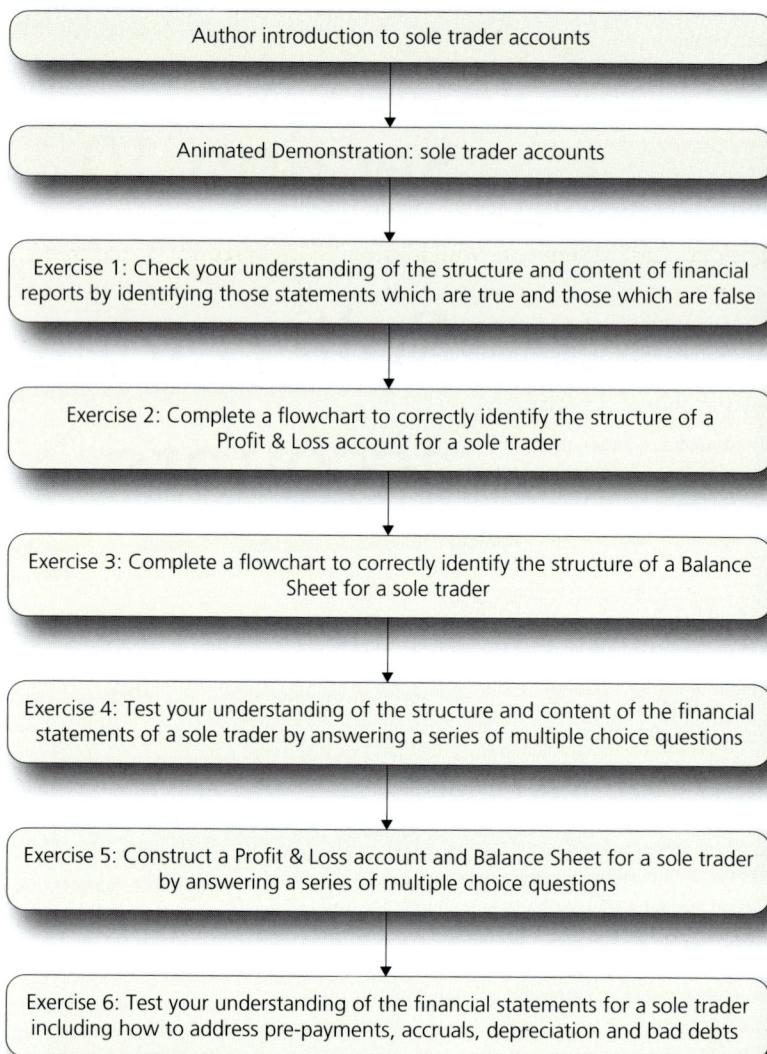

Author introduction to sole trader accounts

Animated Demonstration: sole trader accounts

Exercise 1: Check your understanding of the structure and content of financial reports by identifying those statements which are true and those which are false

Exercise 2: Complete a flowchart to correctly identify the structure of a Profit & Loss account for a sole trader

Exercise 3: Complete a flowchart to correctly identify the structure of a Balance Sheet for a sole trader

Exercise 4: Test your understanding of the structure and content of the financial statements of a sole trader by answering a series of multiple choice questions

Exercise 5: Construct a Profit & Loss account and Balance Sheet for a sole trader by answering a series of multiple choice questions

Exercise 6: Test your understanding of the financial statements for a sole trader including how to address pre-payments, accruals, depreciation and bad debts

Introduction

In the previous section you were introduced to a number of different concepts and principles that you will be applying as you seek to understand and interpret financial statements. The more familiar you become with these concepts and principles, the easier you will be able to understand financial statements, particularly as we begin to consider sole trader financial statements in this section and partnership and company financial statements in subsequent sections.

In this section, we will concentrate on consolidating your knowledge of financial statements and consider those statements which must be prepared for a sole trader. We will introduce the concepts of making adjustments to the trial balance to account for pre-payments and accruals and apply the concept of depreciation and accounting for bad debts. We will also look to see how the sole trader will retain money within the business and update their accounts accordingly.

Adjustments

As we saw in the previous section, at the close of the financial year the business will prepare from that year's ledgers a trial balance, which will need to be reviewed, updated and then closed. It is from these that the Profit & Loss account and Balance Sheet will be prepared.

However, the ledgers may not in fact accurately reflect the true state of affairs. For example, have all invoices been received and paid? Are the Fixed Assets in the Balance Sheet correctly valued? Has the business been paid all the debts owing to it, and is there a reasonable expectation that all such debts will in fact be paid?

In this section we will look at accruals, pre-payments, depreciation and bad debts. For this purpose, and to see how the trial balance is correctly updated and represented, we will use Amanda's financial statements which are set out in Examples 10.1 to 10.5.

Accruals

Accruals represent a liability due in the financial year in question and have not yet been paid by the business. For example, a bill relating to the accounting period in question may have not have been received or if it has been received, it may not have been paid by the business when the trial balance is prepared. Such unpaid items will obviously not have been recorded on the applicable ledger, and as a consequence will require the amount on the trial balance to be updated and increased so as to be an accurate reflection of the true cost to the business of that item in that financial year.

By way of example let's assume that Amanda has an outstanding invoice of £60 for her telephone expenses at the end of the financial year. Whilst this will not be recorded in a ledger, it will still need to be shown as an expense on the Profit & Loss account. Also, as Amanda is yet to pay the outstanding invoice of £60, it will represent an ongoing liability for her business. As such, it will be identified as a Current Liability on the Balance Sheet. To see how this translates on both the Profit & Loss account and Balance Sheet, see Example 10.1.

Example 10.1

Trading and Profit & Loss account for the year ending 31 March 2010

	£	£
Sales		39,000
less Cost of goods sold		
Opening stock	2,475	
add Purchases of stock	18,375	
	20,850	
less Closing stock	2,025	
		(18,825)
Gross Profit		**20,175**
less Expenses		
Bad debt	725	
Depreciation	1,875	
Electricity	600	
Telephone	150	
Rent	4,000	
Wages	1,050	
		(8,400)
Net Profit		**11,775**

Balance Sheet as at 31 March 2010

Employment of Capital	Cost £	Dep'n £	£	NBV £
Fixed Assets				
Equipment	7,500	3,375		4,125
Vehicles	5,625	3,000		2,625
	13,125	6,375		6,750
Current Assets				
Stock	2,025			
Debtors	1,085			
less Provision	125			
	960			
Pre-payment	375			
Cash	825			
		4,185		
less **Liabilities**				
Accruals	60			
Creditors	600			
		(660)		
Net Assets			3,525	10,275
Capital Employed				
Capital			4,500	
Retained Profit to 31 March 2010			5,775	10,275

Calculation of Retained Profit to 31 March 2010

	£
Retained Profit at 1 April 2009	3,750
add Net Profit for the year	11,775
	15,525
less Drawings	9,750
Retained Profit to 31 March 2010	5,775

Accrual: Assuming an unpaid telephone invoice of £60:

- Profit & Loss account: The expense item (i.e. telephone) is increased by the amount of the unpaid sum (i.e. from £90 to £150), so showing the correct/true value for the expense for the accounting period.
- Balance Sheet: The unpaid sum represents a liability for the business for payment in the forthcoming accounting period, and is identified as a Current Liability under the heading 'Accruals'.

> ### Essential Principles
>
> Accruals:
>
> - Profit & Loss account: increases the expense
> - Balance Sheet: shown as a Current Liability

Pre-payments

In contrast to accruals, a pre-payment arises where the business has paid for an item of expense in the current accounting period, but the benefit of which will continue into the next. Accordingly a pre-payment will require the expense to be adjusted down to show the correct/true value, but will also represent an asset for the forthcoming financial year.

For example, suppose that Amanda's ledger shows that she has paid rent of £4,375, but that payment straddles the close of the accounting year and the start of the following year. Accordingly, the sum that is for the current financial year, say £4,000, can only be shown on the Profit & Loss account. The remaining £375, in theory, could be refunded and therefore represents a form of asset for inclusion as such in the Balance Sheet. Example 10.2 illustrates how Amanda's pre-payment has been adjusted and included within both financial statements.

> ### Essential Principles
>
> Pre-payment:
>
> - Profit & Loss account: reduces the expense
> - Balance Sheet: shown as a Current Asset

Depreciation

From the moment a Fixed Asset is purchased, it will start to lose value. There are any number of reasons why an asset will start to fall in value, such as general wear and tear, improvements in technology that make the purchased item obsolete, or even a collapse in the property market.

Depreciation is an annual loss, often referred to as a 'hidden expense', which must be reflected in the business' financial statements. There are a number of accounting concepts that determine what information appears in the financial statements and a number of different means by which depreciation may be calculated. Whilst you will not be expected to calculate depreciation for the purposes of *LPC Accounts Online*, it is important that you appreciate the basis upon which it is determined. For example, two common methods used to calculate depreciation are the straight-line and the reducing balance methods. The

Example 10.2

Amanda Lloyd
Trading and Profit & Loss account for the year ending 31 March 2010

	£	£
Sales		39,000
less Cost of goods sold		
Opening stock	2,475	
add Purchases of stock	18,375	
	20,850	
less Closing stock	2,025	
		(18,825)
Gross Profit		**20,175**
less Expenses		
Bad debt	725	
Depreciation	1,875	
Electricity	600	
Telephone	150	
Rent	4,000	
Wages	1,050	
		(8,400)
Net Profit		**11,775**

Amanda Lloyd
Balance Sheet as at 31 March 2010

Employment of Capital	Cost	Dep'n	NBV
	£	£	£
Fixed Assets			
Equipment	7,500	3,375	4,125
Vehicles	5,625	3,000	2,625
	13,125	6,375	6,750
Current Assets			
Stock	2,025		
Debtors	960	1,085	
less Provision		125	
Pre-payment	375		
Cash	825	4,185	
less Liabilities			
Accruals	60		
Creditors	600	(660)	
Net Assets			**3,525**
			10,275
Capital Employed			
Capital		4,500	
Retained Profit to 31 March 2010		5,775	
			10,275

Calculation of Retained Profit to 31 March 2010

	£
Retained Profit at 1 April 2009	3,750
add Net Profit for the year	11,775
	15,525
less Drawings	9,750
Retained Profit to 31 March 2010	5,775

Prepayment: Assuming a pre-payment on Rent of £375:

- Profit & Loss account: As the benefit of the pre-payment will not be received until the following accounting period, the expense of Rent is reduced by the amount of pre-payment.
- Balance Sheet: Because benefit of the pre-payment will be received in the following accounting period, it represents a Current Asset and it will appear as such under the heading 'Pre-payment'

straight-line method of depreciation anticipates the expected working life span of an asset, determined from its purchase, and its value is reduced in equal portions over that period (e.g. if the expected life of the asset is 5 years, it will therefore lose 20% of its original purchase price each year). By contrast, the reducing balance method of depreciation sees a fixed percentage of the asset's value being deducted each year, with the greatest drop in value occurring at the end of the first year from its purchase and the same percentage being applied year-on-year but to an ever decreasing value.

As depreciation is an annual 'expense' it is first treated as an operating expense and as an accumulative adjustment to the value of assets. Two concepts exist that dictate how depreciation is to be shown on the Balance Sheet - the 'cost' concept states that the actual cost of assets is the basis of the asset's valuation for the Balance Sheet and the 'prudence' concept (Denny, R., *Accounts for Solicitors,* 2003) states that depreciation must be offset against the asset's initial purchase cost in order to record a proper loss to give a true 'Net Book Value' (NBV) – although this is somewhat of an over-simplification for law students, it is sufficient for your Business Accounts course. If we look at the Fixed Assets section of Amanda's Balance Sheet in Example 10.3, we can see how this is represented.

Example 10.3

> **Depreciation and Net Book Value:** the depreciation is the cumulative value since the asset was purchased, and once deducted from the cost price, produces the Net Book Value (i.e. the updated value of the asset).

Employment of Capital	£	£	£
Fixed Assets	Cost	Dep'n	NBV
Equipment	7,500	3,375	4,125
Vehicles	5,625	3,000	2,625
	13,125	6,375	6,750

> Cost: this shows the purchase price of the assets (i.e. the 'cost' concept).

As you can see from the extract of Amanda's Balance Sheet in Example 10.3, two Fixed Assets are used in the business, Equipment and Vehicles. As depreciation is applied to each item year-on-year the depreciation figure will increase, which will in turn reduce the Net Book Value. The trial balance will include as a note the expense of depreciation for the accounting period, as depreciation is a matter that can only be determined 'off ledger'. This 'off ledger' figure (however determined) is then included in the Profit & Loss account as an annual operating expense, and is also then added to the cumulative depreciation for the end of the previous financial year. This is best demonstrated by looking at Example 10.4, where it is possible to see that Amanda has incurred an annual depreciation cost of £1,875.

Example 10.4

Amanda Lloyd
Trading and Profit & Loss account for the year ending 31 March 2010

	£	£
Sales		39,000
less Cost of goods sold		
Opening stock	2,475	
add Purchases of stock	18,375	
	20,850	
less Closing stock	2,025	(18,825)
Gross Profit		**20,175**
less Expenses		
Bad debt	725	
Depreciation	1,875	
Electricity	600	
Telephone	150	
Rent	4,000	
Wages	1,050	(8,400)
Net Profit		**11,775**

Amanda Lloyd
Balance Sheet as at 31 March 2010

Employment of Capital	Cost £	Dep'n £	NBV £
Fixed Assets			
Equipment	7,500	3,375	4,125
Vehicles	5,625	3,000	2,625
	13,125	6,375	6,750
Current Assets			
Stock	2,025		
Debtors	1,085		
less Provision	125	960	
Pre-payment	375		
Cash	825	4,185	
less Liabilities			
Accruals	60		
Creditors	600	(660)	
Net Assets			3,525
			10,275
Capital Employed			
Capital		4,500	
Retained Profit to 31 March 2010		5,775	**10,275**

Calculation of Retained Profit to 31 March 2010

	£
Retained Profit at 1 April 2009	3,750
add Net Profit for the year	11,775
	15,525
less Drawings	9,750
Retained Profit to 31 March 2010	5,775

Depreciation:

- Profit & Loss account: The determined depreciation for the year is a one-off cost and is shown as an expense.
- Balance Sheet: The annual cost depreciation is allocated between assets and added to the cumulative depreciation figure from the previous year. In this instance, at the end of the last financial year cumulative depreciation would have been £4,500, to which this year's cost of £1,875 has been added.

As appropriate, in *LPC Accounts Online* you will be provided with the depreciation figures to use (to be found in the trial balance as 'Provision for depreciation as at [last day of prior year/first day of year in question]'). Note also, the headings used alongside Fixed Assets apply only to this section of the Balance Sheet.

Essential Principles

Depreciation

- Profit & Loss account: shown as an annual expense
- Balance Sheet: shown as a cumulative deduction against the Fixed Assets

---

Bad debts and doubtful debts

It is a harsh commercial reality that not all debts owed to the business will be paid. However, although unpaid debts are an expense for the business, they also represent an asset - in fact, debts are often sold to debt collection agencies, who will then seek to recover the debt for themselves as, unlike a business, they have the expertise, time and inclination to do so; by selling the debt the business will have realised an asset.

All businesses maintain ledgers recording their debtors and the sum owing (see Section 9 for further detail), and will keep this continually under review during the year. When it becomes evident that a debt will not be paid, the business will write that debt off and so it will become an expense for the business and will appear in the Profit & Loss account. Those debts remaining unpaid at the close of the financial year also represent an asset for the business and will be shown in the Balance Sheet.

But this is to assume that all debts owing at the end of the financial year will in fact be recovered by the business. As the business prepares its financial statements it will have to decide if a debt is recoverable and, if they are 'doubtful' this will require an adjustment to both the expense figure in the Profit & Loss account and the asset figure in the Balance Sheet. The Profit & Loss account will see the debt expense increase from that in the trial balance by the addition of the 'doubtful' debt. On the Balance Sheet, the amount of 'doubtful' debtors will be referred to as a 'provision for doubtful debts' and, as this is an adjustment made at the end of the accounting period, will be shown as an 'on sheet' calculation on the Balance Sheet as a deduction from debtors.

To see how this works, let's consider Amanda's bad debts. For this purpose we will assume that Amanda has written off £600 of debts during the year and still has £1,085 outstanding at the end of the financial year. However, as Amanda prepares her financial statements she decides that a further £125 is unlikely to be recovered and will therefore need to write this sum off. To see how this is presented in Amanda's financial statements, consider Example 10.5.

Example 10.5

Amanda Lloyd
Trading and Profit & Loss account for the year ending 31 March 2010

	£	£
Sales		39,000
less Cost of goods sold		
Opening stock	2,475	
add Purchases of stock	18,375	
	20,850	
less Closing stock	2,025	
		(18,825)
Gross Profit		**20,175**
less Expenses		
Bad debt	725	
Depreciation	1,875	
Electricity	600	
Telephone	150	
Rent	4,000	
Wages	1,050	
		(8,400)
Net Profit		**11,775**

Amanda Lloyd
Balance Sheet as at 31 March 2010

Employment of Capital	£	Cost £	Dep'n £	NBV £
Fixed Assets				
Equipment		7,500	3,375	4,125
Vehicles		5,625	3,000	2,625
		13,125	6,375	6,750
Current Assets				
Stock		2,025		
Debtors	1,085	960		
less Provision	125			
Pre-payment		375		
Cash		825	4,185	
less Liabilities				
Accruals		60		
Creditors		600	(660)	
Net Assets				**3,525**
				10,275
Capital Employed				
Capital			4,500	
Retained Profit to 31 March 2010			5,775	**10,275**

Calculation of Retained Profit to 31 March 2010

Retained Profit at 1 April 2009		3,750
add Net Profit for the year		11,775
		15,525
less Drawings		9,750
Retained Profit to 31 March 2010		5,775

Bad debts and doubtful debts: Assuming 'doubtful' debts are £125:

- Profit & Loss account: To £600 debts already written off, the additional doubtful debts of £125 will be added and shown as an expense reducing the Net Profit figure.
- Balance Sheet: The book value of the debtors will be shown as a Current Asset. This will then be reduced by the doubtful debts as an 'on sheet' calculation, and so show the correct/true value.

Essential Principles

Bad debts and doubtful debts:

- Profit & Loss account: added together and shown as an annual expense
- Balance Sheet: shown as a calculation within the Balance Sheet reducing the Current Asset of debtors

Updating the trial balance

Matters such as accruals, pre-payments, depreciation, and provisions for bad debts are often done 'off ledger' and for *LPC Accounts Online* they will be found as notes to the trial balance. From now on you should identify which items on the trial balance need to be adjusted. You should get into the habit of updating the trial balance before you start to compile the financial statements by making these changes directly on to the trial balance – those students who struggle with accounts invariably fail to get into the habit of making changes directly on to the trial balance. You should then tick off each item on the trial balance once used.

Essential Principles

Accruals:

- Profit & Loss account: Increases the expense
- Balance Sheet: Shown as a Current Liability

Pre-payment:

- Profit & Loss account: Reduces the expense
- Balance Sheet: Shown as a Current Liability

Depreciation:

- Profit & Loss account: Shown as an annual expense
- Balance Sheet: Shown as an accumulative expense against the Fixed Assets

Bad debts and doubtful debts:

- Profit & Loss account: Added together and shown as an annual expense
- Balance Sheet: Shown as an calculation within the Balance Sheet reducing the Current Asset of debts

Now watch the Animated Demonstration online. This will build further on the previous section and provide additional commentary on how depreciation and bad debts are treated in both financial statements and demonstrate how the Retained Profit is calculated for a sole trader.

Cynthia Henry
Balance Sheet as at 30 September 2010

Employment of Capital	£	£ Cost	£ Dep'n	£ NBV
Fixed Assets				
Equipment		9,000	3,600	5,400
		9,000	3,600	5,400
Current Assets				
Stock		3,000		
Debtors	6,000			
less Provision	500	5,500		
Pre-payment		1,000		
Cash		16,400	25,900	
less Liabilities				
Accrual		1,000		
Bank loan		2,600		
Creditors		3,300	(6,900)	19,000
Net Assets				**24,400**
Capital Employed				
Capital			9,000	
Retained Profit			15,400	**24,400**

Retained Profit Calculation	
Retained Profit as at Nov 1 2009	2,000
add Profit for the year	31,400
	33,400
less Drawings	18,000
Retained Profit as at Sept 30 2010	15,400

00:36 08:41

Having viewed the Animated Demonstration, now consider undertaking Exercise 1. This exercise will test your understanding of the key principles introduced in both this section and in section 9, and will require you to identify whether a series of statements relating to the structure and composition of the Profit & Loss account and Balance Sheet are true or false.

To continue to help you understand the structure and content of financial reports, set out below are statements relating to different aspects of both Profit & Loss accounts and Balance Sheets. You need to identify which statements are true and which are false. When you have made your selection click the 'submit' button at the bottom of your screen to view your score and receive feedback on your answers.

	True	False
A pre-payment will appear as a Current Liability on the Balance Sheet.	○	○
Employment of Capital is the amount the business owes the proprietor.	○	○
An accrual will increase an item shown in the Profit & Loss account.	○	○
Current Liabilities are all debts owed by the business.	○	○
Capital Employed is the amount the business owes the proprietor.	○	○

Early consolidation

The structure and content of the financial statements for sole traders will not vary greatly from those that you have been preparing to date. As you have seen; you are be required to make more adjustments to the trial balance to ensure that they correctly reflect the true state of affairs of the business. Let's quickly remind ourselves of the differences between the two financial statements.

Profit & Loss account

This summarizes the transactions of the business (both revenue-generating and the expenses of operating the business) to calculate profit or loss over the accounting period. The basic structure of the Profit & Loss account can be seen in Example 10.1.

The first calculation is Gross Profit, i.e. the profit the business has made from sales less the costs directly attributable to sales. From Gross Profit, the business operating expenses will be deducted to calculate Net Profit figure. It is the Net Profit figure that will be carried forward into the Balance Sheet to help determine the Retained Profit of the business.

As regards expenses, after you have made adjustments to the trial balance, items of expense will be reduced to reflect pre-payments, others will be increased to reflect accruals, bad debt and provision for bad debt will be added together and included, as will the hidden expense of depreciation for the accounting period.

Example 10.6

Profit & Loss account		
	£	£
Sales		xxxx
less Cost of goods sold		
Opening stock	xxxx	
add Purchases of stock	xxxx	
	total	
less Closing stock	(xxxx)	(total)
Gross Profit		**Gross Profit**
less Expenses	xxxx	
	xxxx	
	xxxx	
		(total)
Net Profit		**Net Profit**

Once you have refreshed your understanding of the Profit & Loss account attempt Exercise 2 and test yourself on its structure – try to attempt this exercise without reference to your notes to see how much you have already learned.

If you have attempted the exercises in section 9 of *LPC Accounts Online* you will already have seen how a basic Profit & Loss account and Balance Sheet should appear. A Profit & Loss account for a sole trader is the same. In this exercise you are required to place the various headings of a sole trader's Profit & Loss account in the correct order to see how much of the basic structure you can remember. Complete the flowchart below by placing the various headings in the correct order by selecting the correct option from those available. The first and final steps are completed for you. When you are happy with your flowchart, click 'Submit' at the bottom of your screen to see your feedback and score.

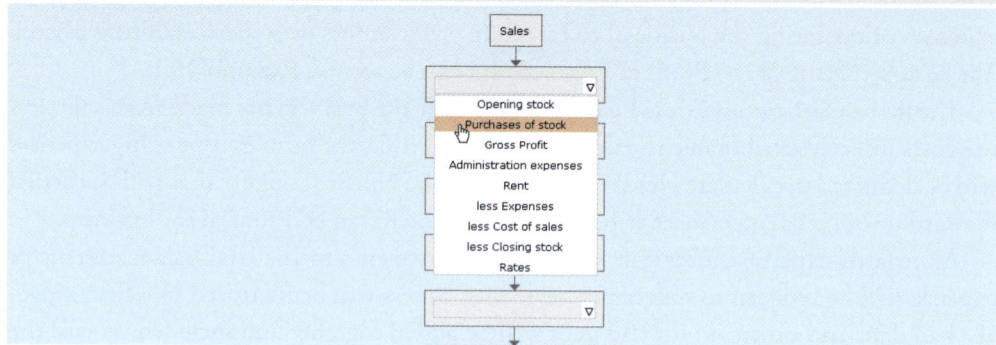

Sales

- Opening stock
- Purchases of stock
- Gross Profit
- Administration expenses
- Rent
- less Expenses
- less Cost of sales
- less Closing stock
- Rates

Balance Sheet

This financial statement provides a snapshot of the business's assets and liabilities 'as at' the end of the accounting period. This is because the assets and liabilities of the business fluctuate continually and so the Balance Sheet can only be accurate for one day. Example 10.7 illustrates the structure of a basic Balance sheet.

Example 10.7

Basic Balance Sheet

Employment of Capital	£	£	£
Fixed Assets	Cost	Dep'n	NBV
			xxxx
			xxxx
			total Fixed Assets
Current Assets			
	xxxx		
	xxxx		
	xxxx	total Current Assets	
less Current liabilities			
	xxxx	(total Current	total Current Asset –
	xxxx	Liabilities)	Current Liabilities
Net Assets			Net Assets
Capital Employed			
		xxxx	
		xxxx	Capital Employed

The Balance sheet comprises two halves:

- **Employment of Capital**: The 'top half' shows how the money owed to the proprietor has been used – such as the business assets, which in turn are offset by what the business owes in liabilities. It is the Net Assets figure that you will be seeking to determine, which if we recall is the sum of:

  Net Assets = Fixed Assets + (Current Assets – Current Liabilities)

From now on you will be required to ensure that the Fixed Assets are shown at their cost value, and then reduced by the cumulative depreciation attributable to those assets to show their current value, the Net Book Value.

For Current Assets, you must remember to list items according to their relative liquidity, with the least liquid listed first, and to include those items that the business has paid for but the benefit of which will not be gained until the following accounting period, i.e. pre-payments. A further 'on sheet' calculation (i.e. undertaken within the Balance Sheet) will also have to be made to adjust the value of bad debts (trade debtors) to account for doubtful debts – something that can only be undertaken on the date at which the Balance Sheet is prepared.

Once Current Assets have been determined, Current Liabilities will need to be deducted before Net Assets may be calculated. For Current Liabilities, all items due for payment within the next 12 months will have to be listed, including items that the business has already received a benefit from in the accounting period, but which have not yet been paid for, i.e. accruals.

It is only after Current Liabilities have been deducted from Current Assets, that you can then add the resulting figure to Fixed Assets and so determine Net Assets.

- **Capital Employed**: The 'bottom half' shows the amount the business owes the proprietor, such as the capital investment in the business and Retained Profit. You must now ensure that this 'balances' with the top half.

One of the components of the Capital Employed section is the Retained Profit of the business, i.e. that money which the proprietor has not withdrawn from the business. It is here that your Net Profit figure from the Profit & Loss account will be used in the following calculation:

Retained Profit for the current year = (Retained Profit from previous year + Net Profit) − Drawings

Once this is added to the capital of the business (determined by reference to the trial balance), you should have a figure that is the same as the Net Assets figure. If you don't then there is a chance that you may have miscalculated earlier on, in which case, check your adjustments to the trial balance and ensure that all items that were to be included in the Expenses section of the Profit & Loss account are listed correctly, that you have calculated the cumulative depreciation of Fixed Assets correctly, and that you have identified all the Current Assets and Current Liabilities.

We have already seen how a basic Profit & Loss and Balance Sheet should look. A sole trader's Balance Sheet becomes slightly more detailed. In this exercise you are required to identify the correct order in which the various headings should appear in a sole trader's Balance Sheet. Complete the flowchart below by placing the various headings in the correct order by selecting the correct option from those available. To help you, the two elements that represent the 'balancing' components of a Balance Sheet are completed for you. When you are happy with your flowchart, click 'Submit' at the bottom of your screen to see your feedback and score.

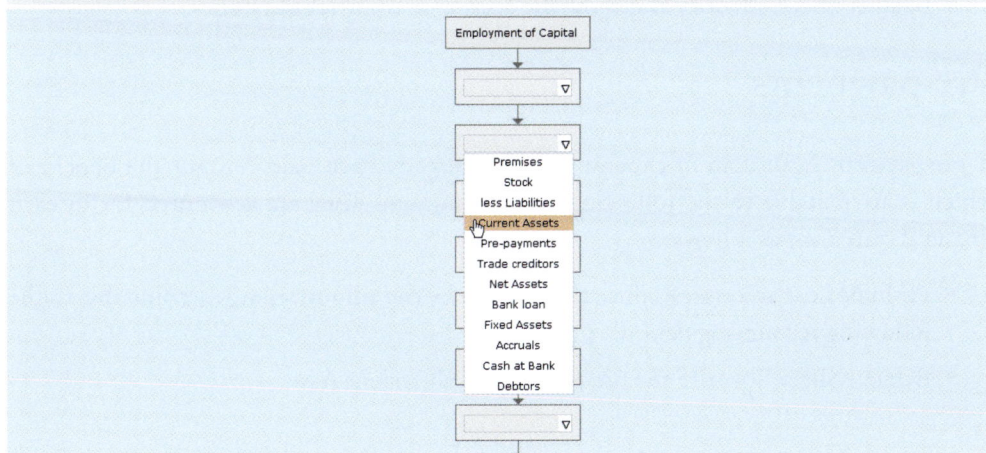

Employment of Capital

Premises
Stock
less Liabilities
Current Assets
Pre-payments
Trade creditors
Net Assets
Bank loan
Fixed Assets
Accruals
Cash at Bank
Debtors

As you did with the Profit & Loss account in Exercise 1, refresh your understanding of the Balance Sheet and attempt Exercise 3 to test yourself on its structure – try to do this exercise without reference to your notes to see how much you have already learned.

Once you have completed Exercise 3, and before you progress further to read the following commentary on adjustments, test your understanding of the Profit & Loss account and Balance Sheet for a sole trader by tackling the multiple-choice questions in Exercise 4.

> (?) **Question 1**
> With reference to the trial balance for Benjamin Hillen, trading as Hillen & Co., which one of the following items will *not* appear on the Profit & Loss account?
> ○ Drawings
>
> ○ Interest
>
> ○ Sales
>
> ○ Expenses
>
> (?) **Question 2**
> With reference to the trial balance for Benjamin Hillen, trading as Hillen & Co., which one of the following items will appear on the Profit & Loss account?
> ○ Debtors
>
> ○ Vehicles
>
> ○ Capital
>
> ○ Purchases of Stock

Adjustments

From now on, you should automatically be making adjustments to the figures provided to you in the trial balance. Matters such as accruals, pre-payments, depreciation and provisions for bad debts are often done 'off ledger' and for *LPC Accounts Online* they will be found as notes to the balance. Each should be treated as follows.

Accruals

An accrual is a liability due in the accounting year but which has not yet been paid by the business. They are accounted for in each financial statement as follows:

- Profit & Loss account: Increase the expense by the amount that has not yet been paid.
- Balance Sheet: Identify and show the accrual as a Current Liability.

Pre-payments

A pre-payment is an item of expense that has already been paid for, but the benefit of which is attributable to the following accounting year. They are accounted for in each financial statement as follows:

- Profit & Loss account: Reduce the expense by the amount that is attributable to the following accounting period.
- Balance Sheet: Identify the pre-payment as a Current Asset.

Depreciation

Depreciation is the hidden cost of the business that reduces the value of Fixed Assets. It is both an annual expense and a cumulative reduction in the value of Fixed Assets. It is accounted for in each financial statement as follows:

- Profit & Loss account: The depreciation for the year in question is an expense.
- Balance Sheet: Add the depreciation for the year to the cumulative depreciation up to the beginning of the year. This cumulative total is then used to reduce the cost value of the Fixed Asset to determine the Net Book Value.

Bad debts and doubtful debts

These are the debts that have been written off during the year as non-recoverable by the business and those that are judged at the end of the accounting period to be unlikely to be recovered. They are accounted for in each financial statement as follows:

- Profit & Loss account: Include bad debts as an expense, and add the figure for doubtful debts if identified.
- Balance Sheet: Show as an 'on sheet' calculation under the provision for doubtful debts reducing the book value of the debts.

Now attempt Exercise 5. In this exercise you will be required to construct a sole trader's financial statement by answering a series of multiple-choice questions.

Question 1
With reference to the trial balance, identify Christopher Hull's business expenses and calculate Net Profit from a Gross Profit figure of £51,000.

Bank interest	300	
Insurance	400	
Misc expenses	1,200	
Rates	3,000	
Rent	6,900	
Utilities	1,700	
Wages	2,300	(15,800)
Net Profit		35,200

Bad debts & provision	1,500	
Bank interest	300	
Insurance	400	
Misc expenses	1,200	
Rates	3,000	
Rent	6,900	
Utilities	1,700	
Wages	2,300	(17,300)
Net Profit		33,700

Bad debts & provision	1,500	
Bank interest	300	
Depreciation	1,800	

You should now attempt the final exercise in this section, Exercise 6, which will require you to answer a series of multiple-choice questions designed to ensure that you understand the construction of both the Profit or Loss account and Balance sheet for a sole trader, and now pre-payments, accruals, depreciation, and bad debts are addressed in both forms of financial statement.

This exercise sets out a number of multiple-choice questions to assist you in further understanding the construction of Profit & Loss accounts and Balance Sheets and how to address pre-payments, accruals, depreciation, and bad debts. Answer each of the questions in turn. When you are happy with your answers, click the 'Submit' button at the bottom of the screen to view your score and receive feedback on your answers.

Question 1
Use the following information to calculate Gross Profit for Gargamel Ltd:

Sales	£150,000
Purchases	£90,000
Opening stock	£56,000
Closing stock	£27,000

○ £32,000

○ £31,000

Question 2
Use the following information to calculate Gross Profit for Harry & Fred:

Sales	£89,000
Purchases	£35,000
Opening stock	£26,000
Closing stock	£28,000

○ £55,000

○ £56,000

Conclusion

This section, along with the previous section of *LPC Accounts Online,* has sought to provide you with a fundamental grounding to the various concepts and principles underpinning the Profit & Loss account and Balance Sheet. Be sure that you do not just apply these concepts and principles automatically; what you must seek to do is understand why they are applied and what they are seeking to do vis-à-vis the financial presentation of the business. As we progress through *LPC Accounts Online,* you will be required to draw upon your understanding as we first move on to consider partnership accounts followed by an examination of company accounts before finally moving on to look at the financial analysis and interpretation of financial statements.

www.**oxford**interact.com

Section 11

Partnership accounts

Exercise map

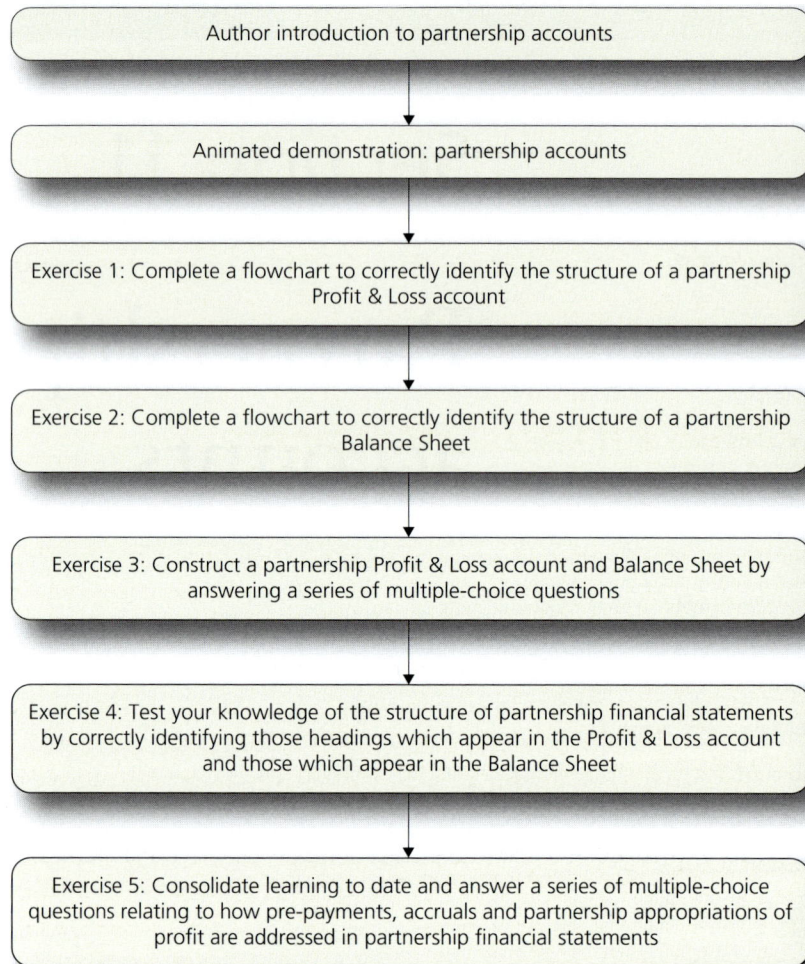

Author introduction to partnership accounts

Animated demonstration: partnership accounts

Exercise 1: Complete a flowchart to correctly identify the structure of a partnership Profit & Loss account

Exercise 2: Complete a flowchart to correctly identify the structure of a partnership Balance Sheet

Exercise 3: Construct a partnership Profit & Loss account and Balance Sheet by answering a series of multiple-choice questions

Exercise 4: Test your knowledge of the structure of partnership financial statements by correctly identifying those headings which appear in the Profit & Loss account and those which appear in the Balance Sheet

Exercise 5: Consolidate learning to date and answer a series of multiple-choice questions relating to how pre-payments, accruals and partnership appropriations of profit are addressed in partnership financial statements

Introduction

In sections 9 and 10 of *LPC Accounts Online* we have concentrated on understanding the basic construction of both forms of financial statements; namely the Profit & Loss account and Balance Sheet. This has required the incorporation of adjustments to the figures for each item as they are derived from the ledgers and appear in the trial balance and the subsequent calculation to determine the profits retained by the business.

In this section we will continue to consolidate your learning and move on to look at the requirements for financial statements that are required by partnerships. As we will see the basic construction of the financial statements for a partnership remains unchanged. However, the difference arises from the need to apportion the profits (or losses) between the partners and to show such apportionments as the capital of the business.

Partnership financial statements

A partnership will consist of two or more individuals who agree to carry on business together, sharing profits and losses in proportions which usually will have been agreed in a partnership agreement.

Whilst in a partnership, each individual partner is not dissimilar to a sole trader. Each will be taxed individually according to his or her income, less any applicable reliefs and charges that may have been apportioned between the partners. As a consequence, each financial statement will have a two-fold purpose: the Profit & Loss account will need to show the profitability of the partnership and how that profit has been apportioned between the partners; the Balance Sheet will show a 'snapshot' of the value of the assets and liabilities of the partnership, together with the contribution by each individual partner in his or her role as proprietor of the business. It is these distinctions that we will now look at.

Once you have read the following sections relating to the partnership Profit & Loss account and Balance Sheet, watch the Animated Demonstration online for a detailed explanation and worked example designed to highlight the key features of partnership financial statements.

Alan & Helen trading as 'Kiddies-Parties-R-Us!'
Trading and Profit & Loss account for the year ending 31 March 2010 together with Profit & Loss Appropriation account

	£	£
Sales		197,000
less Cost of sales		
Opening stock	30,000	
add Purchases	59,000	
	89,000	
less Closing stock	(28,000)	(61,000)
Gross Profit		**136,000**
less Expenses		
Depreciation	9,000	
Insurance (non-vehicular)	3,000	
Market stall rents	6,000	
Marketing & publicity	3,000	
Professional fees	2,000	
Rates	400	
Vehicle expenses	21,000	
Wages	24,600	(69,000)
Net Profit		**67,000**

Profit & Loss Appropriation account	Alan	Helen
Salary	2,000	0
Interest on capital	1,500	2,500
Profit share	30,500	30,500
	34,000	33,000

Partnership Profit and Loss Account

For the purposes of this section, we will be using the financial statements for the partnership, of Tracey, Tricky and Trinny trading as 'The 3T's'. Example 11.1 shows their Profit & Loss account.

Example 11.1

Tracey, Tricky and Trinny trading as 'The 3T's'
Trading and Profit & Loss account for the year ending 31 December 2010

	£	£
Turnover		640,000
less Cost of goods sold		
Opening stock	35,000	
add Purchases	341,000	
	376,000	
less Closing stock	31,000	(345,000)
Gross Profit		**295,000**
less **Expenses**		
Advertising	2,000	
Bad debts & provision	4,000	
Depreciation	19,000	
Distribution costs	15,000	
Insurance	14,000	
Power	16,000	
Rates	14,000	
Wages	40,000	(124,000)
Net Profit		**171,000**

As you can see from Example 11.1, a partnership Profit & Loss account is no different to the Profit & Loss account of a sole trader. From Example 11.1 we can see that The 3T's have made a healthy Net Profit of £171,000. Note however, that under expenses there is a heading for 'Wages' – this does not represent wages that Tracey, Tricky and Trinny may have paid themselves, but rather it represents the payment of wages to any staff they employ. It is important to remember that the partnership is an unincorporated business, and accordingly the partners are all sole traders. As a result, any profits generated by the partnership will be attributed to the relevant partner and it is that partner who is individually responsible for completing their tax returns, including such profits as part of their taxable income.

Provided that Tracey, Tricky and Trinny have been sensible, it will be their partnership agreement that will govern not only their respective roles and responsibilities within the partnership but will also dictate any salaries and interest on capital contributed which each partner will be entitled to. Where a partnership exists without any formal agreement as to profits and losses, any profits or losses will be shared equally.

However, the payment by agreement of any salaries or interest on capital contributed does not amount to a business operating expense incurred by the business, and therefore is not deducted before Net Profit is determined. This is because HM Revenue & Customs rules deem such items as *preferential appropriations of profit*, which may only be made once Net Profit has been determined. As a result, once Net Profit is known, a further calculation will be undertaken to apportion Net Profit between the various partners and this is termed Profit Appropriation. Strictly speaking the Profit Appropriation does not form part of the Profit & Loss account.

So let's assume that Tracey, Tricky and Trinny have a partnership agreement and that Net Profits are shared as follows: Tracey and Tricky each receive £1,000 interest on capital, after which Tracey receives a salary of £3,000 and Tricky receives a salary of £4,000. The balance of Net Profit is shared as follows: Tracey 2/8ths, Tricky 2/8ths and Trinny 4/8ths. When you are required to consider Profit Appropriation in *LPC Accounts Online*, this information will be provided in the notes to the trial balance.

Example 11.2 sets out how The 3T's will apportion their Net Profit of £171,000, in line with their partnership agreement (outlined above). The first item to deduct from Net Profit is salaries, followed by any interest on capital. The remaining Net Profit will be divided as agreed between the partners. The resulting totals should then be equal to the Net Profit.

Example 11.2

Salary: From the £171,000 Net Profit made by the partnership, deduct Tracey and Trickys' salary entitlement (£171,000 – (£3,000 + £4,000) = £164,000). As the agreement does not provide for Trinny to receive a salary, no salary entitlement will be apportioned to her.

Interest: From the £164,000 Net Profit remaining unapportioned, Tracey and Trickys' interest on capital contributions will then be deducted (£164,000 – (£1,000 + £1,000) = £162,000). As the agreement does not provide for Trinny to receive interest, no interest on capital contributions will be apportioned to her.

Profit & Loss Appropriation account	Tracey	Tricky	Trinny
Salary	3,000	4,000	0
Interest	1,000	1,000	0
Profit share	40,500	40,500	81,000
	44,500	45,500	81,000

Total Net Profit of £171,000 now fully apportioned.

Profit Share: As the partnership have decided to apportion their profit, once The 3T's partnership have deducted salaries and interest from Net Profit, the remaining sum is then divided on a basis of eights in accordance with their partnership agreement. Accordingly, of the £162,000 to be shared, Tracey and Tricky each receive £40,500 (2/8ths each) and Trinny £81,000 (4/8ths).

However, in the event that The 3T's Net Profits are insufficient to cover salary and interest payments, the resulting loss this will have caused will be apportioned between the partners in accordance with their profit sharing ratios. To avoid this situation, partnership agreements will often only permit salaries and interest to be paid if Net Profits are sufficient to cover them.

Essential Principles

Profit Appropriation calculation:

Share of Net Profit =

(Net Profit – (Salary and Interest on Capital)) ÷ Agreement on share of remaining profit

---

Other than to determine a partner's entitlement to Net Profit, the resulting totals of the apportioned Net Profit will be carried forwarded into the Capital Employed section of the Balance Sheet to help determine the Closing Balance of Current accounts (see below at page 189).

Now go online and attempt Exercise 1 to test yourself on the structure of a partnership Profit & Loss account ensuring that you correctly incorporate the requirement to apportion profits between the partners. Try to attempt the exercise without reference to your notes to further consolidate your learning to date.

As we move through the various Profit & Loss accounts and Balance Sheets, each becomes slightly more structured. The Profit & Loss account for partnerships is substantially similar to those you may already have prepared in sections 9 and 10 of *LPC Accounts Online*; the only difference is the need to apportion the Net Profit in accordance with the partnership agreement.

In this exercise you are required to place the various headings of a Partnership Profit & Loss account in the correct order to see how much of the structure you can remember. Complete the flowchart below by placing the various headings in the correct order by selecting the correct option from those available. The first and final steps are completed for you. When you are happy with your flowchart, click 'Submit' at the bottom of your screen to see your feedback and score.

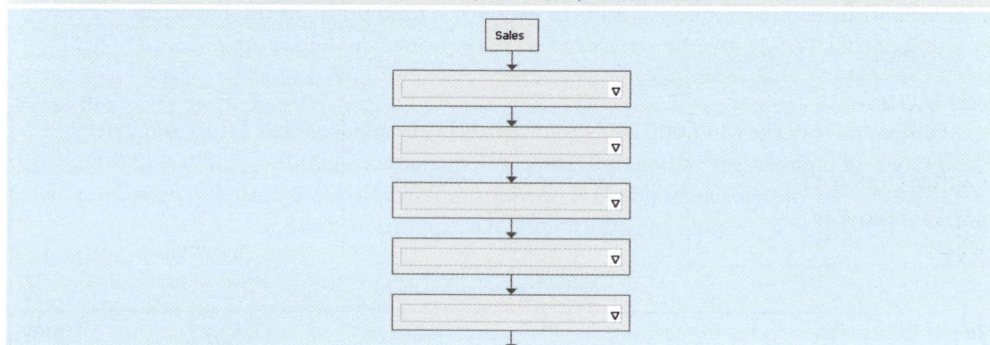

Partnership Balance Sheet

As we have seen with the Partnership Profit & Loss account, it is only the apportionment of the Net Profit that differs from the Profit & Loss account of the sole trader. In a partnership Balance Sheet, the difference appears in the Capital Employed section.

As we recall, the Capital Employed section is the 'bottom half' of the Balance Sheet which shows the amount the business owes the proprietors, i.e. the partners. Each partner's funds will need to be differentiated from the funds contributed by other partners, and the Capital Employed section will therefore detail under two account headings, the Capital account and Current account, the funds each partner has contributed to, and retained within, the business (after drawings). By way of example, consider now The 3T's Balance Sheet set out at Example 11.3.

Example 11.3

> Note how the 'top half' of a partnership Balance Sheet does not differ from a detailed Balance Sheet for a sole trader. Take a moment to consider its content and structure.

Tracey, Tricky and Trinny trading as 'The 3T's' Balance Sheet as at 31 December 2010				
Employment of Capital		£	£	£
Fixed Assets		Cost	Dep'n	NBV
Plant & Equipment		90,000	28,000	62,000
Premises		110,000	-	110,000
Vehicles		40,000	17,000	23,000
		240,000	45,000	195,000
Current Assets				
Stock		31,000		
Debtors	30,000			
less Provision	1,000	29,000		
Pre-payment		6,000		
Cash at Bank		18,000	84,000	
less **Liabilities**				
Accrual		4,000		
HM Revenue & Customs		20,000		
Loan		36,000		
Trade creditors		50,000	(110,000)	(26,000)
Net Assets				169,000
Capital Employed				
Capital accounts				
Tracey			20,000	
Tricky			20,000	
Trinny			50,000	90,000
Current accounts				
Tracey			16,500	
Tricky			21,500	
Trinny			41,000	79,000
				169,000

> **Current accounts:** Represent each partner's apportioned Net Profits, including any salary and interest on capital and after drawings have been accounted for. See Example 11.4 on page XXX for further detail on the process of updating the Current account.

> **Capital accounts:** Represent the capital contribution of each partner to the business. Subject to any agreed sharing ratio, it will also include a partner's share of assets (after depreciation). If there is no agreement, assets will be shared according to the partner's agreed profit sharing ratio.

Movements in Partners' Current Accounts

Partners are not dissimilar to sole traders in that they will take their income from the profits made by the business, and separate records for each partner recording their drawings from the business will be kept and reconciled at the end of the financial year. The partners' Current account is separate to the Capital account to assist in clearly identifying any interest entitlement a partner may have on capital, and to avoid confusion with any subsequent appropriations of profit and drawings. For the purposes of the Balance Sheet and to ensure that it accurately reflects a snapshot of a business at a date, and as the Current accounts will have fluctuating balances, the balance of the Current accounts will need to be calculated to show their final balances. Example 11.4 shows this calculation, provided as an appendix to The 3T's Balance Sheet, and sets out the detailed movements in partners' Current accounts.

Example 11.4

Movement in Current accounts: A calculation required for each partner prior to completing the Balance Sheet (although it does not form part of the Balance Sheet).

Opening balance: The closing balance for the Current accounts at the close of the last financial year and extracted from that year's Balance Sheet.

Movements in Current accounts	Tracey	Tricky	Trinny
Opening balance	2,000	6,000	6,000
Profit share	44,500	45,500	81,000
	46,500	51,500	87,000
Drawings	(30,000)	(30,000)	(46,000)
Closing balance	16,500	21,500	41,000

Closing balance: Transferred to the Capital Employed section under the heading 'Current accounts'.

Drawings: Represent all funds each partner withdrew by way of income from the business during the course of the year (it does not include salary or interest on capital entitlement as this has already been allocated as part of the profit share).

As you can see from Example 11.4, the Movement in Current accounts calculation is undertaken for each partner and requires you to add to the closing balance of the Current account (i.e. that from the previous accounting period) that partner's apportionment of Net Profit before deducting any money that the partner may have withdrawn during the accounting year (i.e. drawings).

Once completed, this will update the balance of the Current account and may then be transferred to the Capital Employed section, under the heading 'Current accounts', of the Balance Sheet.

In practice, in the event that the Capital Employed section of the Balance Sheet fails to balance with the Employment of Capital section, the accountants will look to the Current accounts for an explanation. Should a partner have withdrawn more money from the business than it can afford, it will become evident at this stage and may require the partner concerned to repay the business some of the drawings which he or she took.

Now attempt Exercise 2 and test your knowledge of the structure of the partnership Balance Sheet remembering to correctly incorporate the requirement to calculate the Movements in Current accounts. Try to attempt this exercise without reference to your notes to further consolidate your learning.

As we move through the various Profit & Loss accounts and Balance Sheets, each becomes slightly more structured. The Balance Sheet for partnerships is substantially similar to those you may already have prepared in sections 9 and 10 of *LPC Accounts Online*; the only difference is the need to undertake the Movements in Current accounts calculation before the Balance Sheet can be completed.

In this exercise you are required to place the various headings of a Partnership Balance Sheet in the correct order to see how much of the structure you can remember. Complete the flowchart below by placing the various headings in the correct order by selecting the correct option from those available. The first and final steps are completed for you. When you are happy with your flowchart, click 'Submit' at the bottom of your screen to see your feedback and score.

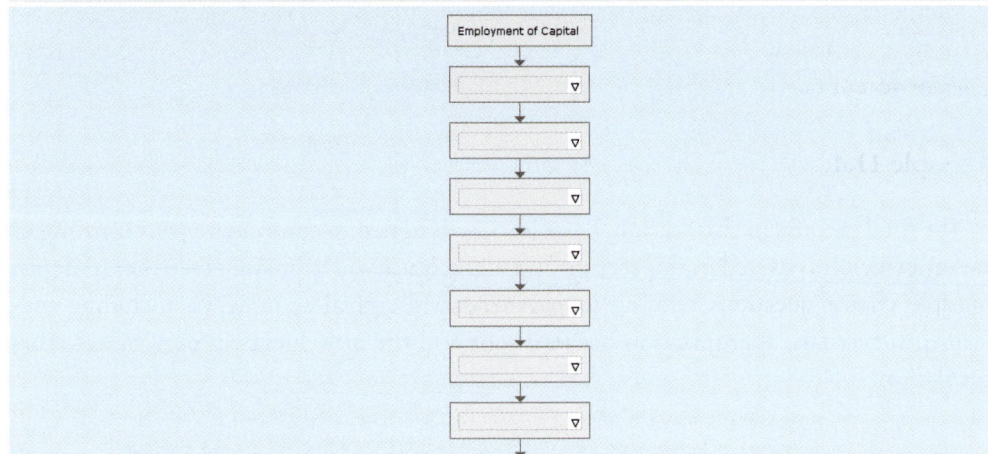

Employment of Capital

Once you have completed Exercise 2, the subsequent exercises will offer you further practicse in consolidating your understanding of partnership financial statements and the principles and concepts upon which they are based. Now attempt Exercise 3 and practise constructing both forms of financial statement by answering a series of multiple-choice questions.

In this exercise we will start to pull together the key principles of Profit & Loss accounts and Balance Sheets learnt to date, and also begin to apply the additional requirements for a Partnership. The only difference is that at the end of the Profit & Loss account you need to apportion the Net Profit in accordance with the partners' agreement, and the calculation to determine the closing balance for the Partners' Current accounts.

Below is a list of income, expenditure, assets and liabilities relating to Leslie and Dipa in partnership trading as 'LesDip Partnership' for the year ending 31 October [year]. Based on this information you are to answer a series of multiple-choice questions relating to the Profit & Loss account and Balance Sheet for the LesDip Partnership. To begin the questions click on the 'Question' tab above or the 'Complete your questions' button below and answer each of the multiple-choice questions in turn. When you are happy with your answers, click the 'Submit' button at the bottom of your screen to view your score and receive feedback on your answers.

LesDip Partnership

	Debit (£)	Credit (£)
Fixed Assets		
Motor vehicles	10,000	
Plant & equipment	62,000	
Leasehold premises	10,000	
Current Assets		
Stock (at 1 November [last year])	6,250	
Debtors	5,150	
Bank	2,750	
Cash	100	
Purchases of Stock	18,700	
Sales		33,550
Expenses		
Wages	2,500	
Postage & stationery	250	
Rent & rates	1,400	

Once you have completed Exercise 3, move on to Exercise 4 to apply all of your knowledge to date by correctly identifying those headings which appear in the Profit & Loss account and those which appear in the Balance Sheet.

This exercise continues to help you consolidate your understanding of the structure of both the partnership Profit & Loss account and the Balance Sheet.

Set out below is a list of headings that you would expect to see in either the Profit & Loss account or the Balance Sheet, with the additional elements that you would associate with partnership accounts. Drag the words 'Profit & Loss' and 'Balance Sheet' and drop them next to the headings to which you think they apply. When you are happy with your selection, click the 'Submit' button at the bottom of your screen to view your score and see feedback on your answers.

Heading		
Pre-payment	Profit & Loss	Balance Sheet
Net Assets	Profit & Loss	Balance Sheet
Gross Profit	Profit & Loss	Balance Sheet
Current Assets	Profit & Loss	Balance Sheet
less Drawings	Profit & Loss	Balance Sheet
Interest on capital	Profit & Loss	Balance Sheet

The final exercise in this section, Exercise 5, is designed to consolidate your learning of the key principles covered in this section and will require you to answer a series of in-depth multiple choice questions relating to partnership financial statements, including pre-payments, accruals, appropriation of Net Profit and the movements in current accounts calculation.

This exercise sets out a number of multiple-choice questions to assist you in understanding further the construction of Profit & Loss accounts and Balance Sheets, and how to address pre-payments, accruals, and partnership appropriation of profits. Some questions will require you to make slightly more detailed calculations than you may otherwise expect — answer each in turn, taking time to select your answer. When you are happy with your answers, click the 'Submit' button at the bottom of the screen to view your score and receive feedback on your answers.

Question 1
A trial balance prepared on June 30 includes the following balances:

	Debit (£)	Credit (£)
Sales		12,000
Electricity	1,800	
Stationery	1,000	

Sales includes £1,000 attributable to the following accounting period. There is an accrued amount for Electricity for £400. There is Stationery stock of £300.

Which one of the following statements is correct?

○ Sales on the Profit & Loss account for year ending June 30 will be £13,000.

○ Sales on the Profit & Loss Account for year ending June 30 will be £12,000.

○ The Balance Sheet as at June 30 will show Sales of £1,000 as a Current Asset.

○ The Balance Sheet as at June 30 will show Sales of £1,000 as a Current Liability.

Conclusion

The only difference for partnership financial statements compared with those that we have looked at in previous sections is the requirement to carefully apportion Net Profit amongst the partners and to update the Current accounts balance. Structurally, both of these calculations do not form part of the financial statement but they will contribute to elements within the Balance Sheet's Capital Employed section.

By the time you have completed the exercises associated with this section, you should have fully consolidated your understanding of the issues we examined in the previous sections, such as the need to make adjustments to the trial balance, and be comfortable with these additional elements.

Section 12

Company accounts

Exercise map

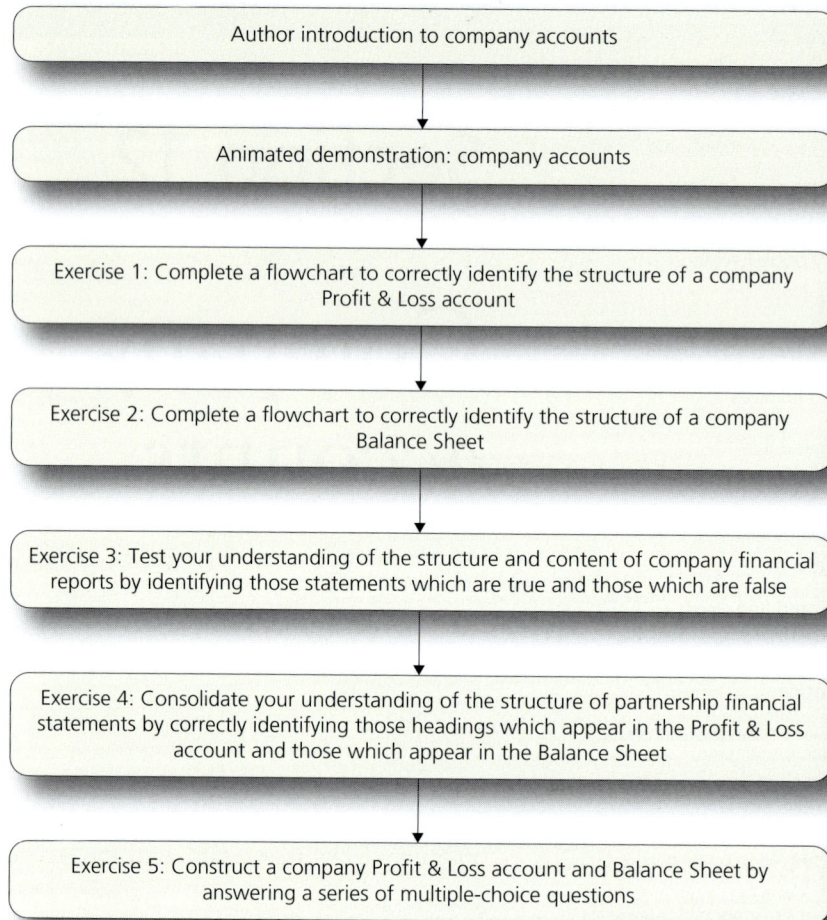

Author introduction to company accounts

Animated demonstration: company accounts

Exercise 1: Complete a flowchart to correctly identify the structure of a company Profit & Loss account

Exercise 2: Complete a flowchart to correctly identify the structure of a company Balance Sheet

Exercise 3: Test your understanding of the structure and content of company financial reports by identifying those statements which are true and those which are false

Exercise 4: Consolidate your understanding of the structure of partnership financial statements by correctly identifying those headings which appear in the Profit & Loss account and those which appear in the Balance Sheet

Exercise 5: Construct a company Profit & Loss account and Balance Sheet by answering a series of multiple-choice questions

Introduction

In this section we will move on to look at the final business entity that needs to be examined as part of *LPC Accounts Online*: companies.

As we work our way through this section we will start to notice the increased burden of regulation placed upon incorporated entities, i.e. companies, in relation to the structure, content and standards applied to the preparation of their financial statements. Whilst similarities still remain when compared to sole traders and partnerships, both of these business entities do however retain a greater degree of privacy in that their financial statements are not published for a wider public to scrutinise. Companies by contrast are creatures of statute run by directors for the benefit of shareholders, and as such their financial statements are subject to greater regulation to ensure transparency and publication.

Accounting Regulation: Companies

In Section 9 of *LPC Accounts Online*, we briefly touched upon the regulation imposed by and on the accountancy profession to ensure financial statements are prepared on a uniform basis, the result of which is that agreed and accepted conventions are applied to allow for the valid comparison of accounts.

Accounting Standards

As we recall, it was the big six UK accountancy firms that established the Accounting Standards Committee and set definitive standards of financial accounting and reporting. It was then the Accounting Standards Board (ASB) who adopted the existing standards and issued its Financial Reporting Standards (FRSs). It is these standards that we will be applying during *LPC Accounts Online*. For further information on the FRSs visit the Financial Reporting Council's website at <http://www.frc.org.uk/>.

Legal force of accounting standards

It is s396(3) Companies Act 2006 that gives the ASB's adopted standards and the FRSs their statutory force. As is common of most new legislation, the Companies Act 2006 grants the Secretary of State the necessary authority to issue secondary legislation to govern the form and content of both the Balance Sheet and Profit & Loss account, and to prescribe that information which is to be included as notes to each financial statement. Accordingly by application of s396(3) Companies Act 2006 (set out below), which mirrors earlier legislation, there exists for the Secretary of State flexibility to adopt new standards and amend existing standards quickly.

Statutory requirements for companies

Before we look more closely at the structure and composition of financial statements for companies, it is worth taking a quick look at some of the statutory requirements imposed by the Companies Act 2006 on directors and companies. This will go some way to help you understand the need for consistency of presentation and content when looking further at company accounts.

Companies Act 2006

Every company must keep accounting records sufficient to show and explain its transactions. There are detailed requirements stating what the accounting records must show; in particular, they must be sufficient to enable the production of final accounts for publication. In fact, these records must be kept for three years for a private company, six for a public company, and be available for inspection.

Companies Act 2006

386 Duty to keep accounting records

(1) Every company must keep adequate accounting records.

(2) Adequate accounting records means records that are sufficient –

    a. to show and explain the company's transactions.

    b. To disclose with reasonable accuracy, at any time, the financial position of the company at any time, and

    c. To enable the directors to ensure that any accounts required to be prepared comply with the requirements of the Act….

(3) Accounting records must, in particular, contain –

    a. Entries from day to day of all sums of money received and expended by the company and the matters in respect of which the receipt and expenditure takes place, and

    b. A record of the assets and liabilities of the company.

However, it is the directors' duty to prepare a set of accounts for the company for each of its financial years which must consist of a Profit & Loss account and a Balance Sheet.

Individual accounts

394 Duty to prepare individual accounts

The directors of every company must prepare accounts for the company for each of its financial years.

Those accounts are referred to as the company's "individual accounts".

396 Companies Act individual accounts

(1) Companies Act individual accounts must comprise –

    a. A balance sheet as at the last day of the financial year, and

    b. A profit and loss accounts.

(2) The accounts must –

    a. In the case of the balance sheet, give a true and fair view of the state of affairs of the company as at the end of the financial year, and

    b. In the case of the profit and loss account, give a true and fair view of the profit or loss of the company for the financial year.

(3) The accounts must comply with provision made by the Secretary of State by regulations as to –

    a. The form and content of the balance sheet and profit and loss account, and

    b. Additional information to be provided by way of notes to the accounts.

As we noted in Section 9, companies are required to present their accounts so as to give a '*true and fair view of the state of affairs of the company*' (emphasis added), a requirement of s396(2) Companies Act 2006 (see above). It is worth noting that this duty falls upon the directors (s394 Companies Act 2006) to ensure compliance, and in the event that in complying with any regulation of the Secretary of State's this duty may result in the company's financial statements failing to give that "*true and fair view*" (either by including or omitting certain information), then the directors may depart from that particular requirement, provided explanations are attached as notes to the accounts. Do consider taking a little time to read fully the provisions of Part 15, Chapter 5 of the Companies Act 2006. Chapter 5 details the information that directors are required to provide in their accompanying statements which, together with the company's financial statements assist shareholders in reviewing the company's performance and the directors ability to promote the success of the company (a duty directors are required to do under s172 of the Companies Act 2006).

But the directors' duties in the preparation of financial statements do not end there; it is their duty to appoint and ensure that the company's financial statements are audited by suitably qualified auditors. Part 16 of the Companies Act 2006 will provide you with more detail about when financial statements are to be audited (unless the company falls within one of the exemptions), and in fact when shareholders may require financial statements to be audited. In any event, within nine months after the end of each financial year for a private company, the directors must ensure that the company's financial statements, together with the auditors' and directors' reports be laid before the company in a general meeting.

It is the combination of these statutory requirements and the FRS (particularly FRS 4) that we will adopt and apply as we examine the financial statements for companies.

By now, you should be familiar with the general structure of both the Profit & Loss account and Balance Sheet. As we move on to consider the more specific requirements of company financial statements, watch the Animated Demonstration provided online for a detailed explanation and worked example designed to illustrate the structure and composition of the financial statements of a company.

J&P Crocco Ltd
Trading and Profit & Loss account for the year ending 31 December 2010

	£	£
Sales		1,394,150
less Cost of goods sold		
Opening stock	45,000	
add Purchases	650,000	
	695,000	
less Closing stock	(25,000)	670,000
Gross Profit		**724,150**
less Expenses		
Administration expenses	78,500	
Bad debts & provision	10,000	
Depreciation	51,750	
Directors' remuneration	195,000	
Wages & salaries	253,450	(588,700)
Operating Profit		**135,450**
less Interest charges		(4,300)
Profit Before Tax		**131,150**
Taxation		(10,000)
Profit After Tax		**121,150**
Interim dividends paid	15,300	
Final dividends	45,900	(61,200)
Retained Profit for the year		**59,950**
Retained Profit brought forward		7,650
Retained Profit carried forward		**67,600**

01:32 08:55

Company Profit & Loss account

A company Profit & Loss account will first differ under the expense items. In contrast to sole traders and partnerships, those that manage the company (i.e. the directors) will be regarded as an expense in recognition of the fact that they are company employees. As an expense, their salaries will be included as a separate entry under the Expenses section of the Profit & Loss account and will be shown separately to the wages of other employees. This is illustrated in the Profit & Loss account for Nash Ltd contained in Example 12.1

Example 12.1

Nash Ltd Trading and Profit & Loss account for the year ending 31 December 2010

	£	£
Sales		179,000
less Cost of goods sold		
Opening stock	23,000	
add Purchases	70,000	
	93,000	
less Closing stock	26,000	67,000
Gross Profit		**112,000**
less Expenses		
Council tax	2,300	
Depreciation	9,000	
Directors remuneration	39,000	
General expenses	11,400	
Motor expenses	2,500	
Wages	33,000	(97,200)
Operating Profit		**14,800**
Interest paid		6,000
Profit Before Tax		**8,800**
Taxation		1,760
Profit After Tax		**7,040**
Interim dividend paid	3,000	
Final dividend	2,000	5,000
Retained Profit for the year		2,040
Retained Profit brought forward		17,040
Retained Profit carried forward		19,040

Directors' remuneration: separately identified as an expense; distinct from other employees whose salaries are identified under the heading 'Wages'

If you have already watched the Animated Demonstration which accompanies this section, you may have noticed a number of further differences between the financial statements for a company and those for other types of business entity. In particular, FRS 4 imposes greater structure to company financial statements and consistency in the accounting treatment of capital instruments, i.e. those items of debt finance. As a result, the term 'Net Profit' is replaced with the term 'Operating Profits'. It is from Operating Profits that the cost of financing debt (i.e. interest charged) is deducted.

Example 12.2

Interest: this relates to interest paid to holders of debentures, i.e. loans made to companies, which entitle the holder to regular interest payments regardless of whether the company has made a profit. As such it is not a business operating expense but a payment against a liability that may only be deducted once Operating Profits have been determined. In contrast to mortgages which will be secured against the company's assets, debentures may be unsecured. For further information see also Company Balance Sheets at page xxx below.

Operating Profit		14,800
Interest paid		6,000
Profit Before Tax		8,800
Taxation		1,760
Profit After Tax		7,040
Interim dividend paid	3,000	
Final dividend	2,000	5,000
Retained Profit for the year		2,040
Retained Profit brought forward		17,040
Retained Profit carried forward		19,040

Retained Profit: represents any Operating Profit not appropriated for tax or dividends and retained within the business. As 'labels' to the financial statements, the directors will indicate why such profits are retained, for example, for expansion, maintaining adequate working capital, payment of preference share redemption. Retained profit could have been distributed as a dividend, but once retained will become part of the company's reserves and represents further shareholders funds – as can be seen here, it is added to the previous year's retained profit and carried forward to the Balance Sheet.

Dividends: once the company's liabilities and taxation have been settled, and provided the directors do not to retain any profits for future purposes, shareholders may be rewarded for their investment in the company by receiving a dividend (or 'distribution' of the Operating Profit). Dividends may only be declared by directors, although shareholders may exert pressure for payment. Two forms of dividend payments may be made:

• **Interim Dividend**: if the company is performing well during the year and prior to finalising the accounts, the directors may declare an interim payment of dividend. As an appropriation of Operating Profit, it will appear in the Appropriation section of the Profit & Loss account rather than in the expenses section; dividends are not operating expenses but rewards on investments which may only be made if the company makes a profit. As an interim dividend is paid during the financial year it is shown only in the Profit & Loss account and not on the Balance Sheet.
• **Final Dividend: Is** that sum yet to be paid to shareholders at the end of the financial year out of Operating Profits (after tax and other liabilities). As the final dividend will be paid after the close of the financial year, it will be identified as an appropriation of Operating Profit and as a Current Liability in the Balance Sheet.

Taxation: Reflecting a company's separate legal personality, companies (e.g. limited or public limited companies) will be required to pay corporation tax on any profits they generated. The amount of tax will appear in both the Profit & Loss account, as an Appropriation, and the Balance Sheet, as a Current Liability. Once the tax liability has been determined, the directors will then be able to declare whether a dividend may be paid to the company's shareholders.

Once Operating Profit has been calculated, further items will be 'appropriated' (i.e. deducted) in accordance with the accounting standards for items such as tax, dividends and reserves. This section of the Profit & Loss account is generally referred to as the 'Appropriation' section, and identifies those items normally paid at the end of the accounting period. It also shows whether the directors have set aside profits for particular purposes. If we now look at the Profit & Loss account for Nash Ltd set out in Example 12.2 we can see those items which are to be deducted from Operating Profit, and how the Appropriation section of the Profit & Loss account is calculated.

Whilst we can see from Example 12.2 that Nash Ltd has appropriated part of its Operating Profit to pay taxation and dividends, and has retained the remaining sum, other items may occasionally appear in the Appropriation section of a company's Profit & Loss account. For example, it may be applied to such items as goodwill purchased on the takeover of a business, company formation expenses, or against future anticipated costs (or extraordinary items) required to cover the potential award made against the company in litigation proceedings.

Now attempt Exercise 1 to test yourself on the structure of a Company's Profit & Loss account ensuring that you correctly incorporate the new headings and the necessary appropriations that are made after Operating Profit has been calculated. Try to attempt this exercise without reference to your notes to further consolidate your learning to date.

As we now move to look at company Profit & Loss accounts, we will again see that new additional elements start to appear in the structure. The first difference is the expense appearing on a company's Profit & Loss account and the appropriation section which shows how profit is used, namely taxation, dividends, and reserves.

In this exercise you are required to place the various headings of a company Profit & Loss account in the correct order to see how much of the structure you can remember. Complete the flowchart below by placing the various headings in the correct order by selecting the correct option from those available. The first and final steps are completed for you. When you are happy with your flowchart, click 'Submit' at the bottom of your screen to see your feedback and score.

Sales

- add Purchases
- Final dividends
- Gross Profit
- Interim dividends paid
- less Closing stock
- less Cost of goods sold
- less Expenses
- less Interest charges
- Opening stock
- Operating Profit
- Profit After Tax
- Profit Before Tax
- Retained Profit brought forward
- Retained Profit for the year
- Taxation

Company Balance Sheet

If you have already viewed the Animated Demonstration online, you may have noticed that again the FRS 4 requires greater formality in the headings contained in the Balance Sheet and demands the identification and separation of long term liabilities owed by the company and capital. The FRS 4 requirements affect both the Employment of Capital and the Capital Employed sections which we will now consider. An example of a company Balance Sheet is set out in Example 12.3

Example 12.3

Nash Ltd Balance Sheet as at 31 December 2010			
Employment of Capital	£	£	£
Fixed assets	Cost	Dep	NBV
Building	150,000	0	150,000
Fixtures & Fittings	40,000	12,000	28,000
Goodwill	20,000	0	20,000
Machinery	25,000	15,000	10,000
	235,000	27,000	208,000
Current Assets			
Stock	26,000		
Debtors	26,500		
Cash	13,200	65,700	
less **Current Liabilities**			
Creditors	19,900		
Dividends payable	2,000		
Taxation	1,760	(23,660)	
Net Current Assets			42,040
Assets *less* **Current Liabilities**			250,040
less **Creditors falling due after 1 year**			
Falling due between 2 & 5 years		5,000	
Falling due after 5 years		35,000	(40,000)
Net Assets			**210,040**
Capital Employed			
Called up share capital (fully paid)			
Equity shares (Ords)		120,000	
Non-equity shares (Prefs)		40,000	160,000
Share Premium Account			16,000
Reserve			15,000
Accumulated Retained Profit			19,040
			210,040

Employment of Capital

From Nash Ltd's Balance Sheet set out in Example 12.3, you will note the first key difference in the Employment of Capital section, namely, a new heading of 'Net Current Assets' representing the sum of Current Assets *less* Current Liabilities.

Essential Principles

Net Current Assets: determined by the following sum:

Current Assets – Current Liabilities = Net Current Assets

You should also note how information contained in the Employment of Capital section of the Balance Sheet relates to the Profit & Loss account. If we consider the Balance Sheet of Nash Ltd contained in Example 12.3 above, and compare it to its Profit & Loss account which we considered earlier at page 199, you will note that the declared final dividend of £2,000 is included under Current Liabilities in the Balance Sheet. As the interim dividend would have been paid during the financial year, it is only the final dividend that remains outstanding and due for payment to shareholders within the following 12 months.

Also included under Current Liabilities is the tax liability of £1,760, representing the apportionment of Operating Profit identified in the Profit & Loss account. Remember, and in contrast to sole traders and partnerships, that as a company is a separate legal entity it is responsible for corporation tax on its profits and the current year's tax will appear as a liability to be settled in the next 12 months – the proprietors of the company (i.e. the shareholders) will remain personally responsible for any tax due on their investment income derived from any dividend payment.

Once Net Current Assets have been calculated, the final calculation which must be undertaken in the Employment of Capital section is to determine Net Assets. By way of example, Example 12.4 shows how Nash Ltd's Net Assets are calculated.

Essential Principles

Net Assets: determined by the following sum:

Fixed Assets + (Current Assets – (all) Liabilities) = Net Assets

---

Example 12.4

> **Assets *less* Current Liabilities**: FRS 4 requires separation of current and long term liabilities and therefore a further heading is included within the Balance Sheet to make this distinction. This is calculated by adding the sum of Net Current Assets (i.e. Current Assets - Current Liabilities) to Fixed Assets (i.e. (Fixed Assets + Net Current Assets).

Net Current Assets			42,040
Assets *less* Current Liabilities			250,040
less Creditors falling due after 1 year			
Falling due between 2 & 5 years		5,000	
Falling due after 5 years		35,000	(40,000)
Net Assets			210,040

> **Liabilities falling due after 1 year:** in complying with FRS 4, company Balance Sheets are required to first identify those debts falling due within 12 months (i.e. Current Liabilities) and those after 12 months from the date of the Balance Sheet (i.e. long-term liabilities). FRS 4 requires such liabilities to be categorised under the following headings:
>
> * in one year or less or on demand;
> * between one and two years;
> * between two and five years;
> * in five years or more.
>
> Items such as long term bank loans and debentures will fall within these headings. In the case of a debenture issued below its nominal value or at a discount, the expense of its issue is included as an expense in the Profit & Loss account to reflect the actual value the company will have to repay on redemption.

Capital Employed

Finally, looking now at the Balance Sheet's Capital Employed section, FRS4 requires that items of long-term debts, share capital and shareholder funds be separately identified. This separation is illustrated in Nash Ltd's Balance Sheet which is set out in Example 12.5.

Example 12.5

> **Called up share capital:** FRS 4 requires that the capital raised by the issue of shares and the different types of shares, and the rights attached to them (e.g. whether voting, redeemable, rights to dividends, priority and entitlement on winding up) be distinguished under the headings of 'equity' capital (i.e. ordinary shares) and 'non-equity' capital (i.e. preference shares with restrictions on the right to participate in profits or in assets on a winding up).
>
> The figure stated is the cumulative nominal or face value of all such shares sold (share may not be sold at a discount, s580 Companies Act 2006), and identified as whether fully or partially paid up (i.e. whether the total of the face value has been paid, or if only part, as is permitted, been paid).

Capital Employed			
Called up share capital (fully paid)			
Equity shares (Ords)		120,000	
Non-equity shares (Prefs)		40,000	160,000
Share Premium Account			16,000
Reserves			15,000
Accumulated Retained Profit			19,040
			210,040

> **Accumulated Retained Profit**: drawn and carried from the Profit & Loss account, representing Operating Profits not distributed by the directors as a dividend.

> **Reserves:** This is any profit retained by the company and representing a shareholder capital. May include such items or funds to settle pending litigation judgements or legal reserve funds required by legislations (depending on the industry sector, e.g. banking) and maintained as a percentage of share capital.

> **Share premium:** Since the Share capital account only shows the nominal value of the shares (or, the amount if only part paid) sold, the Share premium account represents any premium above nominal value made on the sale of shares – the premium is not to be regarded as profit, but as capital of the company and is therefore shareholder's funds. The company may only use such capital for limited purposes, for example, the Companies Act permits this capital to be used for capital maintenance purposes.

Having now looked at the additional requirements for the Balance Sheet to ensure compliance with the FRS 4 and Companies Act 2006, attempt Exercise 2 to test whether you can identify the correct structure of a Company Balance Sheet. Try to attempt this exercise without reference to your notes to further consolidate your learning to date and be sure to incorporate the new headings, showing the greater separation of liabilities and identification of the sources of capital of the business.

Turning now to the company's Balance Sheet, we will again see that new additional elements start to appear in the structure. Greater separation needs to be made in relation to the long-term liabilities of the company and under the Capital Employed section. Separation is also required to show the capital raised from the nominal (face) value of the shares, and any premium acquired from the sale of such shares.

In this exercise you are required to place the various headings of a company Balance Sheet in the correct order to see how much of the structure you can remember. Complete the flowchart below by placing the various headings in the correct order by selecting the correct option from those available. The first and final steps are completed for you. When you are happy with your flowchart, click 'Submit' at the bottom of your screen to see your feedback and score.

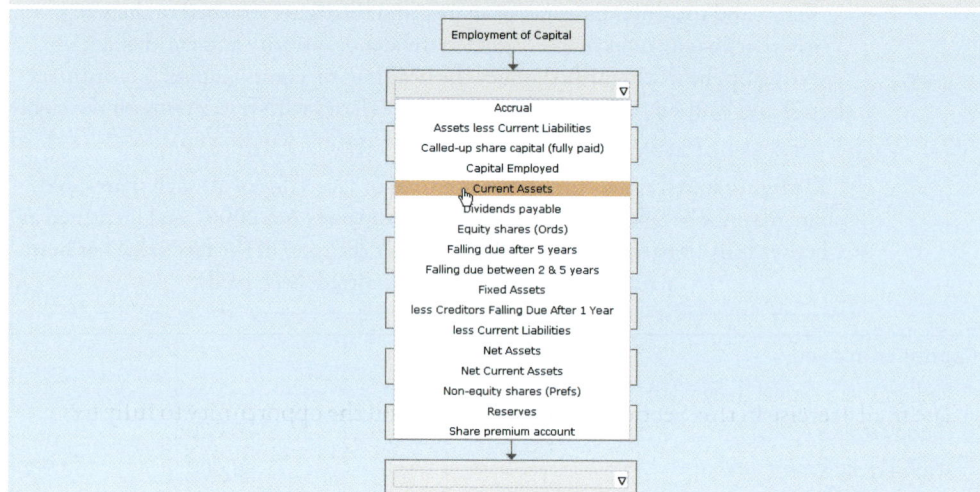

Employment of Capital

Accrual
Assets less Current Liabilities
Called-up share capital (fully paid)
Capital Employed
Current Assets
Dividends payable
Equity shares (Ords)
Falling due after 5 years
Falling due between 2 & 5 years
Fixed Assets
less Creditors Falling Due After 1 Year
less Current Liabilities
Net Assets
Net Current Assets
Non-equity shares (Prefs)
Reserves
Share premium account

Once you have completed Exercise 2, you can further test your understanding of the structure and composition of company financial statements by undertaking Exercise 3 and correctly identifying those statements which are true and those which are false.

To continue to help you understand the structure and content of financial reports, set out below are statements relating to different aspects of both Profit & Loss accounts and Balance Sheets. You need to identify which of the statements are true and which of the statements are false. When you are happy with your selection click the 'Submit' button at the bottom of your screen to view your score and receive feedback on your answers.

	True	False
The Balance Sheet will show the total of all dividends declared by the company as a Current Liability.	○	○
Interest paid to service debentures is an expense of the business and is deducted after Operating Profit.	○	○
Net Current Assets is determined by the following sum: Current Assets – Current Liabilities = Net Current Assets.	○	○
When making adjustments for a further provision for bad debt, it is only the Profit & Loss account that shows this adjustment.	○	○
An interim dividend is shown in the appropriation section of the Profit & Loss account since a portion of the company's profit has already been allocated to this purpose.	○	○
Reserves represents an allocation of profits for distribution to members.	○	○
Net Book Value (NBV) represents that value of a Fixed Asset after annual depreciation has been deducted from its acquisition cost.	○	○

You should then attempt Exercise 4, which requires you to allocate various headings to the correct financial statement.

To continue to help you consolidate your understanding of the structure of the company's Profit & Loss account and Balance Sheet, set out below is a list of headings that you would expect to see in either financial statement, with the additional elements that you would associate with companies. Drag the words 'Profit & Loss' and 'Balance Sheet' and drop them next to the headings to which you think they apply. When you are happy with your selection, click the 'Submit' button at the bottom of your screen to view your score and see feedback on your answers.

Net Current Assets	Profit & Loss	Balance Sheet
Interim dividends paid	Profit & Loss	Balance Sheet
Called-up share capital	Profit & Loss	Balance Sheet
Assets *less* Current Liabilities	Profit & Loss	Balance Sheet
Share premium account	Profit & Loss	Balance Sheet
less Interest charges	Profit & Loss	Balance Sheet
Accrual	Profit & Loss	Balance Sheet

The final exercise in this Section, Exercise 5, offers you the opportunity to fully test your knowledge of the key principles underpinning company financial statements by requiring you to construct a company's Profit & Loss account and Balance Sheet by selecting the correct entries from a series of multiple choice questions.

Question 1
You should now be familiar with how Gross Profit is calculated, from which the business operating expenses are then deducted. What is the title that is now used against the sum of this calculation?

○ Net Profit

○ Profit

○ Operating Profit

○ Retained Profit

Question 2
With reference to the trial balance and from the information provided in the top half of the Profit & Loss account below, complete the remaining part of the Profit & Loss account and calculate North Recruitment Ltd's Retained Profit Carried Forward.

North Recruitment Ltd
Trading and Profit & Loss account for the period ended 31 December [year]

	£	£
Sales		290,000
less Cost Of Sales		
Opening stock	21,000	
add Purchases	110,000	
	131,000	
less Closing stock	23,000	108,000
Gross Profit		182,000
less Expenses		
Bad debts	1,500	
Council tax	3,000	
Depreciation	5,000	

Conclusion

It is the statutory requirement for compliance with accounting standards that differentiates company financial statements from sole traders and partnerships. As company financial statements are documents that may be inspected by the public, including those undertaking investment decisions, there is an obvious need for conformity in the content, presentation, and any notes or reports that are attached to them. If the financial statements prepared deviate from such standards, it becomes much harder to compare the financial statements of companies undertaking similar activities.

Section 13

Interpretation of financial statements

Exercise map

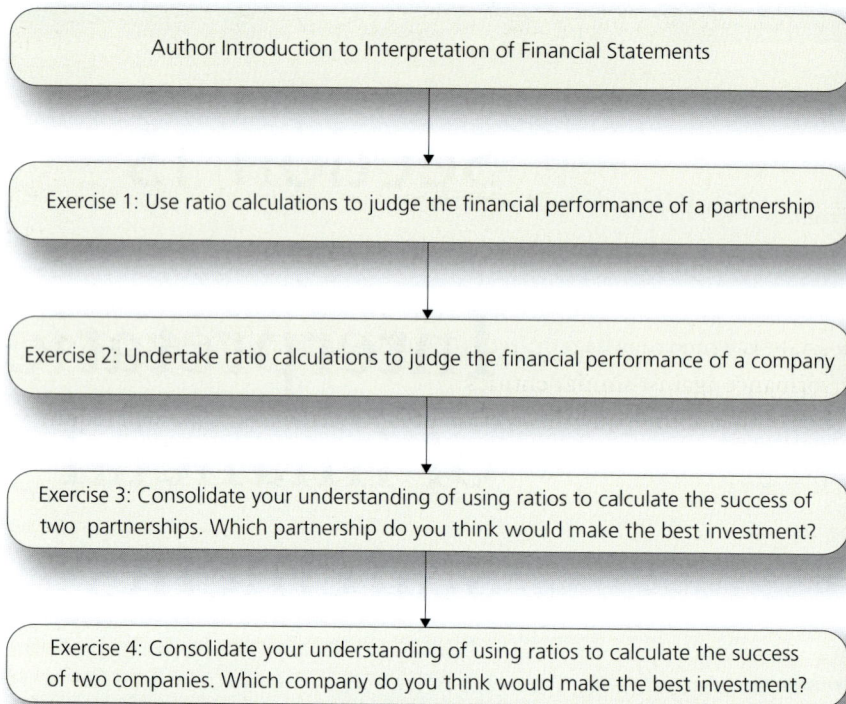

Author Introduction to Interpretation of Financial Statements

Exercise 1: Use ratio calculations to judge the financial performance of a partnership

Exercise 2: Undertake ratio calculations to judge the financial performance of a company

Exercise 3: Consolidate your understanding of using ratios to calculate the success of two partnerships. Which partnership do you think would make the best investment?

Exercise 4: Consolidate your understanding of using ratios to calculate the success of two companies. Which company do you think would make the best investment?

Introduction

In earlier sections of *LPC Accounts Online* we focused on the composition of financial statements for different business entities, namely sole traders, partnerships, and companies. However, this was done without undertaking any analysis of those financial statements to judge the relative performance of the business, both over time and in comparison with other businesses.

The ability to interpret financial statements requires a combination of sound financial judgment and common sense. In this section we will look to apply various ratios to aid in this interpretation and analysis. However, ratios alone do not provide all the answers. At the very least, ratios should, when used in conjunction with other ratios, suggest further avenues of analysis which may be required to establish an overview of the entity concerned and its performance against similar entities.

The exercises that accompany this section of *LPC Accounts Online* will require you to consider financial statements for both partnerships and companies and then draw conclusions about the relative performance of the businesses from those financial statements. But before you start the exercises, let's consider some of the ratios that are employed to aid in interpreting financial statements.

Ratio Analysis

The intention of this section is to introduce you to the purpose and application of ratios in assessing the performance of a business. This will assist you in providing advice to clients within any number of practice areas; not only in commercial transactions and provision of advice to members etc., but also debt collection or even matrimonial practice.

But this is to suggest that you have not already been provided with information to reflect upon the management and performance of the business. You will have noticed from your understanding of how financial statements are constructed that at the end of the business's accounting period, the ledgers used to prepare financial statements are checked to ensure that they accurately reflected the business's actual expenditures. As a consequence, adjustments are made to account for accruals, pre-payments, provision for bad debt and depreciation, and, from this information, it is possible to start to consider how the business manages its cash flow and liabilities and how it values its assets.

For example, if the business has a number of outstanding invoices (i.e. accruals), does this mean that future profits will be needed to pay them? Consider also how the business depreciates its assets; if it fails to reflect a true reduction in the value of assets accurately, the business may, as a consequence, be overvalued or, if the value of depreciation is too much, undervalued. Consider also the amount of dividends being distributed; if too high, is the business failing to retain sufficient profits for future investment?

In addition, it may also be possible to determine from a set of financial statements whether a business entity is on the brink of insolvency. In the context of a company, the statutory definition of insolvency is by reference to s 123 of the Insolvency Act 1986, see extract below. Whilst a company may be deemed insolvent if it fails to satisfy a statutory demand for a debt within 3 weeks of it being served (Insolvency Act 1986, s 123(1)), there are two other tests, which could cause concern for directors as they examine their business's financial statements.

'123. Definition of inability to pay debts

    (1) A company is deemed unable to pay its debts—

        (a) if a creditor (by assignment or otherwise) to whom the company is indebted in a sum exceeding £750 then due has served on the company, by leaving it at the company's registered office, a written demand (in the prescribed form) requiring the company to pay the sum so due and the company has for 3 weeks thereafter neglected to pay the sum or to secure or compound for it to the reasonable satisfaction of the creditor, or . . .

        (e) if it is proved to the satisfaction of the court that the company is unable to pay its debts as they fall due.

    (2) A company is also deemed unable to pay its debts if it is proved to the satisfaction of the court that the value of the company's assets is less than the amount of its liabilities, taking into account its contingent and prospective liabilities . . .

Directors already have statutory duties under the Companies Act 2006 to ensure that they promote the success of the company and that they exercise reasonable care, skill, and diligence (Companies Act 2006, ss 172 and 174, respectively). It is by reference to s 123 of the Insolvency Act 1986 that they will be able to ensure their ongoing ability to do so. Section 123(1)(e) of the Insolvency Act 1986 established the 'cash flow' test whereby if the company is unable to pay its debts as they fall due, it will arguably be insolvent. By examining both the Profit & Loss account to establish the business's turnover and revenue together with an assessment of the business's Current Liabilities and liabilities falling due between 1 and 2 years extracted from the Balance Sheet, it should not be too difficult to determine whether it is in fact impossible for the business to pay its forthcoming liabilities.

But that is not the only test that the Insolvency Act 1986 provides. Section 123(2) also establishes the 'Balance Sheet' test so that a company will again arguably be insolvent should the company's assets be less than its liabilities. But such a test on the face of it may not take into account future revenue, so it will be for the court to be satisfied after judicious examination of the financial statements that the company is indeed insolvent.

Thus far, you should already start to be reflecting on your ability to interpret financial statements to draw conclusions about the relative health and performance of a business, whether it is a sole trader, partnership, or company. By reflecting on information provided in the trial balance and by applying suitable ratios, financial statements may also be examined and compared year-on-year and against other businesses to determine how well the business is performing.

Whilst there are any number of potential ratios that may be applied, LPC Accounts Online will focus on only a few which are suitable for examining partnership and company financial statements. The ratios are grouped into the following categories:

- Profitability ratios;
- Liquidity ratios;
- Efficiency or Activity ratios;
- Gearing ratios; and
- Investment ratios.

If you are unsure which ratios you are to apply on your business accounts course, do consult the tutor responsible for your course for clarification.

Profitability Ratios

Profitability ratios consider the profitability and efficiency of the business to show the return on the long-term investment in the business, i.e. Return on Capital Employed with the return on sales. They seek to show how much sales contribute to business operating costs and their impact on the business's profit margin. As with all ratios, these ratios are not without limitations, and they should not be considered in isolation most profitability ratios do disregard the cost of financing the business, such as long-term interest on debentures and other sources of finance, which will influence profitability.

Return on Capital Employed (ROCE)

ROCE, often referred to as the primary ratio, may be used to show the overall return on the long-term investment in the business and, on a simple comparative basis, is compared with the return that could be earned from 'safer' investments such as interest-earned money held in a bank or building society deposit account.

Ideally, ROCE would be used to determine an average over a 5-year period and compared within its business sector. If the ROCE is too low, then it may be time for proprietors or managers to consider winding the business up and investing the capital elsewhere. However, until that decision is made, a low ROCE would suggest that action is needed to turn the business around and improve the capital return. The ROCE of a business is calculated as follows:

$$\frac{\text{Net Profit (before interest and tax)}}{\substack{\text{Capital Employed} \\ \text{(total assets less Current Liabilities)}}} \times 100\%$$

If we now look at Example 13.1, you will see how to extract the figures and so determine the ROCE ratio for the partnership of Tracey, Tricky, and Trinny trading as 'The 3Ts'.

As to what may be a suitable return on capital may depend on what rate of return investors could get if their capital was invested elsewhere. For example, if the investor put his capital in a bank's high interest deposit account, how would a business's ROCE compare? What the ROCE produces may also be reflective of how new or how risky the business is; the newer the business, the more likely the ROCE will be low, but a risky business investment could see the investor's capital being wiped out as the business fails or it could in fact produce an exceptionally high return. Whilst it appears, from the calculation in Example 13.1, that The 3Ts have achieved a healthy (if exceptionally high) ROCE of 101%, is that ROCE a one-off high or a reflection of consistent performance? The ROCE alone does not define a business's success and even where the ROCE calculated is satisfactory, as in Example 13.1, more will need to be known about the nature of the business carried on by the partnership, how that ROCE compares against previous years, and possibly its performance compared other similar businesses.

Example 13.1

Tracey, Tricky, and Trinny trading as 'The 3Ts' Trading and Profit & Loss account for the year ending 31 December 2010

	£	£
Turnover		640,000
less Cost of goods sold		
Opening stock	35,000	
add Purchases	341,000	
	376,000	
less Closing stock	31,000	(345,000)
Gross Profit		**295,000**
less Expenses		
Advertising	2,000	
Bad debts & provision	4,000	
Depreciation	19,000	
Distribution costs	15,000	
Insurance	14,000	
Power	16,000	
Rates	14,000	
Wages	40,000	(124,000)
Net Profit		**171,000**

Profit & Loss Appropriation account	Tracey	Trickys	Trinny
Salary	3,000	4,000	0
Interest	1,000	1,000	0
Profit share	40,500	40,500	81,000
	44,500	45,500	81,000

Net Profit (before interest and tax): In this instance the partnership does not have any interest liabilities, so the whole of the Net Profit figure should be used.

Capital Employed (total assets less Current Liabilities): This figure may be drawn from the balance or by adding both Fixed Assets and Current Assets together and then deducting any liabilities.

ROCE: $\dfrac{171,000}{169,000} \times 100\% \quad 101\%$

Tracey, Tricky, and Trinny trading as 'The 3Ts' Balance Sheet as at 31 December 2010

Employment of Capital		£	£ Cost	£ Dep'n	£ NBV
Fixed Assets					
Plant & Equipment			90,000	28,000	62,000
Premises			110,000	–	110,000
Vehicles			40,000	17,000	23,000
			240,000	45,000	195,000
Current Assets					
Stock			31,000		
Debtors	30,000				
less Provision	1,000		29,000		
Pre-payment			6,000		
Cash at Bank			18,000	84,000	
less Liabilities					
Accrual			4,000		
HM Revenue & Customs			20,000		
Loan			36,000		
Trade creditors			50,000	(110,000)	(26,000)
Net Assets					169,000
Capital Employed					
Capital accounts					
Tracey				20,000	
Tricky				20,000	
Trinny				50,000	90,000
Current accounts					
Tracey				16,500	
Tricky				21,500	
Trinny				41,000	79,000
					169,000

This is also a suitable point at which to note the need for consistency when conducting ratio analysis. Depending on the figures used, and at which point in the accounting period they are extracted, the resulting ratio may be misleading. For example, the Capital Employed figure could easily be extracted from the beginning of the year, the end of the year, or an average (weighted or otherwise) of the two figures. In each case, how would this distort the resulting ROCE? Convention dictates that either the opening or closing figure for Capital Employed is used but this is not a certainty against the ROCE being misleading if, for example, there has been a substantial increase in capital as a result of an issue of shares or a revaluation of assets. Whichever figure is used, it must be consistently applied to all ratio comparisons, across businesses and year-on-year.

When applying even this first ratio you should be considering further investigations, for example into understanding the business's approach to the valuation of its assets. Most businesses are inclined to state asset values lower than current market value, i.e. depreciating assets by more than the actual amount of depreciation caused by wear and tear. Obviously, depending on the approach to asset valuation, the ROCE ratio may be significantly affected. Again, this demonstrates that ratios alone do not provide the answers. In the case of The 3Ts partnership, Example 13.1, we may need to investigate further the basis upon which the partnership values and depreciate its assets.

Net Profit Percentage (Net Return on Sales)

This ratio produces a representation of the percentage of sales that is left over for profit once all other expenses have been met. It is a ratio used to compare similar businesses and, when compared against an average for the industry over 5 or more years, it is possible to see whether the business is performing better or worse than the average, and whether or not it is improving. This ratio is calculated as follows:

$$\frac{\text{Net Profit}}{\text{Sales}} \times 100\%$$

No ratio should be considered in isolation; accordingly the Net Profit Percentage should be read in conjunction with the Gross Profit ratio (see below at page 216) as both may vary depending on the type of business being conducted. If this ratio were to be applied to The 3Ts partnership which we looked at in Example 13.1, should its Gross Profit ratio remain static, but there is a fall in the Net Profit Percentage when compared to previous years, it may be time to examine the partnership's expenses to see whether they have increased, and if so, why. Comparison against other similar businesses may also show whether the ratio is of a satisfactory level is this a business that operates on a low profit margin but requires a large turnover to achieve its profit, or is the business's management weak?

If The 3Ts are able to achieve percentages above average, this should (generally) infer good management on their part. What is determined to be an average for a business will depend on the sector it operates within. For example, and in contrast with professional services firms, food retailers will seek to sell goods on a continuous and rapid basis, and once they have accounted for the cost of sales, administration costs, selling and distribution costs, and all other costs, they may be happy to have a Net Profit Percentage in a low single figure, but then rely on a large volume of sales to make a sizable profit. However, if the ratio results in an unusually high result, rather than indicating good management, it may be that The 3Ts are the market favourite, which competitors may seek to target.

Again, and as with all other ratios, the Net Profit Percentage does not provide a definitive answer, but indicates where it may be necessary to investigate the business further. For example, even activities such as recruitment and training of staff are inextricably linked with profitability. If a business's existing staff are underemployed, what benefit would be derived from recruiting additional staff who may not be required in either the long or short term or who may require training?

Throughout this section of *LPC Accounts Online* examples of how certain ratios are to be calculated will be provided. For others you should consider attempting these yourself, starting with calculating Net Profit Percentage for The 3Ts using the financial statements in Example 13.1. Once you have completed your own calculation, compare your answer to the calculation available at the end of this section.

Gross Profit Percentage (Return on Sales)

The Gross Profit Percentage is a useful 'control' ratio, in that it represents the difference between the buying price and the selling price of goods. For any business, it reflects the amount added to the cost price of the goods or services provided and the subsequent price that the business then sold those goods or services. In theory, businesses should be using ratio analysis to assess their own business's performance, using that analysis to set achievable targets for the business, which they may either not deviate from or seek to attain over the forthcoming financial periods. The Gross Profit Percentage is calculated as follows:

$$\frac{\text{Gross Profit}}{\text{Sales}} \times 100\%$$

Again, as with any ratio, this ratio should be used with a degree of caution. For example, although the ratio shows the profitability of sales, even if a business's sales have increased it may not mean that overall Gross Profit will also have increased. This may be for any number of reasons, such as the cost of goods sold has increased, but the price at which they are sold has not; that the sale price may have been reduced to encourage sales; that the types of goods themselves have changed or that the profit margin may have been altered.

To give any meaningful interpretation to the Gross Profit Percentage, consideration should be given to that figure in previous years to determine if the ratio has been influenced by the need for the business to undertake activities requiring it to increase its expenditure on certain items that could affect its profitability. Such items of additional expenditure may include increased marketing costs, research, staff recruitment and training etc., which, once identified, may assist in determining whether such expenditure brought the business the returns anticipated or whether it acted as a burden.

Before moving on to look at the various liquidity ratios, try calculating the Gross Profit Percentage for The 3Ts using the financial statements in Example 13.1. Once you have completed your own calculation, compare your answer to the calculations available at the end of this section.

Liquidity Ratios

Liquidity ratios seek to analyse a business's ability to pay its way in the medium and short term. Again, and as you may realize as a general theme when conducting ratio analysis, ratios alone do not indicate much about the business. However, when liquidity ratios are analysed in conjunction with the average for the business sector and general trends, they do provide useful indicators of a business's overall liquidity.

It is important at this stage to make sure that you are aware of the difference between the terms 'solvency' and 'liquidity', which are often confused. *Liquidity* refers to the business's ability to pay its short-term debts from readily realizable assets. By contrast, *solvency* refers to a business's ability to meet all its liabilities from all its assets, i.e. if it sold all of its assets, would it be able to meet (pay) its liabilities? If not, it may be at risk from creditors pushing for it to be wound up or, in the case of a sole traders or partners, made bankrupt. Consider again the provisions of s 123 of the Insolvency Act 1986, discussed earlier.

Current Ratio

The Current ratio seeks to provide an indication of a business's ability to pay its debts in the medium term, normally regarded as between 4 to 9 months into the future. It is expressed as a comparison of Current Assets as a ratio of Current Liabilities, against a mean of 1, as follows:

$$\frac{\text{Current Assets}}{\text{Current Liabilities}} :1$$

The Current ratio for The 3Ts is shown in Example 13.2. Most analysts would expect a cautious business to seek a Current ratio in the region of 1.5:1. However, there may be any number of factors that cause variants in this ratio; for example, a ratio lower than 1.5:1 may suggest that the business is operating in a slightly more risky environment or that it buys goods on credit knowing that it will quickly convert them into cash.

Example 13.2

Tracey, Tricky, and Trinny trading as 'The 3Ts'
Balance Sheet as at 31 December 2010

Employment of Capital		£	£	£
		Cost	Dep'n	NBV
Fixed Assets				
Plant & Equipment		90,000	28,000	62,000
Premises		110,000	–	110,000
Vehicles		40,000	17,000	23,000
		240,000	45,000	195,000
Current Assets				
Stock		31,000		
Debtors	30,000			
less Provision	1,000	29,000		
Pre-payment		6,000		
Cash at Bank		18,000		
			84,000	
less Liabilities				
Accrual		4,000		
HM Revenue & Customs		20,000		
Loan		36,000		
Trade creditors		50,000	(110,000)	
				(26,000)
Net Assets				169,000
Capital Employed				
Capital accounts				
Tracey			20,000	
Tricky			20,000	
Trinny			50,000	90,000
Current accounts				
Tracey			16,500	
Tricky			21,500	
Trinny			41,000	79,000
				169,000

Current Assets: By reference only to the Balance Sheet, use the Current Assets figure.

Current ratio:

$$\frac{84{,}000}{110{,}000} \quad :1 = \quad 0.76:1$$

Current Liabilities: By reference only to the Balance Sheet, use the Current Liabilities figure.

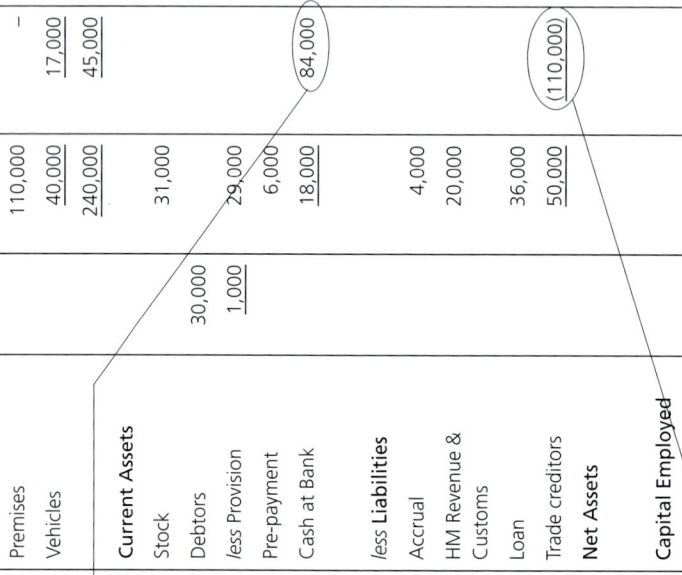

From Example 13.2, we can see that The 3Ts have a Current ratio of 0.76:1. So, what does a ratio of 0.76:1 say about The 3Ts? Thus far we know very little about The 3Ts, but a ratio as low as this may actually suggest that it is operating in the retail sector where it has become common practice to purchase goods on credit which are then sold for cash. We can see just from looking at The 3Ts' Balance Sheet, contained in Example 13.2, that its liabilities exceed it Current Assets by a relatively substantial amount it is only its Fixed Assets that give The 3Ts a healthy looking Balance Sheet. The retail sector is generally in the position of meeting its liabilities as a result of the cash it receives during a day's trading, and can survive with a low amount of additional liquid funds but is this so in the case of The 3Ts? Again, by looking at the Balance Sheet, you will note that The 3Ts do not appear to hold much by way of stock; in fact the level of stock is considerably less than its value of trade creditors. But is this risk offset by the fact that The 3Ts have substantial debtors which, if converted to cash, may be capable of paying creditors as they come knocking at the door? Or is this figure for Debtors too high and an unrealistic sum capable of being recovered?

In any event, a ratio below 1:1 may in fact be one for concern; it may signify that there is only a minimal amount of working capital available for the business should the need for it arise.

Conversely, however, a high ratio, for example a ratio above say 1.80:1 or more may also be of concern it could be an indicator of an unduly cautious business, which is failing to exploit market opportunities to its advantage. Such a ratio may result from too much cash being held on current account or an unreliably high Debtors figure as insufficient bad debts are written off. Excessive stock may also result in a high ratio, but could indicate that the business is unable to sell its products or is unnecessarily accumulating stock. In any event, the nature of the business, the value of its assets, and the manner in which the business treats its liabilities (for example, if the overdraft is shown as a Current Liability, it will be included in the calculation which may not be appropriate in all circumstances) all need to be examined further, and in conjunction with other ratios.

Acid Test

The Acid Test ratio looks at the 'quick' or 'liquid' assets as a ratio of Current Liabilities You should already be reasonably familiar and capable of identifying 'liquid' assets from the examination of the Current Assets listed in the various Balance Sheets you have reviewed as you have progressed through *LPC Accounts Online*. The ratio is calculated as follows:

$$\frac{\text{Liquid Assets (less stock)}}{\text{Current Liabilities}} :1$$

You should note that the ratio excludes Fixed Assets and stock. This is in order to take into account the possible non-saleability of stock, caused as a result of, for example, technological changes or changes in fashions and buying habits. Should the Acid Test ratio result also be low, combined with a low Current ratio, does this mean that the business is at increasing risk of being unable to meet its debts as they fall due?

For some businesses this may be less of a concern, such as for food retailers who will often have very low ratios reflecting the sector's expected high turnover of stock. But what is the nature of the business that you are looking at? At the very least, ratio analysis should be causing you to question more rather than to accept what is presented to you in financial statements. Ratio analysis is one of many tools that will assist you and your clients to examine a business and to determine its financial performance.

Before you attempt the exercises available online, practise calculating the Acid Test ratio by using The 3Ts' financial statements contained in Example 13.2. Once you have completed your own calculation, compare your answer to the calculation available at the end of this section.

Efficiency or Activity Ratios

Efficiency ratios are used to identify how effectively a business manages its stock, creditors, and debtors, i.e. the business's working capital. A lack of working capital could cause the business operational difficulties (and in the case of a bank, affect its ability to lend money) and so cause the management's competencies to come under greater scrutiny. If you have been calculating the various ratios for The 3Ts, this is certainly something that you should start to be questioning.

Average Collection Period

As you may assume from its title, this ratio examines the time it takes the business to collect payment from its debtors for goods or services supplied. The ratio will vary among businesses and so only those of a similar nature should really be compared using this ratio. This ratio is calculated as follows:

$$\frac{\text{(Trade) Debtors}}{\text{Sales}} \times 365$$

Example 13.3 shows the calculation for the Average Collection Period for The 3Ts. As you review the example, consider also the length of time that the debtors are permitted for settling their debts, and any surge in sales immediately before the date of the Balance Sheet. Given The 3Ts' poor showing in the profitability and liquidity ratios, how does the partnership perform in collecting its debts?

From Example 13.3 we can see that The 3Ts' Average Collection Period appears to be 17 days. However, this ratio may not accurately reflect the length of time allowed to debtors, particularly if sales have been strong immediately before the date of the Balance Sheet. But this relatively low collection period does compare well to most terms of sale that would require payment within 28 days of the date of invoice, suggesting that possibly The 3Ts are doing something well by at least managing an efficient collection period.

Example 13.3

Tracey, Tricky, and Trinny trading as 'The 3Ts' Balance Sheet as at 31 December 2010

Employment of Capital		Cost £	Dep'n £	NBV £
Fixed Assets				
Plant & Equipment		90,000	28,000	62,000
Premises		110,000	–	110,000
Vehicles		40,000	17,000	23,000
		240,000	45,000	195,000
Current Assets				
Stock		31,000		
Debtors	30,000	29,000		
less Provision	1,000			
Pre-payment		6,000		
Cash at Bank		18,000	84,000	
less Liabilities				
Accrual		4,000		
HM Revenue & Customs		20,000		
Loan		36,000		
Trade creditors		50,000	(110,000)	(26,000)
Net Assets				169,000
Capital Employed				
Capital accounts				
Tracey			20,000	
Tricky			20,000	
Trinny			50,000	90,000
Current accounts				
Tracey			16,500	
Tricky			21,500	
Trinny			41,000	79,000
				169,000

(Trade) Debtors: Taken from the Balance Sheet, the total value of the Debtors before any adjustment.

Tracey, and Trinny trading as 'The 3Ts' Trading and Profit & Loss account for the year ending 31 December 2010

	£	£
Turnover		640,000
less Cost of goods sold		
Opening stock	35,000	
add Purchases	341,000	
	376,000	
less Closing stock	31,000	(345,000)
Gross Profit		295,000
less Expenses		
Advertising	2,000	
Bad debts & provision	4,000	
Depreciation	19,000	
Distribution costs	15,000	
Insurance	14,000	
Power	16,000	
Rates	14,000	
Wages	40,000	(124,000)
Net Profit		171,000

Sales: By reference only to the Profit & Loss account, this is the total sales figure for the year.

Profit & Loss Appropriation account	Tracey	Trickys	Trinny
Salary	3,000	4,000	0
Interest	1,000	1,000	0
Profit share	40,500	40,500	81,000
	44,500	45,500	81,000

Average Collection Period:

$$\frac{30,000}{640,000} \times 365 = 17 \text{ days}$$

Average Payment Period

The Average Payment Period ratio is one that should most certainly be considered in conjunction with others. In contrast to the Average Collection Period ratio, this ratio will indicate how long the business takes to pay its suppliers. For some businesses, it may be a useful tool for its managers to ensure that they are not paying their suppliers faster than they receive money from their customers. The Average Payment Period is calculated as follows:

$$\frac{\text{(Trade) Creditors}}{\text{Purchases}} \times 365$$

This ratio should also be reviewed against the Average Payment Period from previous years and similar industry standards, together with the terms on which goods are being purchased. Whilst there may be advantages in delaying payment to suppliers for as long as commercially possible (a practice that larger organisations will often impose over smaller suppliers), such a ratio may actually suggest the business has cash flow difficulties or inadequate financial control. If we take the example of The 3Ts, previous ratios that we have applied already hint at a liquidity issue, so would an unduly lengthy period taken to pay trade creditors reinforce this view?

As with all ratios, distortion may arise with this ratio should, for example, a large number of creditors be paid at the close of the financial year or, if immediately before the Balance Sheet is prepared, the pattern of purchase changes.

It is only when you look at these ratios in combination with others, such as the Acid Test ratio, that the above two efficiency ratios start to provide a more useful insight into a business. For example, should a business have a low Acid Test ratio possibly indicating a short-term liquidity problem, if looked at in conjunction with other ratios, such as Average Collection Period, then it be may suggested that it is able to convert sales into cash quickly (and maybe hold off from paying its suppliers for as long as possible). Consequently what may initially appear to be a serious liquidity problem is actually more manageable when additional information is available. No one ratio should therefore be considered in isolation.

Before attempting the exercises available online, try calculating the Average Payment Period for The 3Ts using the financial statements in Example 13.3. Once you have completed your own calculation, compare your answer to the calculation available at the end of this section.

Having considered a number of ratios, now go online and undertake Exercise 1. This exercise will require you to examine a partnership's financial statements and then apply a number of ratios to those financial statements. As you undertake the exercise do take some time to consider whether, from a preliminary examination of the information provided to you, you agree with the resulting ratios. You should also be formulating additional questions which you would want to pose to the partnership as if you were being asked to invest in it you never know, such an exercise may be useful in years to come when you are invited to become a partner of the firm you work for after qualification!

Return on Capital Employed (ROCE)					
Net Profit (before interest)	x 100%		x 100%		
Capital Employed (Total Assets less Current Liabilities)					

Net Profit Percentage					
Net Profit	x 100%		x 100%		
Sales					

Gross Profit Percentage					
Gross Profit	x 100%		x 100%		
Sales					

Current Ratio					
Current Assets	:1		:1		
Current Liabilities					

Acid Test					
Liquid Assets (less stock)	:1		:1		
Current Liabilities					

Average Collection Period					
(Trade) Debtors	x 365		x 365		
Sales					

Gearing Ratios

Whilst liquidity ratios look at the medium to short-term prospects of the business, gearing ratios by contrast look at the long-term solvency. Gearing ratios seek to assess a company's financial structure together with the impact of its borrowing and other financing as a proportion of the total long-term financing of the business.

Unlike the ratios considered earlier in this section, both gearing and investment ratios are primarily suited, and applied, to companies.

Capital Gearing Ratio

The Capital Gearing Ratio looks at how a company is financed, contrasting that part of a company's capital that is borrowed (such as long-term loans and preference shares) with that provided by the proprietors' funds. The ratio is calculated as follows:

$$\frac{\text{Preference shares} + \text{long-term loans}}{\text{All shareholder funds} + \text{long-term loans}} \times 100\%$$

Example 13.4 illustrates how the figures required for this ratio are extracted from Nash Ltd's Balance Sheet.

A company that has most of its finance provided by proprietors, rather than relying on external sources of financing, will be 'low-geared'. Those businesses that rely heavily on debt and have acquired most of their long-term finance by borrowing will be 'highly geared'; a phrase that you will often hear in the context of businesses often regarded as more at risk of failure. What is and isn't a high or low-geared business will obviously depend on the nature of the business and the various market trends. For example, when the availability of credit is in short supply, businesses will turn to their proprietors for more capital.

In relation to Nash Ltd, which we looked at in Example 13.4, does a Capital Gearing Ratio of 31.9% mean that the company is highly geared, i.e. one that has a high proportion

Nash Ltd
Balance Sheet as at 31 December 2010

Employment of Capital	Cost £	Dep'n £	NBV £
Fixed assets			
Building	150,000	0	150,000
Fixtures & Fittings	40,000	12,000	28,000
Goodwill	20,000	0	20,000
Machinery	25,000	15,000	10,000
	235,000	27,000	208,000
Current Assets			
Stock	26,000		
Debtors	26,500		
Cash	13,200	65,700	
less Current Liabilities			
Creditors	19,900		
Dividends payable	2,000		
Taxation	1,760	(23,660)	
Net Current Assets			42,040
Assets *less* Current Liabilities			250,040
less Creditors falling due after 1 year			
Falling due between 2 & 5 years		5,000	
Falling due after 5 years		35,000	(40,000)
Net Assets			210,040
Capital Employed			
Called-up share capital (fully paid)			
Equity shares (Ords)		120,000	
Non-equity shares (Prefs)		40,000	160,000
Share Premium account			16,000
Reserve			15,000
Accumulated Retained Profit			19,040
			210,040

Preference shares + long-term loans: By reference only to the Balance Sheet, this is the total of the nominal value of preference shares, £40,000, plus all debts falling due after 1 year, £40,000.

Capital Gearing Ratio

$$\frac{80,000}{250,040} \times 100\% = 31.9\%$$

All shareholder funds + long-term loans: By reference only to the Balance Sheet, this is the total of Capital Employed, £210,040, plus all debts falling due after 1 year, £40,000.

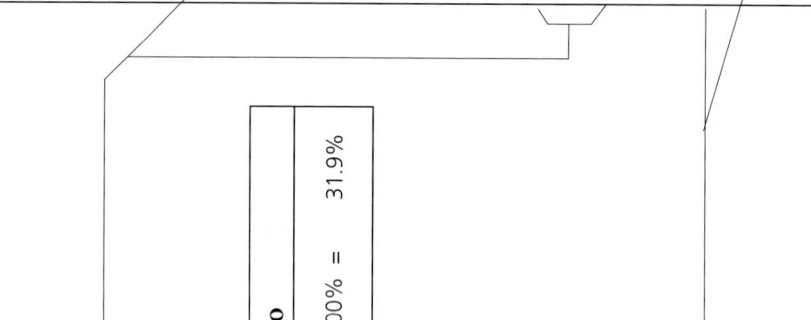

of borrowing? This may be subject to whatever Nash Ltd's business is and whether it is a relatively new entrant into the market. Could it be that this percentage is a relatively highly geared business for its sector, and if so, could it be susceptible to changes in interest rates and any demands for repayment of loans?

The associated risk of highly geared businesses arises from the fact that borrowed capital has to be paid for with interest payments; the more borrowed, the greater the interest payments to be made. Although not necessarily a problem in the good years, in the lean years the constant demand to meet interest payments may cause cash flow problems as profits start to decline. As a result, it is the ability to service interest payments (which in turn reduce profits) and access to insufficient assets to secure against debts that will cause highly geared businesses to be of greater cause for concern.

That said, borrowing should not necessarily be regarded as bad management practice, provided, of course, that there is a readily available source of credit in the market. When it is available, effective use has been demonstrated by the number of successful private equity acquisitions that finance their acquisitions with large-scale borrowing. Businesses will often borrow to finance expansion plans when proprietors are not in a position, or are unwilling, to provide additional funds.

Interest Cover

Interest Cover is another long-term solvency ratio that complements the Capital Gearing Ratio. Having looked to see how heavily (or not) indebted a business is, its ability to service the debt must also be examined. The Interest Cover ratio examines how many times over the business' Net Profit could be used to pay the interest due by the business on its debts. Obviously the more times Net Profits cover interest, the greater the inference that may be drawn that the business is capable of financing its debts. What must also then be considered is when the debts were taken out in relation to when the financial statements were prepared. It may be such that a high Interest Cover ratio could suggest that the debt has only recently been entered into and that interest charges have yet to have much effect. The Interest Cover ratio is calculated as follows:

$$\frac{\text{Net Profit before Interest}}{\text{Interest Charges}}$$

As long as it can be established that a business has available sufficient Net Profit (i.e. Operating Profit) to service its debts, then the Capital Gearing Ratio result may be of less concern.

Before you move on to attempt the online exercises accompanying this section, you may find it useful to practise calculating this ratio using the financial statements for Nash Ltd in Example 13.4. Once you have completed your own calculation, you can compare your answer to the calculation available at the end of this section.

Once you have calculated the Interest Cover, you will also need to examine a number of additional issues. For example, when did the company take out its debt in relation to when its financial statements were prepared? Depending on the proximity of when the debt was incurred and when the financial statement was prepared, the impact of the interest charges against Operating Profit may not yet be evident for the company. In addition, the company would also need to be compared to other companies in its business sector; is the company currently a market leader targeted by competitors seeking to increase their market share and so reduce the availability of profits in future years for the business? Again, it should be evident that ratios alone do not provide the answer; they are only one means by which to conduct an analysis of a business and its performance.

Investment Ratios

Business investors and potential investors will always be concerned with the performance of their investments. A number of ratios may be used by investors to assist them in analysing the performance of their investments, all of which should be used in conjunction with other performance ratios. Such investment ratios include Return on Capital Employed (considered above at page 213), Return on Ordinary Shareholders' Interest, Dividend Yield, and Earnings Per Share. The latter is considered below.

Earnings Per Share

Only once the directors have identified all appropriations (i.e. interest on debts, tax, and contractual debts to preference shareholders) to be deducted from Operating Profit may a dividend be declared. It is the dividend that the ordinary shareholders will be interested in as their reward for investing in the business. Earnings Per Share is calculated as follows:

$$\frac{\text{Net Profit after interest, tax \& preference share dividend}}{\text{Number of ordinary shares}}$$

This ratio also demonstrates that additional information is often required to be able to complete a ratio analysis. For the purposes of applying this ratio, you can see from the equation that it is necessary to know how much dividend was paid to preference shareholders and the number of ordinary shares it has in issue (whilst the Capital Employed section has a figure for the value of the ordinary shares in issue, it will not necessarily state the actual number). Accordingly, if we look at the financial statements for Nash Ltd in Example 13.4 above, we can assume that a final dividend payment of £2,000 was made to preference shareholders and that 120,000 ordinary shares of £1 each are in issue. Based on these figures, Example 13.5 shows the calculation undertaken to ascertain Earnings Per Share.

Nash Ltd's Earnings Per Share ratio will only gain significance once examined against similar businesses to ascertain whether its current dividend payment is acceptable vis-à-vis its competitors. This ratio is also limited in that it only produces a figure for the potential earnings per share for the past financial year not the actual dividend per share which the directors will declare in the forthcoming financial year that will obviously depend on how the business performs. Accordingly, this ratio would be unable to take into account any plans that a company's directors might have regarding future investment for the company, which in fact may reduce the availability of future profits for dividend payments.

In common with all ratios, it therefore becomes necessary to investigate further the company's plans and read any accompanying notes to the published financial statements. If you haven't already, do read the provisions of Part 15, Chapter 5 of the Companies Act 2006 referred to in Section 12 of *LPC Accounts Online*, which details the information that directors are required to provide in their accompanying statements it is this information that will aid in understanding a company's earning potential.

Example 13.5

Nash Ltd
Trading and Profit & Loss account for the year ending 31 December 2010

	£	£
Sales		179,000
less Cost of goods sold		
Opening stock	23,000	
add Purchases	70,000	
	93,000	
less Closing stock	26,000	
		67,000
Gross Profit		112,000
less Expenses		
Council tax	2,300	
Depreciation	9,000	
Directors remuneration	39,000	
General expenses	11,400	
Motor expenses	2,500	
Wages	33,000	
		(97,200)
Operating Profit		14,800
Interest paid		6,000
Profit Before Tax		8,800
Taxation		1,760
Profit After Tax		7,040
Interim dividend paid	3,000	
Final dividend	2,000	
		5,000
Retained Profit for the year		2,040
Retained Profit brought forward		17,040
Retained Profit carried forward		19,040

Net Profit after interest, tax & preference dividend: This is the Operating Profit, £14,800 minus £6,000 for interest, £1,760 for taxation, and £2,000 for preference share dividend.

Number of ordinary shares: This figure may be drawn from the 'lower' half of the Balance Sheet and is the total of the nominal value of ordinary shares.

Earnings Per Share

5,040	0.042 pence per share
120,000	

Nash Ltd
Balance Sheet as at 31 December 2010

Employment of Capital	Cost £	Dep'n £	NBV £
Fixed assets			
Building	150,000	0	150,000
Fixtures & Fittings	40,000	12,000	28,000
Goodwill	20,000	0	20,000
Machinery	25,000	15,000	10,000
	235,000	27,000	208,000
Current Assets			
Stock	26,000		
Debtors	26,500		
Cash	13,200	65,700	
less Current Liabilities			
Creditors	19,900		
Dividends payable	2,000		
Taxation	1,760	(23,660)	
Net Current Assets			42,040
Assets less Current Liabilities			250,040
less Creditors falling due after 1 year			
Falling due between 2 & 5 years			
Falling due after 5 years		5,000	
		35,000	(40,000)
Net Assets			210,040
Capital Employed			
Called-up share capital (fully paid)			
Equity shares (Ords)		120,000	160,000
Non-equity shares (Prefs)		40,000	16,000
Share Premium Account			15,000
Reserve			
Accumulated Retained Profit			19,040
			210,040

In this exercise we will look more at the ratios suited for companies. As previously, you should undertake this exercise with a view to determining the relative success of the business. Consider drawing conclusions about the profitability of the business; is it one that you would want to invest in, or are there further questions that need to be answered?

Using the Profit & Loss account and Balance Sheet for T E Knight Ltd provided in the question below, you are required to complete a number of ratio calculations to draw conclusions relating to its performance. The ratios being used are those suited to companies and the formulae have been provided for you — you only need to extract the correct figures!

Further information that you will need to undertake the ratio calculations is that the company has ordinary shares and preference shares of £1 each, and that it pays 12.5% annually to its preference shareholders.

When you are ready to start the exercise, click the 'Your ledgers' tab above or the 'Complete your ledgers' button at the bottom of your screen to make the necessary entries in the calculations provided. Once you are happy with your calculations click 'Submit' to see your feedback and score.

Please note that when completing your answers, you will need to ensure that you include a '%' sign or the words 'days' where relevant in order for your answers to be marked correct.

Don't forget, you can click 'Save' at any point if you want to come back to this exercise later.

TE Knight Ltd
Trading and Profit & Loss account for the year ending 31 March 2010

	£	£
Sales		365,000
less Cost of goods sold		
Opening stock	19,000	
add Purchases	139,000	
	158,000	
less Closing stock	(21,000)	(137,000)
Gross Profit		**228,000**
less **Expenses**		
Depreciation	7,000	
General expenses	19,000	
Insurance	2,000	
Motor expenses	6,000	

As we have already stated, the Capital Gearing ratio, Interest Cover, and Earnings per shares are more suited for companies. Now go online and undertake Exercise 2 in which you will be required to examine the financial statements of a company and complete a series of ratio calculations to determine the relative success of the business. Again, as you undertake the exercise, try to consider whether you would regard it an entity worthy of investing your own funds.

Once you have completed Exercise 2, attempt Exercises 3 and 4, both of which will require you to apply the ratios set out above to compare two partnerships and two companies. Once you have applied the various ratios to the financial statements of the businesses you will be required to complete a series of multiple-choice questions intended to help you consider further which of the businesses you would view as a suitable investment.

In this exercise we will apply the ratios used in Exercise 2 of this section and compare the performance of two partnerships. As previously, you should undertake this exercise with a view to determining the relative success of the businesses — consider drawing conclusions about the profitability of the businesses; which of the two partnerships would you consider a suitable investment?

Using the Profit & Loss account and Balance Sheet for both the Walton Brittain Partnership and Oxford Dance Academy provided in the question below, you are first required to complete a number of ratio calculations to draw conclusions relating to their performance and decide which partnership is the better investment. Both partnerships undertake similar business activities. When you are ready to undertake these calculations, click the 'Your ledgers' tab above or the 'Complete your ledgers' button at the bottom of your screen to make the necessary entries in the calculations provided.

You are then required to answer a series of multiple-choice questions based on your calculations. When you are happy with your answers, click 'Submit' at the bottom of your screen to view your score and receive feedback on your answers.

Please note that when completing your answers, you will need to ensure that you include a '%' sign or the words 'days' where relevant in order for your answers to be marked correct.

Don't forget, you can click 'Save' at any point if you want to come back to this exercise later.

Emily Walton and Peter Brittain trading as 'The Walton Brittain Partnership'
Trading and Profit & Loss account for the year ending 31 May 2010

	£	£
Turnover		341,000
less Cost of goods sold		
Opening stock	40,000	
add Purchases	169,000	
	209,000	
less Closing stock	35,000	174,000
Gross Profit		**167,000**
less Expenses		
Bad debts & provision	3,500	
Depreciation	10,000	
Insurance	4,000	

Return on Capital Employed (ROCE)		Legal Service Training Ltd		OUP Vocation Ltd	
Net Profit (before interest)	× 100%		× 100%		× 100%
Capital Employed (Total Assets *less* Current Liabilities)					
Capital Gearing Ratio					
Preference shares + long-term loans	× 100%		× 100%		× 100%
All shareholders' funds + long-term loans					
Interest Cover					
Net Profit before interest					
Interest Charges					
Earning per Share					
Net Profit after interest, tax, & preference share dividend					
Number of ordinary shares					
Net Profit Percentage					
Net Profit	× 100%		× 100%		× 100%
Sales					
Gross Profit Percentage					
Gross Profit	× 100%		× 100%		× 100%
Sales					

Conclusion

In this final section of the business accounts part of *LPC Accounts Online*, for convenience, the various ratios have been divided into categories, but you should have an appreciation that no one category should be applied in isolation. It requires considerable additional background information to get a clearer view of the performance of a business, and you may need to consider anything from a business's market reputation and employee relations to an examination of current business activities and existing contracts.

In addition, not just one set of financial statements should be examined; ideally the financial statements of two or more years should be analysed to determine a business's performance year-on-year. It is from these additional years of financial statements that significant changes may be noted, such as sources of new finance (be it new issue of shares or the introduction of new partners), new debt, whether new assets have been acquired, or if the business is selling off its investments. As a result ratio analysis is one of a myriad of methods that may be employed to assist in drawing conclusions about a business, along with a comparison with other similar businesses and looking at or listening to other sources of information about the business.

Solutions for Ratios Suggested in Section 13

At various stages throughout this section it was suggested that you attempt to calculate a number of ratios using the financial statements contained in the examples provided. The solutions to these calculations are set out below.

Tracey, Tricky, and Trinny trading as 'The 3Ts'

Net Profit Percentage (Net Return on Sales)

Net Profit: Taken from the Profit & Loss account.

Net Profit	x 100%	171,000	x 100%	=	26.7%
Sales		640,000			

Sales: Taken from the Profit & Loss account and represents the total sales figure for the year.

Gross Profit Percentage (Return on Sales)

Gross Profit: Taken from the Profit & Loss account.

Gross Profit	x 100%	295,000	x 100%	=	46.1%
Sales		640,000			

Sales: Taken from the Profit & Loss account and represents the total sales figure for the year.

Acid Test

Liquid Assets (*less* stock): Taken from the Balance Sheet, this is Current Assets minus Closing stock.

Liquid Assets (*less* stock)	:1	53,000	:1 =	0.48:1
Current Liabilities		110,000		

Current Liabilities: By reference only to the Balance Sheet, use the Current Liabilities figure.

Average Payment Period

(Trade) Creditors: Taken from the Balance Sheet, the total value of the Creditors (excluding long-term liabilities).

(Trade) Creditors	x 365	50,000	x 365 =	53 days
Purchases		341,000		

Purchases: By reference only to the Profit & Loss account, this is the total purchases figure for the year.

Nash Ltd

Interest Cover

Net Profit before Interest: Taken from the Profit & Loss account, the Operating Profit figure is used.

Net Profit before Interest	14,800		2.47
Interest Charges	6,000		

Interest Charges: Taken from the Profit & Loss account, the Interest Charges figure is used.

Index